T0250657

Research Reports ESPRIT

Project 302 · Vol. 1

Edited in cooperation with
the Commission of the European Communities

J.-P. Banâtre   S.B. Jones   D. Le Métayer

Prospects for Functional Programming in Software Engineering

With the cooperation of P. Fradet and A. Sinclair

Springer-Verlag

Berlin Heidelberg New York London Paris
Tokyo Hong Kong Barcelona Budapest

Authors

Jean-Pierre Banâtre
Daniel Le Métayer
IRISA
Campus Universitaire de Beaulieu
F-35042 Rennes Cedex, France

Simon B. Jones
University of Stirling
Department of Computing Science and Mathematics
Stirling, Great Britain

ESPRIT Project 302 "Prospects for Functional Programming in Software Engineering" belongs to the Subprogramme "Software Technology" of ESPRIT, the European Strategic Programme for Research and Development in Information Technology supported by the European Communities.

Project 302 investigates the functional programming approach for achieving thorough exploitation of the potential of highly concurrent hardware architectures. This involves measurement of the complexity and parallelism of functional programs written in the FP, Lisp, and Me-Too languages. The project aims at: a tool for translating Lispkit and Me-Too to FP; tools to provide a static measure of complexity and potential for parallelism of FP programs; an emulator to emulate parallel execution of functional programs.

CR Subject Classification (1991): D.1-3, F.3

ISBN 3-540-53852-6 Springer-Verlag Berlin Heidelberg New York
ISBN 0-387-53852-6 Springer-Verlag New York Berlin Heidelberg

Publication No. EUR 13016 EN of the
Commission of the European Communities,
Scientific and Technical Communication Unit,
Directorate-General Telecommunications, Information Industries and Innovation,
Luxembourg
Neither the Commission of the European Communities nor any person acting on behalf of the Commission is responsible for the use which might be made of the following information.

© ECSC – EEC – EAEC, Brussels – Luxembourg, 1991
Printed in Germany

Printing and Binding: Weihert-Druck GmbH, Darmstadt
2145/3140 – 543210 – Printed on acid-free paper

PREFACE

During Esprit Project 302, from February 1985 until July 1987, we were primarily concerned with analysing the complexity of functional programs and their potential for parallel execution, and with realizing the analysis methods in the form of a software tool, ACE. However, the interests of the members of the project team, and of their colleagues, were spread rather more widely than the narrow project brief would suggest. Previous work remained influential, inevitably continued in the background during the project, and has been strengthened since the project finished. Our interests are very firmly rooted in the meeting point of the theoretical and pragmatic aspects of functional programming, both their virtues and their problems. For example: programming techniques and style; program transformation, verification and analysis; input/output and systems programming problems; compilation and optimization.

After the project had finished, Mike Coyle (of the Commission for the European Communities) suggested that we draw together our ideas into a book outlining our point of view on functional programming. This seemed like quite an attractive prospect, as it would also give us the opportunity to deal with issues wider than just those of the project. We decided that this goal would be best achieved by attempting to synthesize, from our individual research strands, an illustration of the importance of functional programming in the future of software engineering. Hence, some chapters are about pragmatic aspects of programming, some are about formal techniques which may be turned to good account in the *engineering* of functional programs, and some are about formal techniques and other developments which are important in the *implementation* of functional languages, and are thus making purely functional programming a viable tool (more so than it used to be, for example, with respect to performance).

The book was edited by a team of three comprising Jean-Pierre Banâtre, Simon Jones and Daniel Le Métayer. Several of the chapters were written specially; others are edited versions of papers and reports written for other purposes, in particular chapters 6 and 7 for which we must acknowledge the original joint authors Pascal Fradet (IRISA) and Andrew Sinclair (University of Stirling); Pascal was supported by CNRS and INRIA grants, and Andrew by a SERC research studentship. Roger Oakden and Peter Robinson (STC Technology Ltd) contributed to the early planning stages of the book, and some text contributed by Peter has been included in chapter 6.

We must thank all those who took part in Esprit Project 302, which provided the background for this book, and which fostered the collaboration between the present authors. Those who were involved in Project 302 were:

CAP SOGETI Innovation:
  Olivier Emorine, Christer Fernström, Jean Nsonde, Maurice Schlumberger
IRISA:
  Jean-Pierre Banâtre, Boubakar Gamatie, Daniel Le Métayer
STC Technology Ltd:
  Eleanor Bruce, Peter Davies, Roger Oakden, Peter Robinson, Jonathan Rowles
University of Stirling:
  Peter Henderson, Simon Jones, Paul Williamson

Finally, we must thank Mike Coyle for his support of the Special Interest Group of which this book is the most tangible result, and the CEC for funding our SIG meetings. During one working trip in Rennes, Simon Jones was supported by grants from CNRS, the British Council and the French *Ministère des Affaires Etrangères*.

The opinions contained in this book are those of the named authors, and should not be construed as necessarily in accordance with those of the other members of Project 302, or of the CEC. A similar responsibility lies with the authors for any errors which may be present.

January 1991   The authors

CONTENTS

CHAPTER 1

ABOUT PROGRAMMING ENVIRONMENTS

Jean-Pierre Banâtre

1.1 INTRODUCTION

In this first chapter, we are concerned with the process of developing large software programs. This process cannot be achieved without an appropriate set of tools, usually provided by programming environments. After a brief analysis of the software development process, we identify the principal components of a programming environment and illustrate them with the example of the CEDAR system. Then, we elaborate on system specification and present briefly some specification languages. The next step is the refinement of the specification which amounts to concrete program design. We show how specifications can be refined in the functional and imperative frameworks, and then we compare these approaches. Finally, we give some insight into the desired properties of a functional programming environment and give an overview of the book.

1.2 THE SOFTWARE DEVELOPMENT PROCESS

The complete process of producing a running sofware system from the initial requirements is referred to as the *sofware development process*.

The universally accepted model of software development is called the software life cycle. It describes the evolution in time of a software project (or product). It is divided into six major phases:

(1) *Requirements analysis* (description of the needs). A software system is developed in order to meet the needs of a certain user community. These needs have to be stated in the form of a set of requirements that the system is expected to satisfy. The result of this phase is a document specifying what the system should do, along with performance requirements, development plans, cost statements. However this document does not describe how the system is going to meet these requirements.

(2) *Specification* (what the system should do). Starting from the requirement document, software engineers produce a detailed specification of what the system should do in order to meet the requirements. This specification identifies the major functional components of the software system and describes their relationship.

(3) *Design* (how should it be done). The result of this phase is a complete description of the organization of the software system. A document identifying all the software modules comprising the system is produced.

(4) *Coding* (choice of a programming language and production of the software system). The system is implemented to meet the specifications of phase 2 according to the design of phase 3. At this stage, it is clear that a programming language has to be chosen and this may be a crucial choice.

(5) *Testing* (verification that the developed system meets the specifications). This step assesses the quality of the implementation. In fact this certification activity has to be present at each stage of the software development to check that intermediate deliverables between stages are acceptable. Very often, at the end of the project a certification phase is necessary. This phase, often called quality assurance, measures the quality of the software by running appropriate acceptance tests and checking programs and documentation.

(6) *Operation and maintenance.* Following the delivery of the system, changes may become necessary either because of errors or because of the addition of new capabilities or the modification of existing ones. These aspects are related to what is usually referred to as maintenance.

Several major problems arise when applying the method to real projects :
- the correctness of the output from a previous phase is always assumed and this assumption may turn out to be false,
- every phase requires that the information needed to progress be complete and available.

Thus, the time required to produce a testable system from specification is usually very long, and some backtracking in the development cycle may be necessary. While phase 6 is certainly the most costly, much of its cost can be attributed to failures in early phases of the cycle. Although formal specification techniques do exist, they are not widely used and there is often a severe mismatch between the levels of the languages used in the specification, design and coding phases.

Rapid prototyping is often used to alleviate the temporal distance between requirements analysis and a running system. Such prototypes provide the functionality of the expected final system but in general they do not put much emphasis on performance aspects or user interfaces. Most often they are written in a very high level language such as PROLOG. By producing prototypes at an early stage, the developer can provide a (partial) view of the final system and this may allow him to complement or even correct some aspects of the requirements or the specifications. One can imagine that the development of a sizable project involves the management of a huge number of preliminary or partial documents, the use of many software tools such as text editors, debuggers, compilers etc. Programming environments are designed in order to facilitate the management of software projects by providing appropriate tools. The next section gives an overview of such an environment.

1.3 CHARACTERISTICS OF PROGRAMMING ENVIRONMENTS

This section is concerned with the presentation of the services offered by a programming environment and to the benefits which can be expected from these services. A particular programming environment is quickly sketched in order to show the kind of tools available for software development.

1.3.1 What should be expected from a programming environment?

A programming environment can be seen as an integrated set of tools and techniques that help in the development of software. This environment is used in all phases of the software development. In general the phase supported best is the coding phase, with tools such as text editors, compilers, linkers... However the other phases demand specific tools such as: document handlers, test generators, powerful graphics facilities ...

A good programming environment should produce strong impact on the software development process in several respects :

Higher quality software

By providing flexible program development methodologies, it should be possible to produce robust and reliable software; such methodologies should help in decomposing a problem into sub-problems and in defining clear interfaces between components of an application.

Better programmer productivity

If the environment provides a rich set of tools (editors, compilers, symbolic debuggers, version managers,...), it is most likely that the speed in the production of high quality software will be increased. These tools will relieve the programmer from a lot of time-consuming and error-prone tasks.

Better software integration

By integration, we mean the possibility of building software components which are easily reusable. This amounts to defining appropriate tools for interface description. Of course, integration should facilitate a proper interconnection of programs: the interface offered by a program should be sufficient for it to be used by other programs. In particular, no knowledge of the internal structure of the program should be necessary.

1.3.2 An example of a programming environment: the CEDAR system

CEDAR is an environment for developing and testing large software systems [Swinehart et al. 86]. It was designed at the Xerox Palo Alto Research Center at the beginning of the 80's and has evolved towards a complete and powerful programming environment. The development of CEDAR was closely related to the design of Xerox personal computers such as ALTO, DORADO and DANDELION. So, some of the CEDAR choices were direct consequences of the use of these machines. In particular, the CEDAR programming language is derived from MESA which was developed for the programming of the PILOT operating system [Redell et al. 80]. We have chosen to describe CEDAR as an example of an advanced programming environment providing many sophisticated tools.

1.3.2.1 The CEDAR language

The CEDAR language is a strongly typed language of the PASCAL family. A program consists of separately compiled modules. These modules are of two kinds: interface modules which can be seen as a specification of the data abstraction represented by the module and implementation modules which contain the concrete representation of the data abstraction and the implementation of the functions operating on this abstraction. These two kinds of modules correspond to the definition package and the representation package in ADA [ADA 83].

The CEDAR language offers facilities for process definition and activation. Synchronization is achieved by using the concept of monitors [Hoare 74]. There are also features for exception handling and for safe memory management. The CEDAR language provides automatic storage management: the progammer is no longer in charge of explicitly allocating and deallocating objects with the risk of creating invalid references.

1.3.2.2 Organization of the CEDAR system

CEDAR can be viewed as an operating system as well as a powerful programming environment. It is composed of three main layers :

- The *hardware layer* includes a workstation extended with a set of microcoded instructions for high speed memory allocation, process switching, reference counting and exception handling.
- The *kernel layer* including basic operating system facilities such as storage management, process management, file handling and communication management.
- The *life support layer* which provides the software development tools offered to the CEDAR application programmer. We describe it in some detail:

The CEDAR life support layer

The life support layer incorporates components for the CEDAR user, such as a display manager, a text editor, a command and expression interpreter and also components for software development. We examine some of the major components of this layer:

The abstract machine

The abstract machine provides an interpretation of the semantics of the CEDAR language and is independent of the underlying hardware. This is used for several purposes, such as:

- Program control: it is possible to set up breakpoints and to trace the program execution flow.
- Type information: it is possible to examine at run time the type attributes of any value.
- Value manipulation: at run time it is possible to read a value held by the abstract machine, and to modify it.
- Program and process structure information: it is possible to obtain dynamic information about the program execution itself. For example, one can enumerate the active processes, suspend or activate selected processes. One can also examine every process' current status.

Thus the abstract machine is a very powerful tool for program debugging. Of course, it is intimately related to the CEDAR language and in particular it takes advantage of the elaborate type system of this language.

CEDAR system development tools

We enumerate the set of software tools offered to the CEDAR user.

The imager

The imager is a graphics package for high-quality two-dimensional imaging of the text, drawings and scanned images. It is a device independent tool and as such it can be adapted to a variety of installations: black and white or colour displays, laser printers...

The view manager

The view manager provides each user sharing a real display terminal with a virtual display, a keyboard and a mouse. Each view is like a window whose position and size are managed by the viewer's package and whose contents are entirely determined by the application which created it.

The document composition system

The document composition system (called Tioga) allows document creation and editing. Documents can be of any kind, including CEDAR programs. Tioga documents are structured as trees, and each node may correspond to a paragraph in a document or a statement in a CEDAR program. Nodes may be decorated with user-specified information related to the way the information they represent may be displayed or printed.

Version and release management

A system such as CEDAR is composed of thousands of files. Thus, it is necessary to automate the management of these files. This is done by using the DF (Description File) package which provides operations for organizing a set of files and checking for consistency upon modification of some of them. In order to make this organization manageable, the DF files use a tree-structure to describe the files that compose the system and their relationship.

A CEDAR release is a consistent version of the system (as represented by a set of DF files) containing all the files constituting one release.

CEDAR language-dependent tools

Several tools are directly dependent on the CEDAR programming language. As usual, there is a compiler, a binder, a command interpreter, as well as debugging tools. We will not go into further details here.

Applications provided by the CEDAR system

Above the life support layer, a set of standard facilities are offered to the CEDAR programmer, let us mention some of them:

- electronic mail,
- data base support,
- imaging tools,
- Etherphone, which uses Ethernet communications to transmit digitized voice signals. From a workstation it is possible to make and receive telephone calls, to maintain private telephone directories and to manage a data base of messages.

We have chosen to describe the CEDAR system principally because of the large variety of development tools it offers; however it is rather weak in some other respects such as specification tools. The next sections give a brief insight into specification languages and their use in the software development process.

1.4 THE CHOICE OF THE APPROPRIATE SPECIFICATION LANGUAGE

The system specification is the key document in any software project. All subsequent activities in the project depend on it: design, coding, integration, testing... An error in the specification may lead to a large amount of reworking if it is detected relatively early in the project, or to a disaster if detected once the project is finished. So what should be the properties of a specification? Let us mention the three most important:

- it should be non-ambiguous,
- it should allow reasoning about the properties of the specified system,
- it should be independent of any implementation.

The only formalism allowing us to meet these contraints is mathematics. A mathematical specification can be used as a basis for software development. When a program is produced, it is possible to prove its correctness in order to show that it matches its specification. A mathematical specification language is well suited to describing what a system does rather than how it does it. Let us discuss more precisely some recognized advantages of formal specification techniques:

- *enhancement of clarity and precision*. The formalization of a problem leaves no room for subjective interpretations. This is real progress compared to informal specifications.
- *a basis for communication*. The meaning of a formal specification is not subjective, so it will provide a good basis for communication within a design team.
- *a basis for formal validation*. It should be possible to check mechanically some properties of a specification.

In order to get a feeling for some well-known specification languages, we describe the VDM specification language [Jones 86] and give some insight into Z [Abrial et al. 79, Spivey 89] and OBJ2 [Futatsugi et al. 85].

1.4.1 The VDM specification language

The Vienna Development Method is a mathematically based set of techniques for the specification, development and proof of correctness of computer systems. The basic concept of the specification language is the abstract data type which allows a formal description of information structures and of the operations used to handle them.

1.4.1.1 Basic components of the VDM specification language

The two basic components are propositional logic and set theory. These two theories are well-known, let us only illustrate some formulae which may be used in VDM.

$\{x \in N \mid 0 \leq x \leq 5\}$, the set of integers between 0 and 5, i.e. 0,1,2,3,4,5.

$\{n^2 \mid 0 \leq n \wedge n \in N\}$, the set of squares of natural numbers less than or equal to a given n. N represents the set of natural numbers.

Thus the information structures of a system are defined in terms of sets; what about the operations working on these structures? An operation is defined according to the following scheme :

op_name (...) ... name, arguments and (optional) result
    ext ...   *state description*
    pre ...   *pre-condition on inputs*
    post ...   *post-condition on outputs*

The input values of an operation are its arguments and the initial value of the external state. The outputs of an operation are its result and the final value of the external state. The pre-condition is a predicate on the initial values (inputs) of the operation. The post-condition is a predicate between the input values of the operation and its output values; it specifies the relationship between inputs and outputs. Consider for example the problem of specifying the behaviour of a page allocation procedure in, for example, an operating system:

allocate_page ( ) *p* : *page*

ext wr *free_memory* : *memory*

pre *p* ∈ *free_memory*

post *free_memory* = $\overleftarrow{free\_memory}$ - {*p*}

We assume the declaration *memory* : **set of** *page* and *free_memory* : *memory*. In order to differentiate between input and output values in the post-condition, input values are decorated with a ⟵ (e.g., $\overleftarrow{free\_memory}$). The symbol **wr** in front of *free_memory* means that this value can be transformed within the operation and the symbol **ext** means that it is declared outside the operation.

<u>The notion of mapping</u>

A mapping is composed of two sets and a rule which associates an element from one set with a unique element of the second. A mapping can be represented by a set of pairs, where each pair contains one element of the first set and one element of the second set. So, if *A* and *B* are two sets, the product set of *A* and *B* (denoted *A*×*B*) may be defined as {(*a,b*) | *a*∈ *A* ∧ *b*∈ *B*} and any mapping from *A* to *B* is a subset of *A*×*B* in which all the elements from *A* are unique.

A mapping can be defined explicitly by giving a set of pairs of values: for example {2↦8, 3↦27, 4↦64} defines a mapping associating every number between 2 and 4 with its cube.

It is also possible to define a mapping by giving the first element of a pair satisfying a given predicate and then generating the associated elements by applying a function. For example, the following formulae define mappings :

$$\{x \mapsto x^3 \mid x \in \{2,3,4\}\}$$
$$\{x \mapsto x! \mid x \in \{2,3,4\}\}$$

The first mapping can be explicitly rewritten as {2↦8, 3↦27, 4↦64} and the second as {2↦2, 3↦6, 4↦24}.

The domain of a mapping is the set of the first elements of its component pairs. The set of the second elements is called the range of the mapping. VDM provides the operators *dom* and *range* to extract this information from a mapping. For example:

$$dom \ \{x \mapsto f(x) \mid P(x)\} = \{x \mid P(x)\}$$
$$range \ \{x \mapsto f(x) \mid P(x)\} = \{f(x) \mid P(x)\}$$

Using mappings, let us define two operations dealing with a symbol table represented as a set of pairs (*identifier* ↦ *value*). So a table is simply defined as :

$$table = \textbf{map } identifier \textbf{ to } value$$

and the operators *add* and *look_up* may be defined as:

add (*id* : *identifier*, *v* : *value*)
    ext wr *t* : *table*
    pre *id* ∉ *dom t*
    post $t = \overleftarrow{t} \cup \{id \mapsto v\}$

look_up (*id* : *identifier*) *v* : *value*
    ext rd *t* : *table*
    pre *id* ∈ *dom t*
    post $v = \overleftarrow{t}(id)$

The definition for *add* contains the precondition that a new (*identifier* ↦ *value*) pair may only be added if that identifier is not already present in the table. Similarly, the precondition for *look_up* informs us that we may only look up identifiers which are already present in the table.

Sets versus sequences

Some problems cannot be simply specified using general set theory; it should be possible to describe collections of items containing duplicates and it should also be possible to introduce a notion of ordering. The first requirement may be satisfied by using multisets instead of sets and the second requirement leads to the introduction of sequences.

A sequence of n elements is written as $[s_1, s_2, ..., s_n]$. The order in which the elements are written is significant, thus $[1,2,3] \neq [1,3,2]$, and a sequence may contain several instances of the same element, thus $[1,2,2]$ is an acceptable sequence and is different from $[1,2]$. The usual list operations are available on sequences. In particular, the first element of a sequence is given by applying the *head* operator (e.g., *head* $[3,4,5] = 3$) and the sequence containing all the elements of a given sequence but the first is given by applying the *tail* operator (e.g. *tail* $[3,4,5] = [4,5]$).

Other, more abstract, types may be built up from sets, mappings, sequences and so on, as required.

1.4.2 Other approaches to specification

Several other specification languages have been developed, let us briefly summarize two of them: Z and OBJ2.

1.4.2.1 The Z specification language

Z is a specification language which relies heavily on set theory and propositional logic in the same way as VDM. Furthermore, the language offers a diagrammatic representation for displaying in a clear fashion properties that are used in defining objects and operations. Just to give the flavour of Z, let us redefine the symbol table and the operations *add* and *look_up* from the previous section.

A symbol table is a partial function (in VDM terminology this is a mapping) from identifiers to values. Thus we may define *table*, specifying the type of symbol table objects:

$$table == identifier \nrightarrow value$$

The operations *add* and *look_up* are defined using *schemas*:

$$
\begin{array}{|l}
\hline
add \\
\hline
t, t' : table \\
id? : identifier \\
v? : value \\
\hline
id? \notin dom\ t \\
t' = t \cup \{id? \mapsto v?\} \\
\hline
\end{array}
$$

In this specification *t* and *t'* are respectively the initial and final states of the symbol table, and, by convention, variables decorated with ? are input arguments of the operation. The predicate part of the schema contains both pre- and post-conditions, no distinction being made between them in the notation.

```
┌─look_up ──────────────────────────┐
│  t, t' : table                    │
│  id? : identifier                 │
│  v! : value                       │
├───────────────────────────────────┤
│  id? ∈ dom t                      │
│  v! = t (id?)                     │
│  t' = t                           │
└───────────────────────────────────┘
```

Here, we see that ! is used by convention to decorate the results from an operation. It is common practice in Z to give all operations which are intended for use with external data structures both an initial and a final state; thus *look_up* has both t and t', and we have the additional post-condition that the state does not change during the operation.

Z has been used successfully to specify a variety of applications, some of them being described in [Morgan et al. 84] and [Sufrin 82].

1.4.2.2 The OBJ2 specification language

OBJ2 is a specification language developed at SRI International. This language possesses a formal semantics based on equational logic and an operational semantics based on rewrite rules. An OBJ2 program declares new types and functions which are defined by means of a set of equations. The equations are required to satisfy the Church-Rosser and termination properties which guarantee that repeated rewriting will always terminate with a unique result.

Objects may be parameterized; the range of permissible actual parameters is described by a *requirement theory*. It is necessary to check that the actual parameters satisfy axioms in the requirement theory. Checking properties such as the Church-Rosser property, termination or conformity to a theory requires the use of a theorem proving system.

An object definition contains three main parts : (1) a header specifying the name of the object and the description of its parameters, (2) a signature declaring its new sorts and operations and (3) a body consisting essentially of a set of equations. The object *BOOL* defining the sort *bool* can be written as follows:

```
obj BOOL
        sort bool
        ops true, false : -> bool
        op not : bool -> bool
        eq : not true = false
        eq : not false = true
endo
```

Requirement theories (also called simply theories) have the same form as objects. They define the conditions to be fulfilled by an object to be an admissible actual parameter. In some way, theories can be regarded as interfaces.

This only gives a flavour of OBJ2, which is the result of fifteen years research effort in algebraic semantics. Although originally OBJ was seen as a means of investigation for algebraic abstract data type specification, it soon became a general purpose specification language.

1.5 REFINEMENT OF THE SPECIFICATION

Knowing the specification of a problem, it is necessary to apply some development method in order to produce a correct (executable) program. Usually, such methods are based on the stepwise refinement principle. The main idea is to develop a program P from a specification S_0 by applying a series of small refinement steps. Each step captures a single design decision, for example a choice between several concrete representations for an abstract data type or between several algorithms for implementing a transformation. The whole process can then be pictured as follows:

$$S_0 \rightarrow S_1 \rightarrow S_2 \ldots \rightarrow P$$

where the S_i's represent intermediate refined specifications and P the final executable program. If each intermediate refinement step ($S_i \rightarrow S_{i+1}$) can be proven correct then P is guaranteed correct.

Although this approach may seem attractive, it may be difficult to use it for the development of complex programs starting from large specifications: the correctness proofs may become large and difficult to handle. The usual solution to this problem is based on the decomposition of specifications into smaller and more tractable units: this is the well-known *divide and conquer* principle. These smaller specification units may then be refined independently, thus making the development process easier.

1.5.1 Program development in a conventional language

In this section and the following we focus on the most important part of the programming environment: the programming language. We start with a study of imperative programming languages.

1.5.1.1 About conventional languages

Conventional programming languages can be seen as abstractions of the von Neumann architecture. This architecture is based on three elements: a memory that contains data and instructions, a control and processing unit and a bus connecting the two previous elements. The control unit is responsible for fetching instructions from the memory. The execution of an instruction requires the extraction of data from the memory, their handling by the processing unit via logical and arithmetic operations and the writing of results back to the memory.

The design of conventional languages has been greatly influenced by this model; in particular, two fundamental concepts are present in all conventional languages: the sequential step-by-step execution of instructions and the modifiable store of values. The step-by-step execution of instructions is expressed through control structures which range from the very low-level **goto** instruction to more sophisticated control structures. The variable, which can be modified by an assignment statement, reflects the behaviour of memory cells in von Neumann computer architectures. The assignment statement, as well as the **goto** statement have been central to a hot debate: Backus [Backus 78] argues that these conventional program structures are harmful because they enjoy few useful mathematical properties.

1.5.1.2 How can we develop imperative programs from specifications?

The objective should be to produce a program correct according to an initial specification. So, once the program is produced, no more effort is needed to prove that it meets its specification. Thus, "a program and its proof should be developed hand-in-hand, with the proof usually leading the way" [Gries 81]. Actually, it has been recognized that proving an already existing program is a very difficult task; it is certainly far better to build a program with the proof of correctness in mind at each step of the development process. To illustrate this approach, let us develop a program summing the elements of an array:

We want to develop a program that, given a positive integer n and an integer array t [0:n-1], produces a result representing the sum of the elements of t. The precondition is $n \geq 0$ and the postcondition is $s = \sum_{i=1,n} t[i]$.

The usual strategy for deriving a program consists in putting the specification in conjunctive normal form, and then *weakening* the specification in order to develop a loop. The most useful ways of weakening a specification are: (i) deletion of a conjunct and (ii) replacement of a constant by a variable. Let us use (ii) in order to weaken the postcondition; we obtain: $I = (\, 0 \le j \le n \wedge S = \sum_{i=1,j} t[i]\,)$ which can be chosen as the *invariant* of the loop. Introducing two variables j and s to represent respectively the index and the sum, the assignments $j:=0$; $s:= 0$ establish this invariant. The strategy consists now in developing a loop with I as *invariant* and the property $(j = n)$ as *variant*. I is true before and after each iteration of the loop and the variant is true only after the last iteration of the loop. The general form of the loop is then: **while not** $(j = n)$ **do** C. The purpose of the body of the loop is to make progress towards the validation of the variant while preserving the invariant. This progress is measured by an integer function of the state called *termination function* which represents an upper bound of the number of iterations still to be performed. Each iteration must strictly decrease the value of the termination function. In this example, termination is characterized by the variant $(j = n)$ and j is initially set to 0, so a possible termination function is $f(s, j, n) = n\text{-}j$. Since n is fixed, a natural way to decrease the value of f is to increment j. An obvious choice is $j := j+1$ but this would invalidate the invariant; in order to reestablish it $t[j]$ has to be added to s.

Finally the resulting program is:

$$j := 0;\ s := 0;$$
$$\textbf{while } j \ne n \textbf{ do } j := j + 1;\ s := s + t[j]\ \textbf{od}$$

This development process can be seen as a rigorous transformation from the specification to the program itself. As soon as the program has been successfully derived, no more correctness proof is necessary: in fact the program and the proof have been developed simultaneously. One can also realize that, in general, there are several decompositions of the specification into (invariant, variant) and that each decomposition can possibly lead to a different solution.

1.5.2 Program development in a functional language

We consider now the program development process in the context of functional languages.

1.5.2.1 About functional languages

Functional programs are built from functions which may be applied to arguments. Functions operate on general data structures such as lists or sequences. They may be combined in order to form powerful expressions; they may also be recursive and inductive proofs are often used in order to establish their properties. These are the only elements that are necessary to understand this short section about functional program development; they will be discussed in more detail in chapter 2.

1.5.2.2 How can we develop functional programs from specifications?

Starting from a specification, we want to derive a functional program satisfying it. The idea is to develop functional programs using reasoning based on inductive proof techniques. Let us take a simple example developed in [Bird et al. 88]:

We want to find a function *init* which, applied to a non-empty sequence of n elements, delivers the first n-1 elements of this sequence. Assuming the following specification S of *init*:

$$S = (init\ xs = take\ (\#xs - 1)\ xs)$$

where $\#l$ represents the length of l, and *take* is a predefined function taking two arguments, an integer n and a sequence l, and delivering the first n elements of l or all the elements of l if $n > \#l$. The program development technique is based on appropriate instantiation of xs.

First case: xs contains only one element, so $xs = [x]$.
  The specification S can be instantiated as:

$$init\ [x] = take\ (\#[x] - 1)\ [x]$$
$$= []$$

Second case: The argument sequence is of the form $(x : x': xs)$, so it contains at least two
  elements x and x'. We assume as inductive hypothesis that S applies for $x': xs$.
  The specification S can be instantiated as:

$$init\ (x : x': xs) = take\ (\#(x : x': xs) - 1)\ (x : x': xs)$$
$$= take\ (\#xs + 1)\ (x : x': xs)$$
$$= x : take\ (\#xs)\ (x': xs)$$

$$= x: take \ (\#(x': xs) - 1) \ (x': xs)$$
$$= x: init \ (x': xs) \qquad\qquad \text{by inductive hypothesis}$$

Finally, we get the following program for *init*:

$$init \ [x] = []$$
$$init \ (x: x': xs) = x: init \ (x': xs)$$

Note that the derived program is expressed in the same formalism as the specification. This is an important point, and is the principal difference from the derivation of conventional programs.

1.6 TOWARDS A FUNCTIONAL PROGRAMMING ENVIRONMENT

There are a number of questions that the two previous sections have left open and which have to be answered for any realistic programming environment. The three major questions concern languages: What is the *specification* language? What is the *programming* language? What is the *program development method*?

1.6.1 The choice of a language

From the above section on program development one may realize that conventional languages suffer from two major shortcomings:
- they cannot be directly used as specification languages, because of their imperative view of the world,
- there are not recognized methods for program transformation which can easily be proven correct. The example of the CEDAR system is clear in this respect: there are many useful facilities, but there is no tool to check program correctness or to perform program transformation.

An interesting aspect of functional languages is that they enjoy useful mathematical properties which make them attractive as *specification* languages, but also they may be used efficiently as *programming* languages. Furthermore there exist well-known transformation techniques which may be used readily in the refinement process.

Assuming a *single functional language* used for specification and programming, what kind of tools should a programming environment provide in order to make the programmer's task easier? It is clear that this environment should include tools facilitating program refinement.

This means that the major results of transformational "technology" have to be included. It is necessary to offer the user a set of tools which allow him to interact easily with the transformation process. The question arises about the degree of automation that ought to be implemented in the transformation process; it is clearly not possible to automate a wide range of transformations at present, however it is also clear that, if some transformations are automated, then some additional effort from the program developer may increase the effective power of the system.

Along the same lines, as suggested in [Darlington et al. 89], it would be necessary to allow the user to manipulate transformations as special objects: a *transformation* would be a function from *programs* to *programs*.

1.6.2 Current research on functional programming environments

Some research projects are presently developing methods and tools for functional program development. We have already mentioned [Darlington et al. 89], which aims, under the Alvey project Flagship, to design and develop a functional programming environment and has led to the development of a range of transformation techniques for functional programming.

An ambitious project, named *ToolUse*, supported by ESPRIT, aims at a formal description of the derivation process and a partial automation of this process. The basis of the program derivation technique is still transformation and refinement [Jähnichen et al. 86]. The approach is based on the application of inference rules; design decisions are expressed as deduction rules, objects can be methods, strategies, specifications, programs... Interesting results have already been produced concerning the formalization of the program development process [Sintzoff 87].

Another project, PROSPECTRA [Krieg-Brückner 89] aims at developing programs by specification and transformation. Specifications are given in an algebraic form and are refined towards a program by appropriate transformation steps. The project also tackles the problem of meta-program development, that is the application of algebraic specification and functionals to the definition of program transformation tactics. This amounts to the formalization of the program development process itself.

The CENTAUR system [Borras et al. 89] can be seen as a meta-programming environment. It is intended to produce a specific language-dependent environment from the description of the syntax and semantics of this language. This environment contains a set of tools such as an interpreter, a debugger, an editor, etc. In CENTAUR, a kernel supports symbolic manipulation of structured objects; there is an abstract machine that handles tree structures and a logical machine that handles semantic aspects. A specification level provides tools for the formal description of the syntax and the semantics of programming languages.

The concrete syntax of the language is described in Backus-normal form as usual. This syntax is used to generate the lexical analyser and the parser. The abstract syntax is concerned with the tree representation of the program. Semantic actions are described using this abstract tree. Concrete and abstract syntax and their relationship are described in a formalism called METAL [Kahn et al. 87], developed for the MENTOR system [Donzeau-Gouge et al. 84]. A METAL specification is a set of grammatical rules, with annotations specifying the abstract trees to be generated. Finally, in order to produce a language-specific programming environment, it is necessary to introduce a description of the language semantics. This is achieved with the language TYPOL [Despeyroux 88].

1.7 OVERVIEW OF THE BOOK

The thesis of this book is that the functional paradigm could form the basis of a broad spectrum language which could be used in all stages of the software development process.

How can this proposal be defended?
- the notion of function is very general and simple, and is widely applicable;
- the semantics of functional languages are essentially quite simple;
- there can be a close relationship between the programming language and the specification language - if specifications are in the style of VDM or Z;
- there exist well-known powerful transformation techniques which can be readily applied.

So why don't people use functional languages? Several reasons are usually put forward; let us mention some of them:
- the efficiency problem: functional languages have a bad reputation concerning efficiency. We observe that, due to technological progress, efficiency is not so critical as it used to be and most likely it will not be a problem any more in the near future;
- the input/output problem: a possible answer to this criticism is described in chapter 7 where it is shown that conventional applications such as operating systems may well be programmed in a functional style.

Chapter 2 describes the main characteristics of functional languages and illustrates them with two widespread languages: LISP [McCarthy 60] and ML [Wikström 87]. Chapter 3 introduces the abstract interpretation technique which may be used for program analysis, and as a means of improving the compilation process. Abstract interpretation is used in chapter 4 ato optimize memory management. Chapter 5 introduces program transformation techniques and applies them to program complexity evaluation. In particular, it describes the static evaluation of time and memory complexity of functional programs. A complexity evaluator which has been developed in ESPRIT 302 is also presented and its performance is analysed. Chapter 6 shows how the compilation process can be described completely by program transformation in the functional framework. Chapter 7 tackles the problem of input/output in functional languages and shows how the use of streams and lazy evaluation may lead to purely functional solutions. In the same vein, chapter 8 shows how history-sensitivity (a characteristic of imperative languages) can still be expressed within the functional framework. In conclusion, we defend the idea that functional programming is not unrealistic and that functional programming environments can be completely described in the functional framework.

REFERENCES

[Abrial et al. 79] J. R. Abrial, S. A. Schuman, B. Meyer. Specification language Z. Massachussetts Computer Associates Inc., 1979.

[ADA 83] The programming language ADA reference manual. LNCS 155, Springer Verlag, 1983.

[Backus 78] J. Backus. Can programming be liberated from the von Neumann style? A functional style and its algebra of programs. CACM Vol. 21, No. 8, pp. 613-614, August 1978.

[Bird et al. 88] R. Bird, P. Wadler. Introduction to functional programming. Prentice Hall International, Series in Computer Science, 1988.

[Borras et al. 88] P. Borras, D. Clement, T. Despeyroux, J. Incerpi, G. Kahn, B. Lang, V. Pascual. CENTAUR: the system. Proc. of ACM SIGSOFT'88: 3rd Symposium on Software Development Environments, November 1988.

[Darlington et al. 89] J. Darlington, P. Harrison, H. Khoshnevisan, L. McLoughlin, N. Perry, H. Pull, M. Reeve, K. Sephton, L. While, S. Wright. A functional programming environment supporting execution, partial execution and transformation. Proc. PARLE 1989, LNCS 365, Springer Verlag, pp. 286-305, 1989.

[Despeyroux 88] T. Despeyroux. TYPOL: a formalism to implement natural semantics. In Manual for the version 0.5 of CENTAUR. INRIA Sophia Antipolis report, February 1988.

[Donzeau-Gouge et al. 84] V. Donzeau-Gouge, G. Kahn, G. Huet, B. Lang, J.-J. Levy. Programming environments based on structured editors: the MENTOR experience. In Interactive Programming Environments. D. R. Barstow, H. E. Strobe and E. Sandewall (Eds.), McGraw-Hill, 1984.

[Futatsugi et al. 85] K. Futatsugi, J. A. Goguen, J.-P. Jouannaud, J. Messeguer. Principles of OBJ2. Proc. of the 12th ACM Symposium on Principles of Programming Languages, pp. 52-66, 1985.

[Gries 81] D. Gries. The Science of programming. Springer Verlag, 1981.

[Hoare 74] C.A.R. Hoare. Monitors: an operating system structuring concept. CACM Vol. 17, No. 10, pp. 549-557, October 1974.

[Jähnichen et al. 86] S. Jähnichen, F. Ali Hussain, M. Weber. Program development by transformation and refinement. Proc. of Int. Workshop on Advanced Programming Environments. LNCS 244, Springer Verlag, pp. 471-486, 1986.

[Jones 86] C. B. Jones. Systematic program development using VDM. Prentice Hall International, Series in Computer Science, 1986.

[Kahn 87 et al.] G. Kahn, B. Lang, B. Melèse. METAL: a formalism to specify formalisms. Science of Computer Programming, Vol. 3, North Holland, pp. 151-188, 1983.

[Krieg-Brückner 89] B. Krieg-Brückner. Algebraic specification and functionals for transformational program and meta program development. Proc. of TAPSOFT'89, LNCS 352, Springer Verlag, pp. 36-59, 1989.

[McCarthy 60] J. McCarthy. Recursive Functions of Symbolic Expressions and their Computation by Machine. CACM Vol. 3, pp. 184-195, April 1960.

[Morgan et al. 84] C. C. Morgan, B. A. Sufrin. Specification of the UNIX file system. IEEE Trans. on Software Engineering, Vol. 10, No. 2, pp. 128-142, 1984.

[Redell et al. 80] D. Redell, Y. Dalal, T. Horsley, H. Lauer, W. Lynch, P. McJones, H. Murray, S. Purcell. Pilot: an operating system for a personal computer. CACM Vol. 23, No. 2, February 1980.

[Sintzoff 87] M. Sintzoff. Expressing program developments in a design calculus. In Logic of Programming and Calculi of Discrete Design. M. Broy (Ed.), NATO ASI Series, Vol. F36, Springer Verlag, pp. 343-365, 1987.

[Spivey 89] Spivey J.M. The Z notation: a reference manual. Prentice Hall International, Series in Computer Science, 1989.

[Sufrin 82] B. Sufrin. Formal specification of a display-oriented text editor. Science of Computer Programming, Vol. 1, North Holland, 1982.

[Swinehart et al. 86] D. Swinehart, P. Zellweger, R. Beach, R. Hagmann. A structural view of the Cedar programming environment. ACM TOPLAS Vol. 8, No. 4, pp. 419-490, October 1986.

[Wikström 87] A. Wikström. Functional programming using standard ML. Prentice Hall International, Series in Computer Science, 1987.

CHAPTER 2

ASPECTS OF FUNCTIONAL PROGRAMMING

Jean-Pierre Banâtre

2.1 INTRODUCTION

A functional program consists of a set of function definitions which may be eventually evaluated by a computer. Given a problem, the task of a programmer is to build the function which solves this problem, that is a rule relating the input of the program to the output. This function may be a combination of primitive or user-defined functions. Functional languages are widely appreciated for their semantic simplicity and their power of expression. However, they have long been regarded as highly inefficient (in execution time) and their use has been limited to academic circles. Quite recently, advances in hardware design, as well as progress in functional program evaluation techniques, make it look as if functional programming may become a widely used style of programming. Furthermore, a lot of new application fields, often related to artificial intelligence, require new programming tools possessing facilities similar to those offered by functional programming. This chapter is a brief survey of the properties of functional languages: after a presentation of the main characteristics of functional languages, we describe two widespread languages, LISP and ML. Then we give some insight into the usual implementation techniques and elaborate on the major advantages of a functional programming style. Finally, the reference language used throughout this book is given in the concluding section.

2.2 THE MAIN CHARACTERISTICS OF FUNCTIONAL LANGUAGES

Functional languages are generally characterized by four main properties:

- the absence of explicit sequencing,
- the absence of the assignment statement,
- referential transparency,
- the prominent role of functions.

This section details these four characteristics and particularly emphasizes the notion of function which constitutes the basic building block of functional programs.

2.2.1 Absence of explicit sequencing

As opposed to imperative languages where the control is entirely described with primitive commands such as **goto** or **exit** or with more elaborate commands such as conditionals or loops, functional languages do not provide tools for the description of control. The execution order is determined by the implementation according to such criteria as correctness or efficiency. Let us consider for example the expression:

$g(x)= +(u(x), v(x))$

where + is the ordinary addition operator and u and v are integer functions. The unique constraint to be respected while evaluating the expression $g(n)$ is that $u(n)$ and $v(n)$ must be evaluated before applying +. Several evaluation orders may be chosen, for example:

- first $u(n)$, then $v(n)$, and finally +,
- first $v(n)$, then $u(n)$, and finally +,
- first a simultaneous evaluation of $u(n)$ and $v(n)$ and finally evaluation of +.

A few imperative languages, such as Algol 68, allow the programmer to specify that expressions are independent and thus that the order of evaluation has to be chosen by the implementation. However caution has to be taken in order to avoid side-effects, which amounts to adopting a functional style of programming.

2.2.2 Absence of the assignment statement

The notion of "variable" is strongly connected to the loop control structure. As there is no control structure in the functional world, there is no reason for the existence of the notion of variable. As a consequence, there are no side-effects in functional programs.

2.2.3   Referential transparency

A system is said to be referentially transparent if the entire meaning of an expression can be stated as a function from the environment to a value; in other words, if the only effect of an expression is to return a result. One of the most important consequences of this is that in a referentially transparent system, two syntactically identical expressions always have identical values. For example, the expression $= (f(x), f(x))$ can safely be replaced by *true* in a referentially transparent system. This replacement would not always be valid in an imperative language as function f could use and modify global variables. In the imperative world the meaning of an expression depends on, and can modify, the history of the computation; in the functional world, it does not.

2.2.4   Functions: the essence of functional programming

The most important type of object in the functional world is the *function*. In mathematical terms, a function is a rule of correspondence between members of one set (the domain set) to those of another set (the range set). For example, the function *double* maps members of the integer set to the same set. A function definition specifies the domain, the range and the correspondence rule for the function. In mathematical texts, it is usual to find a sentence such as "consider the function $f(x)$", when what is really meant is "the function f". In such texts, functions are never considered as values and there is no confusion between the function and its application to an argument. This is not the case in the functional programming world. Functions are values and have the same status as other values such as integers, reals, etc. In particular, they can be passed as arguments and returned as results. So, we have to be careful to avoid a confusion between a function value and its application to an argument.

2.2.4.1 Function definition

The expression $\lambda x.x+x$ denotes a function value which accepts an argument called x and yields a value which is the double of the value of this argument. Expressions of this sort are usually called *lambda-abstractions* [Church 41]. Such a function may be applied to an argument, for example, the expression $((\lambda x.x+x)\ 3)$ returns 6.

2.2.4.2 Programming with functions

Now that we know how we can build function values, we may want to give them a name. This is for two reasons:

(1) to simplify the texts of programs, as the whole text of a function will be given a name which will then be used in place of this text,

(2) to be able to define recursive functions.

It is possible to define a function *double* as *double* = $\lambda x.x+x$ and apply this function as follows: *double* (3).

Let us now try to define the factorial function applicable to an integer n and returning as result the integer $n!$. The mathematical definition of this function is:

$$0! = 1$$
$$n! = n \times (n-1)!$$

We would like to write this nice definition in a functional style. This implies the possibility of defining the factorial function in terms of itself. This is possible thanks to the above naming facility:

$$factorial = \lambda n.\ \textbf{if}\ n = 0\ \textbf{then}\ 1\ \textbf{else}\ n \times factorial(n-1)$$

The application of factorial to the argument 2 results in the following computation:

$$
\begin{aligned}
factorial(2) &= (\lambda n.\ \textbf{if}\ n = 0\ \textbf{then}\ 1\ \textbf{else}\ n \times factorial(n-1))(2) \\
&= 2 \times factorial(1) \\
&= 2 \times (\lambda n.\ \textbf{if}\ n = 0\ \textbf{then}\ 1\ \textbf{else}\ n \times factorial(n-1))(1) \\
&= 2 \times 1 \times factorial(0) \\
&= 2 \times 1 \times (\lambda n.\ \textbf{if}\ n = 0\ \textbf{then}\ 1\ \textbf{else}\ n \times factorial(n-1))(0) \\
&= 2 \times 1 \times 1 \\
&= 2
\end{aligned}
$$

2.2.4.3 Higher order functions

Let us now introduce higher order functions which are functions taking functions as arguments or returning them as results. In order to simplify our presentation, we introduce the sequence data structure which allows us to define collections of items. These items may be either atoms or sequences. For example:

A B C 10 105 *LAPHROAIG* are atoms,

[*A*, *B*, *C*] [*A*, [*B*, 5], *C*] are sequences,

[] is a special atom called the empty sequence.

Three functions are necessary in order to handle sequences:

- the *construction* function which can be defined as:

$$cons(x, [y_1, ..., y_n]) = [x, y_1, ..., y_n]$$

- the *head* function which can be defined as:

$$head([x, y_1, ..., y_n]) = x$$

- the *tail* function which can be defined as:

$$tail([x, y_1, ..., y_n]) = [y_1, ..., y_n]$$

We can define a general purpose function, called *map*, which takes a sequence *s* and a function *f* as arguments and returns a sequence whose elements result from the application of *f* to the elements of *s*. It can be defined as follows:

$$map = \lambda(f, s). \text{ if } s = [] \text{ then } [] \text{ else } cons(f(head(s)), map(f, tail(s)))$$

Consider the sequence *s* = [7, 2, 9, 18], the application *map(double, s)* results in a sequence [*double*(7), *double*(2), *double*(9), *double*(18)] = [14, 4, 18, 36].

Another well-known function is the *reduce* function which can be defined as:

$$reduce = \lambda(f, i, s). \text{ if } s = [] \text{ then } i \text{ else } f(head(s), reduce(f, i, tail(s)))$$

This function may be used as follows: consider the sequence *s* = [7, 2, 9, 18] and the function *sum* = $\lambda(x, y). x+y$, the expression *reduce(sum, 0, s)* produces the sum of the elements of *s*.

Finally we show how a function value may be produced as the result of a function application. The most well-known function of this kind is the composition function which takes two function arguments, *f* and *g*, and produces as its result the function which is the mathematical composition of its arguments (*f* o *g*). This function may be defined as follows:

$$comp = \lambda(f, g). (\lambda x. f(g(x)))$$

Thus the application *comp(double, double)* results in the function $\lambda x.\ double(double(x))$ and *comp(double, double)*(3) applies $\lambda x.\ double(double(x))$ to the argument 3 and returns 12.

2.2.4.4 Is it possible to express imperative control structures in functional terms?

Let us see how the function concept may be used in order to model the control structures usually found in imperative languages.

The most well-known imperative control structure is the loop structure. It can be expressed simply with recursion. The usual loop takes the following form:

while *b* **do** *s* **od**

It can be translated as follows:

while = $\lambda(b, s, v)$. **if** $b(v)$ **then** *while(b, s, s(v))* **else** v

where *b* is a boolean function, *s* the function representing the body of the loop and *v* the value of all the state variables involved in the loop.

One may also notice that the sequence of states computed by the **while** is represented here by the sequence of *v* arguments of the successive calls. Consider the following loop:

var integer *x* **init** 0;
while $x < 20$ **do** $x := x+1$ **od**

It will be translated into:

lessthan20 = $\lambda x.\ x < 20$
inc1 = $\lambda x.\ x+1$
while(lessthan20, inc1, 0)

This last call results into a succession of recursive calls taking as third argument successively 0, *inc1*(0), *inc1(inc1*(0)), ..., which is the sequence of values taken by the variable *x* in the original imperative program.

2.2.4.5 Continuations

A continuation is a function ψ which is passed as parameter to another function φ and which is intended to be applied after completion of φ. For example, consider the following function:

$$f = \lambda\,(x, y, g).\ g(x+y)$$

This function may be called as follows:

$$f(a, b, \lambda x.f(x, c, \lambda y.y))$$

This call is interpreted as:

$$(\lambda x.f(x, c, \lambda y.y))(a+b) = f(a+b, c, \lambda y.y)$$
$$= (\lambda y.y)((a+b)+c)$$
$$= a+b+c$$

Functions $\lambda x.f(x, c, \lambda y.y)$ and $(\lambda y.y)$ are continuations. Initially continuations were introduced to give formal mathematical semantics for imperative programming language control structures such as **goto** [Schmidt 86] rather than as a programming language tool. However, continuations may also be used as a programming tool although their use may appear as tricky in some situations.

Consider for example this version of the *factorial* function:

$$fact = \lambda(n, c).\ \text{if } n = 0 \text{ then } c(1) \text{ else } fact\ (n\text{-}1, \lambda x.\ c(n \times x))$$

In order to better understand the behaviour of this function, let us detail the computation of *fact* (3, c):

$fact\ (3, c) = \text{if } 3 = 0 \text{ then } c(1) \text{ else } fact\ (2, \lambda x.\ c(3 \times x))$
$\quad = fact\ (2, \lambda x.\ c(3 \times x))$
$\quad = \text{if } 2 = 0 \text{ then } (\lambda x.\ c(3 \times x))\ 1 \text{ else } fact\ (1, \lambda y.\ (\lambda x.\ c(3 \times x))\ (2 \times y))$
$\quad = fact\ (1, \lambda y.\ (\lambda x.\ c(3 \times x))\ (2 \times y))$
$\quad = \text{if } 1 = 0$
$\qquad \text{then } (\lambda y.\ (\lambda x.\ c(3 \times x))\ (2 \times y))\ 1$
$\qquad \text{else } fact\ (0, \lambda z.\ (\lambda y.\ (\lambda x.\ c(3 \times x))(2 \times y))(1 \times z))$
$\quad = fact\ (0, \lambda z.\ (\lambda y.\ (\lambda x.\ c(3 \times x))\ (2 \times y))\ (1 \times z))$
$\quad = \text{if } 0 = 0 \text{ then } (\lambda z.\ (\lambda y.\ (\lambda x.\ c(3 \times x))\ (2 \times y))\ (1 \times z\ ))\ (1)\ \text{else } ...$

$$= (\lambda z. \,(\lambda y. \,(\lambda x. \,c(3 \times x)) \,(2 \times y)) \,(1 \times z)) \,(1)$$
$$= (\lambda y. \,(\lambda x. \,c(3 \times x)) \,(2 \times y)) \,(1 \times 1)$$
$$\cdots$$
$$= c(3 \times (2 \times (1 \times 1)))$$
$$= c(6)$$

If the function c is the identity function $\lambda x.x$, then the function *fact* is the usual *factorial* function. However, c may be any other function such as $\lambda x. \,square \,(x)$, and in this case the call *fact* $(3, \,c)$ delivers the square of 3!.

2.3 PRESENTATION OF TWO WIDESPREAD FUNCTIONAL LANGUAGES

The very first functional programming language was really invented by Alonzo Church in the 1930's through his lambda calculus [Church 41]. However, at this time there was no computer to run this formalism. The advent of electronic computers initiated the development of a long series of programming languages, most of them belonging to the imperative world, for example Fortran, Cobol, the Algol family, Pascal, ADA. Nevertheless, several functional languages appeared during the same period, the most famous one being LISP (a contemporary of Fortran) that we shall present later in this section. The driving force behind the development of these languages was their conceptual simplicity and their tractable mathematical semantics. Later, progress in the field of programming in general led functional language designers to incorporate new powerful capabilities in these languages, the most important one being the notion of strong polymorphic typing. An example of a strongly typed language is ML, which we shall briefly describe later. LISP and ML are representative of two cultures in the functional programming world: untyped and typed functional languages; let us briefly summarize them.

2.3.1 LISP

LISP (for LISt Processing) was introduced by John McCarthy in 1960 [McCarthy 60]. This original LISP is completely functional, as it does not contain any imperative features, and as such is often referred to as *pure LISP*. Let us describe the major features of LISP.

2.3.1.1 Data structuring facilities

LISP objects are symbolic expressions that are either atoms or lists. An atom is a string of characters (letters, digits or other special symbols). Here are some examples of LISP atoms:

A
178
LSP
MACCALLAN

Lists are sequences of atoms or lists, separated by spaces and bracketed by parentheses. Here are some examples of lists:

(IL FAIT BEAU EN BRETAGNE)
(1 (2 3 4) 17 68 3)

There exists a special list, the empty list, represented as ( ) or as *NIL*.
A LISP program is itself represented as a list. For example, the list *(MULT X Y)* represents a call to the function *MULT* with two arguments *X* and *Y*.

2.3.1.2 Functions

LISP offers a few primitive functions from which it is possible to construct new functions. Let us describe these primitive functions: *QUOTE* is the identity function. It returns its single argument. In some ways, the *QUOTE* function allows its argument to be treated as a constant. Here are some examples using the *QUOTE* function:

(QUOTE X) which evaluates to *X*,
(QUOTE (A B C)) which evaluates to *(A B C)*.

The most common functions are those dealing with lists. The *CONS* function is the list constructor; it appends a new element in front of a list. For example:

(CONS (QUOTE (A B C))(QUOTE (X Y Z))) evaluates to *((A B C) X Y Z)*.

Two functions are provided in order to extract information from lists. The function *CAR* returns the first element of a list and the function *CDR* returns all the elements except the first. For example:

(CAR (QUOTE (X Y Z))) evaluates to *X*,

(CDR (QUOTE (X Y Z))) evaluates to *(Y Z)*.

Some predicates are also available. The value true is represented by the atom *T* and the value false by *NIL*. The function *ATOM* returns *T* if its argument is an atom and *NIL* otherwise. The function *EQ* compares its two atom arguments and returns *T* if they are equal and *NIL* otherwise. The function *NULL* returns *T* if its argument is *NIL* and *NIL* otherwise. The function *COND* takes a set of pairs (predicate expression) and returns as its result the expression in the first pair (from left to right) with its predicate true. Here are some examples:

(ATOM (QUOTE A)) evaluates to *T*,
(ATOM (QUOTE (X Y))) evaluates to *NIL*,
(EQ (QUOTE X)(QUOTE X)) evaluates to *T*,
(EQ (QUOTE X)(QUOTE Y)) evaluates to *NIL*,
(COND ((EQ (QUOTE X)(QUOTE Y))(QUOTE A))(T (QUOTE B)))
     evaluates to *B*.

The last important point concerns the definition of functions; it is based on lambda expressions as in the lambda-calculus. For example, the function $\lambda(x, y).\ x \times y$ is rewritten as follows in LISP notation:

(LAMBDA (X Y)(MULT X Y))

and this function may be applied in an expression such as:

((LAMBDA (X Y)(MULT X Y)) 4 5) which evaluates to 20.

Such a lambda expression is anonymous and using it may become awkward. So LISP offers the possibility of naming a function by using the pseudo-function *DEFINE*. Furthermore, the ability to name a function is absolutely necessary for defining recursive functions. For example:

(DEFINE (REVERSE (LAMBDA (L)(REV NIL L))))
(DEFINE (REV (LAMBDA (X Y)
    (COND ((NULL Y) X) (T (REV (CONS (CAR Y) X) (CDR Y))))))))

As a conclusion, in pure LISP functions are first class citizens; they may be defined, applied and passed as arguments. There are no traditional variables and no assignment. LISP variables are identifiers which can be bound to a value and retain this value throughout their lifetime.

2.3.2 ML

The name ML stands for Meta Language because ML was originally designed as the command language in the LCF system, a system for proving properties in a theory of programs called PPλ [Gordon et al. 79]. ML is a strongly typed and polymorphic functional language. A ML program is a sequence of expressions containing definitions of variables (in the LISP sense) and function applications. In this section, we use the notation of [Wikström 87].

2.3.2.1 Data structuring facilities

Basic objects are integers, reals, booleans and characters. One way of combining objects to form new ones is by grouping them into pairs, triples, quadruples, etc. For example, (3, "e") and (17.5, "r") are pair values. Functions allowing the selection of elements of a tuple will be defined later.

Another way of grouping elements together is by using lists. A list is an homogeneous sequence. This means that all elements of a list possess the same type. For example [1,2,3,4] is a list of integers and ["e","r","s"] is a list of characters. List construction and selection operations are presented later.

2.3.2.2 Functions

It is possible to define functions using the **fn** construct. For example (**fn** $x \Rightarrow x+2$) is equivalent to the usual lambda-expression $\lambda x.\ x+2$. It may be applied directly to an argument in the following way: (**fn** $x \Rightarrow x+2$) 3 which evaluates to 5. Of course it is possible to name functions, this is done with the **fun** construct:

fun *plus*1 $x = x + 1$

This function could have been written in another way:

val *plus*1 $=$ **fn** $x \Rightarrow x + 1$

This function may now be applied, for example:

*plus*1 (5)

Functions may also take several arguments, for example let us define the multiplication function as follows:

fun *mult* (*x*: *int*) (*y*: *int*) = $x \times y$

Here we have given the types of the two arguments of mult; ML deduces that the result is also an integer. Now, we may apply this function as follows:

mult 4 5

which is interpreted in the following way: *mult* takes an argument 4 of type integer and produces as result a function (*mult* 4) which takes one argument of type integer and produces a result of type integer. This device whereby any function of two or more arguments is treated as a higher-order function is called "currying", after the logician H. B. Curry. Actually, the following expression is perfectly valid:

val *mult4* = *mult* 4

thus making clear that *mult4* is a function in its own right.

It is also possible to define functions by cases. Let us for example define the logical implication:

fun *implies*   (*true, true*) = *true*
     | *implies* (*true, false*) = *false*
     | *implies* (*false, true*) = *true*
     | *implies* (*false, false*) = *true*

We enumerate all possible pairs and for each one we give the result of the implication. Finally let us define in ML two well-known recursive functions, *factorial* and *ackermann*:

fun *fact* 0 =   1
     | *fact n* = $n \times fact(n\text{-}1)$

and

fun *ackermann* 0 *m* = *m*+1
     | *ackermann n* 0 = *ackermann* (*n*-1) 1
     | *ackermann m n* = *ackermann* (*m*-1) (*ackermann m* (*n*-1))

2.3.2.3 Polymorphic strong typing

ML is a strongly typed language. This means that every expression and subexpression possesses a type, which can be either explicit or deduced by the compiler. Any inconsistency in the type structure of an expression results in a compile-time error.

The four primitive types are *int, real, bool* and *char*. The type construction can be summarized as follows:

- if *t* is a type, then *t list* is the type of the list whose elements are of type *t*.
- if t_1, ..., t_n are types, then $t_1 \times ... \times t_n$ is the type of a *tuple* with objects of those types as components.
- if t_1 and t_2 are types, then $t_1 \rightarrow t_2$ is the type of a function with argument of type t_1 and result of type t_2.

Here are the types of functions presented in the above section:

> *plus*1: (*int -> int*)
> *mult* : (*int -> int -> int*)
> *mult*4 : (*int -> int*)
> *implies* : ((*bool* × *bool*) -> *bool*)
> *fact* : (*int -> int*)
> *ack* : (*int -> int -> int*)

It is possible, in ML, to use types involving variables (usually called polymorphic types) which can be instantiated to different types. Consider for example, the projection functions *first* and *second* delivering respectively the first and second element of a pair; they can be defined as follows:

> **fun** *first* (*x, y*) = *x*
>   **val** *first* = *fn* : '*a* ×'*b* -> '*a*
> **fun** *second* (*x, y*) = *y*
>   **val** *second* = *fn* : '*a* ×'*b* -> '*b*

The text starting with **val** is output by the ML evaluator; only the type of a functional value is printed. The symbols '*a* and'*b* represent generic type variables: one can think of *first* and *second* as having many types obtained by substituting arbitrary types for '*a* and '*b*. For example, the following expressions are acceptable:

> *first* (2, *true*) which produces the result:
>   2 : *int*

or   *second (2, true)* which produces:

        true : bool

As a conclusion on this topic, let us give the composition function which takes two functions *f* and *g* as arguments and produces a new one behaving as *f* o *g*.

     fun *comp (f, g) x = f(g(x))*
        val *comp* = *fn*: $((('a \rightarrow 'c) \times ('b \rightarrow 'a)) \rightarrow 'b \rightarrow 'c)$

The user may also introduce his own types. New types are defined by giving a set of value constructors that can be used to build objects of that type, for example:

     datatype *suit = Heart* | *Diamond* | *Club* | *Spade*

It is also possible to define abstract data types whose implementation details are hidden from the rest of the program. Such abstract data types become important in building large programs which may evolve over time. We do not discuss this aspect here.

2.4 BRIEF SURVEY OF IMPLEMENTATION TECHNIQUES

In this section we are going to discuss two well-known approaches to the implementation of functional languages. It is not our intention to give an exhaustive presentation of the topic, we only want to give an insight into the most widely used implementation techniques.

2.4.1 The SECD machine

The SECD machine is an abstract machine architecture proposed by P. Landin in order to evaluate lambda-expressions [Landin 64]. It defines an operational semantics for the lambda-calculus and implements call-by-value and static binding. The SECD machine uses four stacks which are called the *Stack*, the *Environment*, the *Control* and the *Dump*. At any time, the state of the machine is represented by the values of these stacks:

- The *Stack* is used to store the partial results while evaluating an expression, and holds the final result of the execution.
- The *Environment* consists of a series of pairs (*identifier, value*) that give the values of the free variables of an expression.
- The *Control* stores the expression currently being evaluated.

- The *Dump* is used to store copies of the stacks while evaluating a subfunction.

The machine is described in terms of state transitions based on the form of the first element of the control store. The interested reader may refer to [Landin 64] for a comprehensive presentation of the SECD machine.

2.4.2 Graph reduction

A simple way of representing the structure of expression is a *graph*. The advantage of this representation is that an occurrence of a variable may be shared by several expressions, so when substitutions have to be performed, there is only one copy to be modified. Reductions usually consist of replacing a subgraph with a new graph containing pointers to parts of the old graph.

The evaluation mechanism has to be committed to some reduction strategy that prescribes a certain order in which reductions have to be carried out. Among the well-known strategies, let us mention *normal order reduction*, which always reduces the leftmost reducible expression (called a *redex*). This reduction strategy is similar to the *call-by-name* mechanism of conventional languages. Another well-known strategy is *applicative order reduction* which reduces the leftmost redex free of internal redexes. This strategy corresponds to the *call-by-value* mechanism of conventional languages. There are occasions when the arguments do not need to be evaluated as they will never be used and this may cause differences in the result depending on the reduction strategy which is used. In particular when the argument has no normal form and the reduced abstraction makes no use of it in its body, we have a situation where normal order reduction succeeds while applicative order fails. Thus when dealing with non-strict functions (which may not need all their arguments) it may be interesting to adopt a reduction strategy known as *lazy evaluation*, which has the property of delaying the evaluation of both the arguments of user-defined functions and the arguments to *cons* [Henderson et al. 76]. In fact, lazy evaluation is not really another strategy, it is *normal order reduction with update*, sometimes referred to as *call-by-need*.

2.5 WHY IS FUNCTIONAL PROGRAMMING RELEVANT?

Before entering the technical part of the document, we justify our choice of functional languages. In chapter 8, this matter is reexamined in the light of the material presented in this book.

2.5.1 Semantic simplicity

The purpose of defining the semantics of a language is to assign a meaning to any expression in the language. Two ways of defining the semantics of a function are operational semantics and denotational semantics. Operational semantics consist of defining the behaviour of the function as a sequence of execution steps operating on a global state. The SECD machine presented above can be considered as an operational semantics of a functional language. Denotational semantics is a method of specifying the meaning of programs in terms of mathematically defined functions acting on particular domains [Schmidt 86]. This semantics provides a static view of the programs: they are seen as fixed sets of associations between arguments and the corresponding results.

2.5.1.1 Semantics of functional languages

An expression is a syntactic object formed according to the syntax rules of the language. A denotational semantics of a functional language can be seen as a function (called **E**) from the set of expressions into the set of values that expressions may yield. Let us give the definition of **E** for a simple functional language, the lambda calculus. Several situations have to be considered, depending on the form of the expression:

(1) *The expression is a variable*
A variable cannot be interpreted without considering the environment in which it is defined. This environment can be modelled by a function (usually called ρ) which maps identifiers into their values. Thus the semantics of an expression consisting of a variable x can be expressed as:

$$\mathbf{E} \, [\![x]\!] \, \rho = \rho \, x$$

(2) *The expression is a lambda expression $\lambda x. \, e$*
The value of ($\lambda x. \, e$) is a function which can be defined by specifying its behaviour when applied to an argument. Actually, we have to formally rewrite the following informal rule: "The value of a lambda expression, applied to an argument y, is the value of the text of the lambda expression, in a context where the formal parameter is bound to y". This can be simply written as:

$$\mathbf{E} \, [\![\lambda x. \, e]\!] \, \rho \, y = \mathbf{E} \, [\![e]\!] \, (\rho \, [y \, / \, x])$$

where the notation $\rho\,[y\,/\,x]$ means that the function ρ is extended with the information that y is bound to x. We have the following properties: $(\rho\,[y\,/x])\,x = y$ and $(\rho\,[y\,/\,x])\,z = \rho\,z$, if z is a variable different from x.

(3) *The expression is a function application of the form* $e_1\,e_2$

We have to define $\mathbf{E}\,[\![e_1\,e_2]\!]\,\rho$. The simple way to proceed is to say that the value of the above expression is the value of e_1 applied to the value of e_2. More precisely:

$$\mathbf{E}\,[\![e_1\,e_2]\!]\,\rho = (\mathbf{E}\,[\![e_1]\!]\,\rho)\,(\,\mathbf{E}\,[\![e_2]\!]\,\rho)$$

(4) *The expression is a built-in function or a constant*

The problem here is to define the correspondence between lambda expressions and abstract mathematical objects used to define the semantics, for example consider the binary $\times$ operator:

$$\mathbf{E}\,[\![\times]\!]\,x\,y = \textit{multiply}(x, y)$$

where $\times$ is the primitive lambda calculus function for multiplication and *multiply* the usual mathematical multiplication operation.

This constitutes a simplified version of denotational semantics for the lambda calculus as we have not taken recursion into account. Stoy's book [Stoy 81] and Schmidt's book [Schmidt 86] on denotational semantics are highly recommended to interested readers.

2.5.1.2 Denotational semantics of a simple imperative language

We shall focus here on the translation rules allowing us to derive a function from an imperative program, this function being considered as the meaning of the program. Let us consider some elements of the syntax of a small imperative language:

$$C ::= C_1\,;\,C_2 \mid I := E$$
$$E ::= E_1 + E_2 \mid I \mid N$$

I stands for an identifier and N for an integer constant. An imperative language splits the world into a domain of commands (C) and a domain of expressions (E). The effect of a command is to modify an implicit data structure called the *store* which maps identifiers to values. So its semantics is given by a function from the domain of stores to itself:

Store = Identifiers -> D

C: *Command -> Store -> Store*

$$\text{C } [\![C_1 ; C_2]\!] = \lambda s. \text{ C } [\![C_2]\!] \text{ (C } [\![C_1]\!] \text{ s)} \qquad (1)$$

$$\text{C } [\![I := E]\!] = \lambda s. \text{ } (\lambda i. \text{ if } i = [\![I]\!] \text{ then (E } [\![E]\!] \text{ s) else } (s \text{ } i)) \qquad (2)$$

D is the domain of values. In (1), the argument *s* denotes a store which is first modified by C_1, then by C_2. In (2) the store is modified to take into account the new value associated with *I*. **E** is the semantic function for expressions; it can be defined in the same way as in section 2.5.1.1.

The application of these rules to the program $X := 4; X := 5$ yields:

$$\text{C } [\![X := 4; X := 5]\!] = \lambda s. \text{ } (\lambda i. \text{ if } i = [\![X]\!] \text{ then 5 else } (s \text{ } i))$$

We can already draw two conclusions from the small semantics presented here:
- the semantics of an imperative program is more complicated than the semantics of a functional program because it involves states and state modifications.
- the denotational semantics can be seen as a way of translating imperative programs into functional programs: the state is expressed as a function from identifiers to values and commands are functions from states to states.

Chapter 8 presents the denotational semantics of a more realistic imperative language and uses it to perform a detailed comparison of the imperative and the functional programming styles.

2.5.2 Correctness aspects

Even if the semantic simplicity of functional languages is attractive, this quality may not seem strong enough to convince the software engineer of the potential benefits of this style of programming. We show in this section that it is also easier to prove properties of programs in the functional framework.

Consider the definition of *length*, the usual function computing the length of a sequence:

length [ ] = 0

length (x:s) = 1 + *length* s

The ":" is another notation for the *cons* function which inserts a new first element in front of a list. The *length* function has some interesting properties, in particular it is well known that the length of the concatenation of two sequences l_1 and l_2 is the sum of the lengths of l_1 and l_2. Let us formulate and prove this property.

$$\forall s_1, s_2 \in \Sigma, \ length \ (concat \ (s_1, s_2)) = (length \ s_1) + (length \ s_2) \qquad (1)$$

where Σ is the domain of sequences and the function *concat* is recursively defined as:

$concat \ ([], xs) = xs$
$concat \ (x:xs, ys) = x:concat(xs, ys)$

The proof of property (1) uses the well-known induction principle on sequences. We perform induction on sequence s_1:

base step:

$$(length \ [\ ]) + (length \ s_2) = 0 + (length \ s_2) \qquad \text{definition of } length$$
$$= \ length \ s_2 \qquad \text{property of } +$$
$$= \ length \ (concat \ ([\ ], s_2)) \qquad \text{property of } concat$$

induction step:
induction hypothesis: $length(concat(s, s_2)) = length(s) + length(s_2)$

$$(length \ (x:s)) + (length \ s_2) = (1 + (length \ s)) + (length \ s_2) \qquad \text{definition of } length$$
$$= 1 + ((length \ s) + (length \ s_2)) \qquad \text{property of } +$$
$$= 1 + (length \ (concat \ (s, s_2))) \qquad \text{hypothesis}$$
$$= \ length \ (x: (concat \ (s, s_2))) \qquad \text{property of } length$$
$$= \ length \ (concat \ (x:s, s_2)) \qquad \text{property of } concat$$

This example suggests that it is easier to prove properties in the functional framework than in the imperative framework. The interested reader is encouraged to rewrite *length* and *concat* in an imperative style and to use classical methods such as Hoare's axiomatic approach [Hoare 69] to perform the proof. The important thing here is that proofs are carried out in the same language as the program on which they operate. On the other hand, in the imperative framework, it is necessary to introduce a new assertional language in order to prove programs; this, of course, adds more complexity and makes imperative program proving hard to achieve.

2.5.3 Program transformation

Chapter 5 contains a survey of program transformation techniques. Here, we only give an insight into the possibilities offered by transformation techniques in a functional framework. Let us take a simple example from [Henson 87] dealing with the *length* function.

Imagine that you have often to compute the total length of two lists l_1 and l_2. It could be interesting to write a special function for this purpose. This new function, called *length2*, possesses the following property:

$$length2 \; l_1 \; l_2 = (length \; l_1) + (length \; l_2)$$

Let us transform this property into a program form by specializing it to the cases $l_1 = [\;]$ and $l_1 = x:l$:

$$
\begin{aligned}
length2 \; [\;] \; l_2 &= (length \; [\;]) + (length \; l_2) \\
&= 0 + (length \; l_2) &&\text{as } length \; [\;] = 0 \\
&= length \; l_2 \\
length2 \; (x:l) \; l_2 &= length \; (x:l) + (length \; l_2) \\
&= (1 + (length \; l)) + (length \; l_2) &&\text{def. of } length \\
&= 1 + ((length \; l) + (length \; l_2)) &&\text{property of } + \\
&= 1 + (length2 \; l \; l_2) &&\text{property of } length2
\end{aligned}
$$

So:

$$
\begin{aligned}
length2 \; [\;] \; l_2 &= length \; l_2 \\
length2 \; (x:l) \; l_2 &= 1 + (length2 \; l \; l_2)
\end{aligned}
$$

Thus, by straightforward transformations we have obtained a new version of *length2*. This very simple example shows that program transformation may be used for program synthesis. It can also be used for several other purposes such as program analysis or the improvement of program efficiency. Chapter 5 contains a survey of program transformation techniques and applies them to the complexity analysis of functional programs; chapter 6 describes a method of compilation by program transformation.

2.6 THE REFERENCE LANGUAGE

We introduce now the source language that is used in the remainder of the book. Since some sections assume a first order language and others a higher order language, we present separately the two versions of the language. In both versions, programs are defined as collections of functions in the following way:

$$Prog::=\{f_1(x_{11},...,x_{1k1})=e_1$$
$$f_2(x_{21},...,x_{2k2})=e_2$$
$$...$$
$$f_n(x_{n1},...,x_{nkn})=e_n\}$$

We give now the syntax of expressions in the first order version of the language:

$e ::=$ x |	identifiers
k |	constants
$cond(e_1,e_2,e_3)$ |	conditional
$op^k(e_1,...,e_k)$	operator application
$f(e_1,...,e_n)$ |	function application

This syntax is extended in the following way for the higher order version of the language:

$e' ::= e$ |	
$e'(e'_1,...,e'_n)$ |	expression application
$\lambda(x_1,...,x_n).e'$	functional expression

The concrete syntax is very similar to this abstract syntax with the following exceptions:
  (1) the usual **if then else** notation is generally used instead of *cond*,
  (2) infix notation may be used for operators,
  (3) the expression (**let** $x = e_1$ **in** e_2) or (e_2 **where** $x = e_1$) may be used for $((\lambda x. e_2) e_1)$,
  (4) (**letrec** $f = e$) is a shorthand notation for $Y(\lambda f. e)$ where Y is a fixed point combinator.

Definition of the traditional functions *factorial* and *length* in this language are:

letrec *fact* = $\lambda x.$ *cond* (*eq* (0, *x*), 1, *mult* (*x* , *fact* (*sub* (*x*, 1))))
letrec *length* = $\lambda s.$ *cond* (*null* (*s*), 0, *add* (1, *length* (*tail* (*s*))))

REFERENCES

[Backus 78] J. Backus. Can programming be liberated from the von Neumann style? A functional style and its algebra of programs. CACM Vol. 21, No. 8, pp. 613-641, August 1978.

[Bird et al. 88] R. Bird, P. Wadler. Introduction to functional programming. Prentice Hall International, Series in Computer Science, 1988.

[Church 41] A. Church. The calculi of lambda conversion. Princeton University Press, 1941.

[Gordon et al. 79] M. J. Gordon, R. J. Milner, C. P. Wadsworth. Edinburgh LCF. LNCS 78, Springer Verlag, 1979.

[Henderson et al. 76] P. Henderson, J. H. Morris. A Lazy Evaluator. Proc. 3rd ACM Symposium on Principles of Programming Languages, pp. 95-103, 1976.

[Henson 87] M. C. Henson. Elements of functional programming. Blackwell Scientific Publications, 1987.

[Landin 64] P. Landin. The mechanical evaluation of expressions. The Computer Journal, Vol. 6, pp. 308-320, 1964.

[McCarthy 60] J. McCarthy. Recursive functions of symbolic expressions and their computation by machine. CACM Vol. 3, No. 4, pp. 184-195, April 1960.

[Schmidt 86] D. A. Schmidt. Denotational Semantics. Allyn and Bacon, 1986.

[Stoy 81] J. E. Stoy. Denotational semantics. MIT Press, 1981.

[Wikström 87] A. Wikström. Functional programming using standard ML. Prentice Hall International, Series in Computer Science, 1987.

CHAPTER 3

PROGRAM ANALYSIS BY ABSTRACT INTERPRETATION

Simon B. Jones

3.1 THE NEED FOR A METHOD OF PROGRAM ANALYSIS

In Chapters 1 and 2 we were introduced to the idea that functional programming languages form an excellent basis for a broad spectrum language which could be used in all stages of the software development process; benefits will be derived from the use of functional languages in the design and implementation of both the applications software and the program development environment itself.

One of the major benefits of functional languages is that programs are expressed at a high level of abstraction; this allows the software engineer to concentrate on the *primary* task of ensuring the *correctness* of programs. However, this is, at the same time, the root of a major problem: the run time *performance* characteristics of programs are far from evident from their source text (this is especially true if the functional program is to be executed using *lazy evaluation*). Thus a software engineer will find it difficult to be confident that programs produced are as efficient as required; and compilers have a difficult task generating efficient code. This problem is not unique to functional languages: imperative languages suffer from essentially the same problem, but to a lesser degree since they are closer to machine language and the mode of expression is not at such an abstract level.

Thus, in the context of professional software engineering, we may identify two major measures of software *quality*: correctness and performance. The former should clearly be the primary concern, but the latter cannot be dispensed with. We should regard an inefficient program as lacking in quality, and we should attempt to improve it in this respect.

It is not clear that it is the sole responsibility of either the software engineer or the compiler to ensure the efficiency of a program. It seems reasonable to adopt the point of view that the responsibility is a joint one, and so we should assume a hybrid approach to solving the efficiency problem: the software engineer needs tools in the programming environment to help in assessing the quality of programs and improving them where necessary, and compilers need sophisticated optimization techniques to improve run time performance of the code which they generate.

Functional languages suffer from three main sources of inefficiency:

- "good" programming style often encourages the use of functionally modularized code and many intermediate data structures; this improves the readability of a program, at the expense of run time efficiency if the program is executed literally;
- they generally need a heap storage management system; this is well known to be a considerable expense, since decisions must be taken at run time based on information gathered dynamically, and lengthy sweeps of the store may be performed occasionally which destroy real time response and predictability; this will clearly interact badly with the problem noted above;
- lazy evaluation may introduce run time overheads due to the construction of closures for delayed computations, and to repeated testing of values to determine whether or not they are closures that need forcing.

Various approaches to solving these problems are being investigated:

- program transformations can be applied to eliminate unnecessary functions, to specialize functions and hence to produce more optimal forms [Burstall et al. 75], and to eliminate the computation of unnecessary intermediate data structures [Wadler 88];
- the use that executing programs make of the store is being improved through more sophisticated basic implementation techniques, and through optimizations which avoid some of the expense of dynamic storage allocation and deallocation operations, for example see Chapter 4 and [Hudak 87, Jones et al. 89a];
- *strictness analysis* can be applied to (lazy) functions to determine whether or not their arguments can be evaluated safely *before* (or *in parallel with*) the function call without changing the outcome of the program, for example see [Mycroft 80, Wadler 87, Jones et al. 89b]; where this is found to be possible, a faster evaluation strategy such as call-by-value or parallel evaluation can be exploited.

Each of these methods is best supported by some form of *formal program analysis*, in order to place the judgements made and the improvements or optimizations carried out on a firm foundation; in this way we can truly refer to software *engineering*. Much of the formal analysis and program transformation which can be carried out is much easier (though still not trivial) if the programming language is a functional language, and this is one reason for choosing such a language for software engineering.

In this chapter we will examine the method of *abstract interpretation* [Cousot et al. 77, Abramsky et al. 87], which is a unifying basis for the program analysis techniques required in software engineering tools and compilers. Chapter 4 shows the application of abstract interpretation to the optimization of storage management.

Abstract interpretation is a formal mathematical method based on the formal semantics of programming languages. With careful application it can be automated, and thus be incorporated into software tools and compilers. Very roughly speaking: from a formal standard semantics of the language in which we are interested (concerned with the actual output from programs), we proceed to a formal non-standard semantics in which a program is interpreted as yielding as result some property of the actual output (other than, or in addition to, its value), or some property of the computation that would have led to that output. As an example of the former, in the next section we look at the arithmetic of odd and even numbers, in which a program is interpreted to determine how the parity (oddness or evenness) of its output is dependent on the parity of its input; as an example of the latter, in Chapter 4 we interpret programs so as to determine how the sharing of data structures arises during program execution.

3.2 THE BASIC PRINCIPLES OF ABSTRACT INTERPRETATION

It is common to illustrate the basic principles of abstract interpretation with the *rule of signs* learnt by children (at least implicitly). The rule of signs tells us how to determine the arithmetic sign of the result of a calculation from the signs of the operands: for example, "*positive* + *positive* gives *positive*", "*positive* × *negative* gives *negative*", "*negative* × *negative* gives *positive*", and so on. From these rules we can deduce general properties such as that "$x + x$ has the same sign as x", "$x \times x$ is always *positive*", and so on. However, analyses such as these are not perfect: note that "*positive* + *negative* may be either *positive* or *negative*"; hence the abstraction from numbers to signs has lost some information: our prediction of the result is sometimes inexact, but never incorrect (where *correct* means that the actual result is always amongst the predicted outcomes). A full treatment of the rule of signs may be found in [Burn 87].

In this chapter we will illustrate the basic principles of abstract interpretation by looking at how we may re-interpret arithmetic expressions over the integers as abstract computations involving only the *parity* of those integers: that is, the property of integers that we will be interested in is whether they are *even* or *odd*. We will not worry here about whether or not such information can be used in program optimization, but will concentrate simply on the principles involved.

3.2.1 Standard semantics

We consider a restricted version of the functional language introduced in Chapter 2, restricted to integer arithmetic and the operators +, ×, =. Note that subtraction of constants is still possible since we have negative integers. Here is an example function in this language:

$$square(x) = \textbf{if } x = 0 \textbf{ then } x \textbf{ else } square(x + (-1)) + (2 \times x) + (-1)$$

This computes the arithmetic square of any positive integer (including 0) by a rather indirect means, and is undefined (does not terminate) for negative integers. The function has the interesting property, proved below, that $square(x)$ has the same parity as x provided that the computation terminates.

We start from a standard, call-by-value, denotational semantics of the language:

Semantic domains:

$\quad Z = \{\bot\} \cup \{..., -1, 0, 1, ...\}$ Integers, with $\forall\ i \in Z: \bot \leq i$

$\qquad\qquad\qquad\qquad\qquad\qquad\qquad$ ($\bot$ is pronounced "undefined" or "bottom")

$\quad F = Z^* \rightarrow Z$ Functions from tuples of integers to integers

$\quad Fve = Fv \rightarrow F$ Function variable environments

$\quad Bve = Id \rightarrow Z$ Argument (bound) variable environments

Semantic functions:

$\quad \mathcal{P}. \ Prog \rightarrow Fve$

$\quad \mathcal{E}: Exp \rightarrow Fve \rightarrow Bve \rightarrow Z$

$\quad \mathcal{K}. \ Con \rightarrow Z$

$\mathcal{P}[\![\{f_i(x_1,...,x_n) = e_i\}]\!] = \textbf{letrec } fve = [strict(\lambda\ v_1 \ ... \ v_n. \ \mathcal{E}[\![e_i]\!] \ fve \ [v_j/x_j])/f_i]$

$\mathcal{E}[\![x]\!] \ fve \ bve = bve[\![x]\!]$

$\mathcal{E}[\![k]\!] \ fve \ bve = \mathcal{K}[\![k]\!]$

$\mathcal{E}[\![\textbf{if } e_1 \textbf{ then } e_2 \textbf{ else } e_3]\!] \ fve \ bve =$

$\qquad\qquad\qquad cond(\mathcal{E}[\![e_1]\!] \ fve \ bve, \ \mathcal{E}[\![e_2]\!] \ fve \ bve, \ \mathcal{E}[\![e_3]\!] \ fve \ bve)$

$\mathcal{E}[\![e_1 + e_2]\!] \ fve \ bve = \mathcal{E}[\![e_1]\!] \ fve \ bve + \mathcal{E}[\![e_2]\!] \ fve \ bve$

$\mathcal{E}[\![e_1 \times e_2]\!] \ fve \ bve = \mathcal{E}[\![e_1]\!] \ fve \ bve \times \mathcal{E}[\![e_2]\!] \ fve \ bve$

$\mathcal{E}[\![e_1 = e_2]\!] \ fve \ bve = (\mathcal{E}[\![e_1]\!] \ fve \ bve = \mathcal{E}[\![e_2]\!] \ fve \ bve)$

$\mathcal{E}[\![f(e_1,...,e_n)]\!] \ fve \ bve = (fve[\![f]\!])(\mathcal{E}[\![e_1]\!] \ fve \ bve,..., \mathcal{E}[\![e_n]\!] \ fve \ bve)$

On the right hand sides of the equations note the use of the ordinary arithmetic operators + and ×, comparison =, and the conditional operator *cond*. Since we only have integers as expressible values, we encode the logical values false and true as 0 and 1; thus = yields either 0 or 1 (or $\bot$ if either operand is $\bot$), and *cond* selects the first branch or the second depending on whether its first operand is 1 or 0 (or yields $\bot$ if the first operand is $\bot$). We assume the usual least fixed point interpretation for these recursive semantic equations; in particular for the meaning of a program, which is a self-referential function environment. Each function in a program is interpreted strictly (giving call-by-value); this is indicated in the first semantic equation.

3.2.2 Non-standard semantics and abstract interpretation

Now we need to consider abstracting the integer domain Z to just represent the odd and even properties of the integers. We wish to interpret expressions as yielding a value indicating the parity of the integer that would be computed by the concrete semantics in 3.2.1. Our aim is thus to define systematically modified versions, $\mathcal{P}^{oe}$ and $\mathcal{E}^{oe}$, of the semantic functions $\mathcal{P}$ and $\mathcal{E}$, which will yield results in a new domain Z^{oe} rather than in Z.

What kinds of results can expressions have? In the standard semantics each expression has a *concrete* value which is either undefined, even or odd. In the non-standard, or abstract, semantics we may not have full information about the values of free variables, and hence we may only be able to say that the value of an expression will be one of a particular set of values. There are four possibilities in the interpretation that we consider here:

- "the result is undefined"; for example: the value of *square*(−3)
- "the result is even or undefined"; for example: **if** $x = 0$ **then** 2 **else** *square*(−3)
- "the result is odd or undefined"; for example: **if** $x = 0$ **then** 3 **else** *square*(−3)
- "the result is even or odd or undefined"; for example:
  if $x = 0$ **then** 2 **else if** $y = 0$ **then** 3 **else** *square*(−3)

We do *not* include the additional possibilities "the result is even" and "the result is odd"; for example, the value of the expression 3+2 is "odd or undefined". This is explained below.

In our abstract domain we take one element to represent each of the possibilities; thus we have the four point domain:

$Z^{oe} = \{\bot^{oe}, \text{even, odd, } \top\}$ ($\top$ is pronounced "top")

where

     $\bot^{oe}$ represents   "the result is undefined"

     even represents   "the result is even or undefined"

odd	represents	"the result is odd or undefined"
$\top$	represents	"the result is even or odd or undefined"

Note the decoration on $\perp^{oe}$ to distinguish it from the bottom element of Z. We may describe the correspondence between the elements of the concrete domain and the elements of the abstract domain in two ways: by giving an elementwise *abstraction map*, *abst*, from Z to Z^{oe}, and by giving a *concretization map*, *Conc*, from Z^{oe} to sets of elements of Z:

$$abst: Z \to Z^{oe} \qquad\qquad Conc: Z^{oe} \to \mathbb{P}(Z)$$
$$abst(\perp) = \perp^{oe} \qquad\qquad Conc(\perp^{oe}) = \{\perp\}$$
$$abst(x) = \textbf{even} \;\; \text{if } x \text{ is even} \qquad Conc(\textbf{even}) = \{\perp\} \cup \{...,-2,0,2,...\}$$
$$abst(x) = \textbf{odd} \;\;\; \text{if } x \text{ is odd} \qquad Conc(\textbf{odd}) = \{\perp\} \cup \{...,-1,1,...\}$$
$$\qquad\qquad\qquad\qquad\qquad Conc(\top) = \{\perp\} \cup \{...,-2,-1,0,1,2,...\}$$

The function *abst* tells us, for each possible concrete value of an expression, what the corresponding abstract value is; and *Conc* tells us which concrete values are abstracted by each abstract value.

The domain Z^{oe} is a lattice, ordered as follows:

$$
\begin{array}{c}
\top \\
/ \quad \backslash \\
\textbf{even} \quad \textbf{odd} \qquad\qquad a \leq b \text{ iff } Conc(a) \subseteq Conc(b) \\
\backslash \quad / \\
\perp^{oe}
\end{array}
$$

The intuition behind this ordering is, roughly speaking, that, as we carry out the analysis of any particular expression to determine what its result may be, we start in a state of "ignorance" and proceed by accumulating the information that certain results are possible; accumulating information corresponds to moving upwards through the lattice. At each stage we represent the available information by the element of Z^{oe} which includes in its concretization all the possible results that we know about, but excludes as many as possible of the results that we do not know about. In terms of the abstract domain ordering this element is thus as high as possible but no higher than it needs to be; these attributes can be understood informally as "safety" and "usefulness" respectively. Formally, the element that we choose is the *least upper bound* in Z^{oe} of the abstraction of all the possible concrete results, x_i, that we know about (including $\perp$):

$$lub \; \{ \; abst \, (x_i) \; \}$$

This is the reason that there are no elements in Z^{oe} whose concretization contain only the even numbers and only the odd numbers: they would be inaccessible by the procedure described above.

Thus we start an analysis with $\perp^{oe}$, which promises no defined result at all; as the analysis proceeds we may discover that the result might be even and so we move up to the element **even**, which includes $\perp$ and all even numbers in its concretization, but no odd numbers; perhaps the analysis terminates here, or perhaps we discover subsequently that the result might also be odd, and our analysis then yields $\top$. Alternatively the analysis may proceed via **odd** rather than **even**. Note that $\top$ conveys no useful information at all, since it simply represents the fact that the result will be one of the complete set of possibilities (which is not surprising).

To complete the abstraction: the standard forms of the semantic operators combine and/or yield elements of Z; we must introduce abstract forms of these which combine and/or yield elements of Z^{oe}. In the simple language here we have just $\mathcal{K}$, $+$, $\times$, $=$ and *cond* on the right hand side of semantic equations. We did not give explicit definitions of these operators, since they are clear enough, but we must now give explicit, and justified, definitions for the abstract forms $\mathcal{K}^{oe}$, $+^{oe}$, $\times^{oe}$, $=^{oe}$ and *cond*^{oe}.

The interpretation of constants is straightforward:

$$\mathcal{K}^{oe}: Con \to Z^{oe}$$
$$\mathcal{K}^{oe}[\![k]\!] = abst(k)$$

So: $\quad \mathcal{K}^{oe}[\![0]\!] = \textbf{even} \qquad \mathcal{K}^{oe}[\![2]\!] = \textbf{even} \qquad \mathcal{K}^{oe}[\![-2]\!] = \textbf{even} \quad$ ....
$\qquad \mathcal{K}^{oe}[\![1]\!] = \textbf{odd} \qquad \mathcal{K}^{oe}[\![-1]\!] = \textbf{odd} \quad$ ....

For the abstract arithmetic operators $+^{oe}$ and $\times^{oe}$ we encode the familiar rules, taking into account that operands may take *any* value from Z^{oe}:

$+^{oe}$		$\perp^{oe}$	**even**	**odd**	$\top$
$\perp^{oe}$		$\perp^{oe}$	$\perp^{oe}$	$\perp^{oe}$	$\perp^{oe}$
even		$\perp^{oe}$	**even**	**odd**	$\top$
odd		$\perp^{oe}$	**odd**	**even**	$\top$
$\top$		$\perp^{oe}$	$\top$	$\top$	$\top$

$\times^{oe}$		$\perp^{oe}$	even	odd	$\top$
$\perp^{oe}$		$\perp^{oe}$	$\perp^{oe}$	$\perp^{oe}$	$\perp^{oe}$
even		$\perp^{oe}$	even	even	even
odd		$\perp^{oe}$	even	odd	$\top$
$\top$		$\perp^{oe}$	even	$\top$	$\top$

Note that we take *strict* definitions of these operators, so that if either operand of $+$ and $\times$ is $\perp$ then the result is $\perp$; this is reflected in the tables for $+^{oe}$ and $\times^{oe}$. We should perhaps comment on the logic of some of the entries: "**even** $+^{oe}$ $\top$ = $\top$" since "adding undefined or even to undefined or even or odd gives undefined or even or odd"; but "**even** $\times^{oe}$ $\top$ = **even**" since "multiplying undefined or even by undefined or even or odd gives undefined or even". It is interesting to note that $\top$ does not occur in the central 2×2 square of these tables; hence there is no loss of information through these operators (contrast "**positive** + **negative** may be either **positive** or **negative**" in the sign abstract interpretation).

We will not use $=^{oe}$ in the example that follows, but we may build the defining table: knowing that two numbers have the same parity tells us nothing about whether they are equal, though they are certainly not equal if they are of different parity (recall that false is encoded as 0, hence the **even** entries in the table):

$=^{oe}$		$\perp^{oe}$	even	odd	$\top$
$\perp^{oe}$		$\perp^{oe}$	$\perp^{oe}$	$\perp^{oe}$	$\perp^{oe}$
even		$\perp^{oe}$	$\top$	even	$\top$
odd		$\perp^{oe}$	even	$\top$	$\top$
$\top$		$\perp^{oe}$	$\top$	$\top$	$\top$

In order to interpret a conditional choice abstractly it is usual to *ignore the test* and to specify that the result may be *any* result produced by either branch of the conditional. We can justify this in the following way: the usual aim in abstract interpretation is to determine information about the result of an expression which is is valid for *all* evaluations of that expression; thus we must consider equally the case that the conditional test is true and that it is false, and so we make the simplification that the test expression itself contributes nothing to the analysis. In the domain Z^{oe} this corresponds to taking the *least upper bound* of the two branches, and in terms of Z to taking their union; note that this may entail a loss of information. For example, if the **then** branch is **even** and the **else** branch is **odd** then the result in the domain Z may be either undefined or even or odd, which gives $\top$ in Z^{oe}. Since the abstract interpretation of the conditional will not depend on the test expression, that is, the first argument of *cond*, we shall drop it from the semantic metasyntax and write simply $cond^{oe}(e_2,e_3)$:

$cond^{oe}$		$\perp^{oe}$	*even*	*odd*	$\top$
$\perp^{oe}$		$\perp^{oe}$	*even*	*odd*	$\top$
even		*even*	*even*	$\top$	$\top$
odd		*odd*	$\top$	*odd*	$\top$
$\top$		$\top$	$\top$	$\top$	$\top$

We must be careful in building these abstract operators: they must be consistent with the concrete definitions. This means simply that if we take a concrete expression e and abstract each constant and operator to obtain e^{oe}, then the value of e^{oe} contains the value of e in its concretization. For example, we require that:

$$x + y \in Conc(\ abst(x) +^{oe} abst(y)) \qquad \forall\ x, y \in Z$$

We may now give the full non-standard semantics for our functional language, simply by substituting the abstract constants, domains and operators, and doing some renaming:

Semantic domains:

$$F^{oe} = Z^{oe}* \to Z^{oe}$$
$$Fv^{oe} = Fv \to F^{oe}$$
$$Bv^{oe} = Id \to Z^{oe}$$

Semantic functions:

$$\mathcal{P}^{oe}: Prog \to Fv^{oe}$$
$$\mathcal{E}^{oe}: Exp \to Fv^{oe} \to Bv^{oe} \to Z^{oe}$$

$\mathcal{P}^{oe}[\![\{f_i(x_1,...,x_n) = e_i\}]\!] = \textbf{letrec } fve = [strict(\lambda\ v_1\ ...\ v_n.\ \mathcal{E}^{oe}[\![e_i]\!]\ fve\ [v_j/x_j])/f_i]$

$\mathcal{E}^{oe}[\![x]\!]\ fve\ bve = bve[\![x]\!]$

$\mathcal{E}^{oe}[\![k]\!]\ fve\ bve = \mathcal{K}^{oe}[\![k]\!]$

$\mathcal{E}^{oe}[\![\textbf{if } e_1 \textbf{ then } e_2 \textbf{ else } e_3]\!]\ fve\ bve = cond^{oe}\ (\mathcal{E}^{oe}[\![e_2]\!]\ fve\ bve,\ \mathcal{E}^{oe}[\![e_3]\!]\ fve\ bve)$

$\mathcal{E}^{oe}[\![e_1 + e_2]\!]\ fve\ bve = \mathcal{E}^{oe}[\![e_1]\!]\ fve\ bve +^{oe} \mathcal{E}^{oe}[\![e_2]\!]\ fve\ bve$

$\mathcal{E}^{oe}[\![e_1 \times e_2]\!]\ fve\ bve = \mathcal{E}^{oe}[\![e_1]\!]\ fve\ bve \times^{oe} \mathcal{E}^{oe}[\![e_2]\!]\ fve\ bve$

$\mathcal{E}^{oe}[\![e_1 = e_2]\!]\ fve\ bve = (\mathcal{E}^{oe}[\![e_1]\!]\ fve\ bve = \mathcal{E}^{oe}[\![e_2]\!]\ fve\ bve)$

$\mathcal{E}^{oe}[\![f(e_1,...,e_n)]\!]\ fve\ bve = (fve[\![f]\!])(\mathcal{E}^{oe}[\![e_1]\!]\ fve\ bve,...,\ \mathcal{E}^{oe}[\![e_n]\!]\ fve\ bve)$

3.2.3 Application of the abstract interpretation

Consider the function:

$$square(x) = \textbf{if } x = 0 \textbf{ then } x \textbf{ else } square(x + (-1)) + (2 \times x) + (-1)$$

The abstract interpretation $\mathcal{P}^{oe}$ associates with the identifier *square* the abstract function which is the *least fixed point* of the following recursive definition:

$$square^{oe}(x) = cond^{oe}(x, square^{oe}(x +^{oe} \textbf{odd}) +^{oe} (\textbf{even} \times^{oe} x) +^{oe} \textbf{odd})$$

in which x takes values from Z^{oe}.

To complete the analysis of *square* we must actually calculate the least fixed point of $square^{oe}$. We apply the standard technique of using the recursive definition to iterate towards the least fixed point starting from the totally undefined function. We recast the definition as:

$$square^{oe}_{i+1}(x) = cond^{oe}(x, square^{oe}_i(x +^{oe} \textbf{odd}) +^{oe} (\textbf{even} \times^{oe} x) +^{oe} \textbf{odd})$$
with $\quad square^{oe}_0(x) = \bot^{oe}$

and successively calculate $square^{oe}_{i+1}$ from $square^{oe}_i$ until the fixed point is reached. This iteration is guaranteed to terminate because the domain Z^{oe} is finite. The iteration converges quickly in this example, and the iterates of $square^{oe}$ are tabulated below:

	$square^{oe}$		$\bot^{oe}$	argument even	odd	$\top$
	0	|	$\bot^{oe}$	$\bot^{oe}$	$\bot^{oe}$	$\bot^{oe}$
iterate	1	|	$\bot^{oe}$	even	odd	$\top$
	2	|	$\bot^{oe}$	even	odd	$\top$

Thus the first iterate reached the least fixed point, although we needed the second before we could know this. The least fixed point tells us what we intuitively expect about *square*: the square of a number has the same parity as the number, provided that it is defined (remember that the definition of *square* that we are using is undefined for negative integers, and note that **even** and **odd** both contain $\bot^{oe}$ to deal with this case).

It is interesting to consider an alternative definition of *square* (which is equivalent in terms of the concrete results that it calculates):

$$square'(x) = \textbf{if } x = 0 \textbf{ then } 0 \textbf{ else } square'(x + (-1)) + (2 \times x) + (-1)$$

We have simply replaced x in the **then** branch with the value that we know that it will have. The abstract form of this definition is:

$$square'^{oe}(x) = cond^{oe}(\textbf{even}, square'^{oe}(x +^{oe} \textbf{odd}) +^{oe} (\textbf{even} \times^{oe} x) +^{oe} \textbf{odd})$$

and calculation of the least fixed point gives us:

	$square'^{oe}$	argument			
		$\perp^{oe}$	even	odd	$\top$
	0	$\perp^{oe}$	$\perp^{oe}$	$\perp^{oe}$	$\perp^{oe}$
iterate	1	even	even	even	even
	2	even	$\top$	$\top$	$\top$
	3	even	$\top$	$\top$	$\top$

This fixed point for $square'^{oe}$ appears rather strange: we cannot be sure that the result is undefined if the argument is undefined, and in all other circumstances we cannot be sure of the parity of the result. This is a very weak conclusion to reach about $square'$; we have lost a lot of information in this analysis. It is weak, but nonetheless it is safe: it has not ignored any possible outcomes. Note that each element in the fixed point of $square'^{oe}$ is greater than (or the same as) the corresponding element of $square^{oe}$. Since $square$ and $square'$ clearly compute the same function, the least fixed points of $square^{oe}$ and $square'^{oe}$ are both safe abstractions of that function. We may say that $square'^{oe}$ is "more safe", but it is more useful to say that $square^{oe}$ is "more accurate" (since it contains less overestimation of the sets of outcomes).

The source of the loss of information is in the treatment of the conditional: it ignores the test expression completely, and so does not distinguish between the alternative branches (in addition it *always* takes the branches into account even if the test expression itself is undefined). This is a standard way of treating conditionals, and it could well be argued that improvements in technique are required in this respect.

There are two lessons to be learnt here: firstly, that the abstract interpretation is performed on the syntactic form of the program (rather than the function that it denotes), and the precise form chosen may affect the analysis dramatically; and secondly, that unless great care is taken in setting up an abstract interpretation we may lose so much information that any analysis performed may be useless!

3.3 RESTRICTING THE INTERPRETATION TO FINITE DOMAINS

In the previous section we analysed two functions to determine a certain property by interpreting them through a non-standard or abstract semantics. The important step in the analysis of a function was the calculation from the re-interpreted form of the function of its least fixed point as an *explicit tabulation* of the argument/result relationship of the function. One simple way that such a method could be used in a compiler would be for the compiler to explicitly calculate this table, and to determine from it whether the function had any universal property which could be exploited in compiling a better version of it. This approach clearly depends on the feasibility of the least fixed point calculation, and this in turn depends on the nature of the domains in the abstract interpretation. In the case of functions from $Z^{oe}*$ to Z^{oe} there was no problem since the domain Z^{oe} is finite (and also quite small), and this is sufficient to guarantee termination of the iteration. If our abstract domain were large and finite then it would still be possible, in principle, to calculate the least fixed points of abstract functions, but there would be practical problems. The finiteness of the abstract domains is often an immediate consequence of the abstract model chosen for the property to be analysed; for example, for strictness analysis on flat domains (such as Z) we only need the abstract elements $\bot$ and $\top$, giving a two point domain.

However, it is sometimes the case that the non-standard interpretation that immediately suggests itself does not have pleasantly finite domains, and we need to devise special treatment for these cases.

In Chapter 4, which follows, we analyse programs to determine the degree of sharing between data structures; this is subsequently used to optimize storage management. The abstract domain which comes to mind is one in which each element represents the degree of sharing of a data structure; unfortunately data structures are arbitrarily large, and they can have arbitrarily shared substructures, and hence the abstract domain of sharing patterns is *infinite* and a least fixed point iteration may not terminate. In this case what we do is to artificially reduce the domain to a finite one by choosing a suitable grouping of the elements into a finite number of classes; this may mean keeping the full abstract information about some elements, and having one or more elements to represent "all other cases".

REFERENCES

[Abramsky et al. 87] S. Abramsky, C. Hankin (editors). Abstract interpretation of declarative languages. Ellis Horwood Series in Computers and their Applications, 1987.

[Burn 87] G. L. Burn. Abstract interpretation and the parallel evaluation of functional languages. PhD thesis, University of London, March 1987.

[Burstall et al. 75] R. M. Burstall, J. Darlington. A transformation system for developing recursive programs. JACM, Vol. 24, No. 1, pp. 44-67, 1975.

[Cousot et al. 77] P. Cousot, R. Cousot. Abstract interpretation: a unified lattice model for static analysis of programs by construction or approximation of fixpoints. Proceedings of 4th Conference on the Principles of Programming Languages, pp. 238-252, 1977.

[Hudak 87] P. Hudak. A semantic model of reference counting and its abstraction. In [Abramsky et al. 87], pp. 45-62, 1987.

[Jones et al. 89a] S. B. Jones, D. Le Métayer. Compile time garbage collection by sharing analysis. Proc. of 4th International Conference on Functional Programming Languages and Computer Architecture, pp. 55-74, September 1989.

[Jones et al. 89b] S. B. Jones, D. Le Métayer. A new method for strictness analysis on non-flat domains. Proc. of 4th IEEE TENCON Conference, November 1989.

[Mycroft 80] A. Mycroft. The theory and practice of transforming call-by-need into call-by-value. Proc. of 4th International Symposium on Programming, LNCS 83, Springer Verlag, 1980.

[Wadler 87] P. L. Wadler. Strictness analysis on non-flat domains. In [Abramsky et al. 87], pp. 266-275, 1987.

[Wadler 88] P. L. Wadler. Deforestation: transforming programs to eliminate trees. Proc. of European Symposium on Programming, March 1988.

CHAPTER 4

COMPILE-TIME GARBAGE COLLECTION
BY
SHARING ANALYSIS

Simon B. Jones
Daniel Le Métayer

4.1 INTRODUCTION

Functional programs are profligate consumers of processing time spent on the management of heap storage. It is important to find ways to reduce this storage management overhead. The extravagance with memory can be traced to two causes: firstly, the pursuit of clarity often leads to programs which are far from optimal, and which require much repeated reconstruction of data structures; secondly, the constraints of purely functional semantics prevents the programmer from expressing explicitly that memory can be reused.

Correspondingly, there are two approaches to improving the performance of functional programs with respect to memory management: the greatest gains may probably be obtained by techniques which seek to reduce the algorithmic complexity of programs [Burstall et al. 77], [Wadler 88]; for example, transformations which introduce accumulating parameters can change "quadratic" programs into "linear" programs. However, such improved programs may still imply a large storage management overhead. An orthogonal approach is to analyse, at compile-time, the run-time storage management of a program; the aim is to identify where run-time storage management decisions can be made at compile-time; this information can then be used to generate more efficient compiled code. The effect here is to reduce the cost in processing time of the storage management operations implied by a program (possibly to zero); such optimization cannot alter the order of complexity of a program, only decrease it by a (hopefully large) linear factor. Clearly these two approaches complement each other, and should be used together.

In this chapter we address the latter of the two optimization techniques discussed above. Specifically, we consider the problem of optimizing heap management for a simple first order, strict, functional language with lists, executed using call-by-value with arguments evaluated from left to right. We present a new garbage collection technique based on sharing information. In contrast to reference counting, this technique is not complete (even in the absence of cycles) but possesses two major advantages: it allows the collection of certain structures earlier than reference counting (namely cells that are still accessible from the stack but that will never be accessed by the computation) and, more importantly, it is a better basis for compile-time optimizations. In some sense, sharing may be seen as an abstraction of reference counting: this explains the fact that the method is not complete (some knowledge has been lost) and is more suited to static analysis. The goal of the compile-time optimizations is to replace as much as possible of the allocation of new cells by the reuse of previously deallocated cells; this technique is called in place updating. We show that familiar list manipulation programs such as *reverse* and *quicksort* exhibit the interesting property that all cell allocations involved in their execution can be implemented as in place updating. These programs can be efficiently implemented using our method because garbage collection can be completely compiled.

Section 4.2 contains some examples illustrating the kind of optimization dealt with by our method. We introduce in section 4.3 the semantics of the first-order language with non-flat lists used in this chapter. We describe in section 4.4 several non-standard interpretations allowing us to deduce information about the sharing of list structures. Section 4.5 introduces a new garbage collection technique based on the semantics described in section 4.3 and the sharing interpretations presented in section 4.4. Section 4.6 shows how the infinite domains introduced in the previous sections can be mapped onto finite domains in order to allow the compile-time analysis of sharing and the compilation of garbage collection. We present in section 4.7 a comparison with previous work and some prospects for further research.

4.2 THE TARGET FOR OPTIMIZATION

Let us look at some examples which illustrate the kind of optimization dealt with by the method proposed in this chapter. First we give a brief summary of the basic storage management that we are adopting. We assume a standard implementation of a heap: we have a store of locations each of which can hold a pair of values (one *cons* cell); each location has a unique address. Locations are used to build list structures, and it is their allocation and deallocation with which we are concerned. Atomic values (including location addresses) are held either in the evaluation state (machine registers, stack or graph), or in the fields of the pair stored in a location; hence they do not themselves need to be allocated store locations, and they are copied whenever required.

When a location is first allocated there is a single reference to it. If that reference is subsequently passed as an argument to a function whose body contains more than one use of the argument, then the reference is duplicated. As an expression accesses a location to which it holds a reference, the reference is lost; thus a multiply referenced location may become completely unreferenced (not accessible).

The concept of sharing which we wish to identify is defined with respect to the accessibility of cells. We say that a structure (which may be the component of a larger structure) is shared if either its root cell, or some other cell which directly or indirectly references its root cell, is multiply referenced; hence every substructure of a shared structure is itself shared (although there may only be one reference to each cell of the substructure). We say that a structure is unshared if its root cell and all cells which reference its root either directly or indirectly are singly referenced; a structure may be unshared but nevertheless have shared substructures.

Consider evaluating the expression $f(cons(88, nil))$ where $f(x) = cons(head(x), tail(x))$. We can make two observations:

(1) One cons cell will be allocated to construct the actual parameter for the call of f; there will be a single reference to this cell; it is unshared;

(2) Let us assume that f is called with an unshared argument x. On entering the definition of f, we lose one reference to x (its job as parameter is over), and we gain two references (it will be needed twice during evaluation of the body of f). Therefore x becomes shared at this point. After the evaluation of $head(x)$, x becomes unshared again; one implication of this is that the root cell of x can be deallocated after the execution of $tail$; however we can notice that a new cell is required just afterwards to build the result of $cons$; instead of performing a deallocation and an immediate allocation we can reuse the cell corresponding to the root of x.

Putting these two observations together, we see that we can specialize the implementation of f to reuse its parameter cell directly when the new cons cell is required. Overall, only one allocation step is performed, rather than two (zero rather than one within f). Of course, this is a trivial example. Consider, instead, naïve reverse:

$reverse(l) = $ **if** $l = nil$ **then** nil **else** $append(reverse(tail(l)), cons(head(l), nil))$
$append(l_1, l_2) = $ **if** $l_1 = nil$ **then** l_2 **else** $cons(head(l_1), append(tail(l_1), l_2))$

Granted, this is a very poor solution to the list reversal problem, but let us ignore that and examine the storage use of the functions as given. Reasoning in a similar fashion to above, we discover that

(1) if the spine (that is to say the cells accessible by successive applications of *tail*) of the argument l_1 of *append* is unshared, then its first cell is reusable when a new *cons* cell is required in the **else** part;

(2) if the spine of the second argument of *append* is unshared, then the spine cells of the result of *append* are unshared;

(3) if the spine of the argument of *reverse* is unshared, then its first cell is reusable in the **else** part;

(4) if the argument *l* of *reverse* is unshared, then the argument of the recursive call (*tail(l)*) is shared only with an expression which will not access it during its evaluation;

(5) the spine cells of the result of *reverse* are unshared.

From these observations we can deduce that *reverse* and *append* may indeed be optimized as described in (1) and (3). Hence if we know that its argument is unshared, then we may compile a specialized form of *reverse* which reverses an unshared list "in place" by directly reusing the spine cells of the list (rather than by making a number of cell allocations quadratic in the length of the list). Depending on the relative costs of other aspects of the program execution, we would expect this to reduce the overall execution time by a substantial factor. Similarly quicksort:

$$qs(l) = \textbf{if } l = nil \textbf{ then } nil$$
$$\textbf{else let } x = head(l)$$
$$(l_1, l_2) = split(x, t \ ail(l), nil, nil)$$
$$\textbf{in } append(qs(l_1), cons(x, qs(l_2)))$$
$$split(x, l, le, gr) = \textbf{if } l = nil \textbf{ then } (le, gr) \textbf{ else}$$
$$\textbf{if } head(l) \leq x \textbf{ then } split(x, tail(l), cons(head(l), l \ e), gr)$$
$$\textbf{else } split(x, tail(l), le, cons(head(l), gr))$$

A version of *qs* specialized to sorting unshared lists can reuse its argument's spine cells, and can employ similarly specialized versions of *append* and *split*. The optimized version of *qs* would perform zero allocation steps, rather than $O(length(l)^2)$. Even in an unspecialized version of *qs*, we can still use a specialized version of *append* (since its first argument is unshared); this can be determined by static analysis.

The key component in the analysis required to achieve the optimizations discussed above is determining how the sharing of structure in the result of a function depends on the sharing in its arguments. In the following sections we show how this property can be calculated by static analysis of the program code.

4.3 LANGUAGE SYNTAX AND SEMANTICS

We consider in this chapter the first-order version (with non-flat lists) of the language defined in section 2.6. We add to this definition a syntax for programs, which are collections of functions:

$$Prog ::= \{f_1(x_{11}, ..., x_{1k1}) = e_1$$
$$f_2(x_{21}, ..., x_{2k2}) = e_2$$
$$...$$
$$f_n(x_{n1}, ..., x_{nkn}) = e_n\}$$

The syntactic domains are called respectively *Con* (constants), *Bv* (bound variables), *Fv* (function variables), *Exp* (expressions) and *Prog* (programs). The formal semantics is basically an adaptation of Hudak's definition [Hudak 87] to allow the treatment of general lists. The semantic definition covers both the standard semantics of the language (the "results" of any program), and a non-standard component describing how a store of cells is used to implement list structures. For the moment, no garbage collection is made explicit within this semantics. The equations can be read both as a semantic definition, and as an emulation of a real interpreter or as a specification of the actions to be compiled into the object code for any program.

Let *Db* be some suitable domain of basic values (integers, booleans, value *nil*). There is no explicit domain of lists; instead, elements of the domain of store locations, *Loc*, identify the root of a list structure, built of pairs, in a state of the store (an element of the domain of stores, *St*). As the domain of expressible values, we set $E = Db + Loc$, and we assume that the operations *cons*, *head* and *tail* are available on the appropriate domains; we make no syntactic distinction between the occurrences of these primitives in the syntax of our source language and as semantic functions on the domains: there should be no confusion from the context. In the following we assume (as in [Hudak 87]) that basic objects (elements of *Db* here) are passed by value and lists are passed by reference (elements of *Loc* in our setting). Furthermore we assume a call-by-value evaluation of the language, with arguments evaluated from left to right.

We give now the complete list of the semantic domains:

Db	basic values
Loc	locations
$E = Db + Loc$	expressible values
$Bve = Bv \rightarrow E$	bound variable environments
$L = E \times E$	list pairs
$St = Loc \rightarrow L$	stores
$Fve = Fv \rightarrow E^* \rightarrow St \rightarrow (E \times St)$	function variable environments

A store maps locations to a list pair, since basic values are not stored. Note that the value *nil* is considered as a basic value (element of *Db*). We use the primitives *head* and *tail* to access the different fields of a value of *L*.

We can now introduce the semantic functions:

$$\mathcal{R}p: \quad Prog \rightarrow Fve$$
$$\mathcal{R}: \quad Exp \rightarrow Fve \rightarrow Bve \rightarrow St \rightarrow (E \times St)$$
$$\mathcal{K}\beta: \quad Con \rightarrow Db$$

$\mathcal{R}p$ yields functions which are supposed to emulate the behaviour of an interpreter; $\mathcal{R}p$ gives the meaning of a program, $\mathcal{R}$ the meaning of an expression and $\mathcal{K}\beta$ interprets basic values (constants). Before describing the semantic equations we introduce function *alloc* which allocates a new location in the store:

$$alloc: St \rightarrow L \rightarrow (Loc \times St)$$
$$alloc\ st\ v = \textbf{let}\ loc\ \text{be some location}\ \textbf{such that}\ (st\ loc) = \bot\ \textbf{in}\ (loc, st[v/loc])$$

$st[v/loc]$ is a shorthand notation for the expression $\lambda l.\ \textbf{if}\ l = loc\ \textbf{then}\ v\ \textbf{else}\ (st\ l)$.

The semantic equations can now be expressed:

$$\mathcal{R}p \,[\![\, \{f_i(x_1, ..., x_n) = e_i\} \,]\!] = \textbf{letrec}\ fve = [strict(\lambda v_1\ ...\ v_n\ st.\ \mathcal{R}[\![e_i]\!]\ fve\ [v_j/x_j]\ st)\ /f_i]$$
$$\mathcal{R}[\![x]\!]\ fve\ bve\ st = (bve\ [\![x]\!], st)$$
$$\mathcal{R}[\![k]\!]\ fve\ bve\ st = (\mathcal{K}\beta\,[\![k]\!], st)$$
$$\mathcal{R}[\![\textbf{if}\ e_1\ \textbf{then}\ e_2\ \textbf{else}\ e_3]\!]\ fve\ bve\ st =$$
$$\textbf{let}\ (v, st') = \mathcal{R}[\![e_1]\!]\ fve\ bve\ st$$
$$\textbf{in}\ (\textbf{if}\ v\ \textbf{then}\ \mathcal{R}[\![e_2]\!]\ fve\ bve\ st'\ \textbf{else}\ \mathcal{R}[\![e_3]\!]\ fve\ bve\ st')$$

$$\mathcal{R}[\![+(e_1, e_2)]\!] \; fve \; bve \; st = \quad \textbf{let} \; (v_1, st_1) = \mathcal{R}[\![e_1]\!] \; fve \; bve \; st$$
$$(v_2, st_2) = \mathcal{R}[\![e_2]\!] \; fve \; bve \; st_1$$
$$\textbf{in} \; (v_1 + v_2, st_2)$$

$$\mathcal{R}[\![eq \; (e_1, e_2)]\!] \; fve \; bve \; st = \quad \textbf{let} \; (v_1, st_1) = \mathcal{R}[\![e_1]\!] \; fve \; bve \; st$$
$$(v_2, st_2) = \mathcal{R}[\![e_2]\!] \; fve \; bve \; st_1$$
$$\textbf{in} \; (v_1 = v_2, st_2)$$

$$\mathcal{R}[\![cons \; (e_1, e_2)]\!] \; fve \; bve \; st = \textbf{let} \; (v_1, st_1) = \mathcal{R}[\![e_1]\!] \; fve \; bve \; st$$
$$(v_2, st_2) = \mathcal{R}[\![e_2]\!] \; fve \; bve \; st_1$$
$$\textbf{in} \; alloc \; st_2 \; (v_1, v_2)$$

$$\mathcal{R}[\![head \; (e)]\!] \; fve \; bve \; st = \textbf{let} \; (loc, st_1) = \mathcal{R}[\![e]\!] \; fve \; bve \; st \; \textbf{in} \; (head \; (st_1 \; loc), st_1)$$

$$\mathcal{R}[\![tail \; (e)]\!] \; fve \; bve \; st = \quad \textbf{let} \; (loc, st_1) = \mathcal{R}[\![e]\!] \; fve \; bve \; st \; \textbf{in} \; (tail \; (st_1 \; loc), st_1)$$

$$\mathcal{R}[\![null \; (e)]\!] \; fve \; bve \; st = \quad \textbf{let} \; (loc, st_1) = \mathcal{R}[\![e]\!] \; fve \; bve \; st \; \textbf{in} \; (loc = nil, st_1)$$

$$\mathcal{R}[\![f(e_1, ..., e_n)]\!] \; fve \; bve \; st = \quad \textbf{let} \; (v_1, st_1) = \mathcal{R}[\![e_1]\!] \; fve \; bve \; st$$
$$(v_2, st_2) = \mathcal{R}[\![e_2]\!] \; fve \; bve \; st_1$$
$$....$$
$$(v_n, st_n) = \mathcal{R}[\![e_n]\!] \; fve \; bve \; st_{n-1}$$
$$\textbf{in} \; fve \; [\![f]\!] \; v_1 \; ... \; v_n \; st_n$$

strict is used to make a function strict (we consider a call-by-value semantics here). The only place where the allocation primitive is called is in $\mathcal{R}[\![cons \; ...]\!]$. No deallocation is expressed in this semantics for the moment. The garbage collection technique will appear in section 4.5 after the introduction of sharing interpretation in the next section.

4.4 DETECTION OF SHARING IN FUNCTIONAL EXPRESSIONS

We start with the following remark: the garbage collector may collect a cell when this cell is dereferenced (during the evaluation of a primitive *head, tail, null, eq, cond* or at a function call) and is not shared. So sharing is relevant information for the design of a memory manager. [Stoye et al. 84] describes a one bit reference count technique which turns out to be very effective in the context of combinator graph reduction (it is claimed that 70 percent of wasted cells are immediately reclaimed).

We take a different approach here and we consider sharing as a compile-time abstraction of reference counting. We define a non-standard interpretation $\mathcal{S}$, which yields information about the sharing in the result of an expression in the standard semantics. This information can then be used to infer statically that a dereference always happens in a context where the cell is not shared; when it is possible to infer that a further cell must be allocated in the same context, then no collection and reallocation need occur, instead the cell may be reused destructively.

The sharing interpretations introduced in this section are defined on a domain of patterns P; the values of P represent different kinds of information according to the interpretation considered. In the interpretation S, patterns represent the known degree of sharing in a structure. To be more precise, a sharing pattern denotes the extent to which we are certain that a structure is unshared. The sharing patterns do not capture precise reference count information; they are an abstraction indicating only whether a structure is accessible in exactly one or possibly more than one way. The least element of the domain is 0, which denotes that neither the structure it is associated with, nor any of its substructures, is shared. The greatest element is 1, which denotes that the structure it is associated with might be shared; note that since each substructure of a shared structure is itself shared, we need only keep this single item of information about the entire structure. Between these extremes we have elements denoting partial information about sharing. We may know that the root cell of a structure, and possibly some of the cells accessible from it, are unshared, but that some of its substructures might be shared. To represent this we use binary trees (represented syntactically by nested pairs) built in the following way: each node in the tree corresponds to a cell in the structure which is known to be unshared; leaves are either 0 or 1, corresponding to totally unshared and shared substructures respectively. Let us take two simple examples:

(1) the sharing pattern $(1,1)$ is the greatest element below 1 and represents a structure in which the root cell is unshared but the *head* and *tail* structures are both shared; a structure having this sharing could be created by evaluating the expression $f(cons(5,9))$ in an environment in which $f(l) = cons(l,l)$.

(2) evaluating the expression $g(l)$ in an environment in which $g(l)=cons(5,cons(27,l))$ and $l = cons(2,7)$ yields the result $cons(5,cons(27,cons(2,7)))$; if the argument l is shared then the sharing of the result is represented by $(0,(0,1))$. If the argument l is unshared then the sharing of the result is 0 (which means that the result itself is completely unshared).

Note that patterns $(0, 0)$ and 0 represent the same information for interpretation S (absence of sharing); therefore elements of the form $(0,0)$ will never arise in the interpretation S. However other interpretations give different meanings to $(0,0)$ and 0 (see $\mathcal{N}$ below for example), so they appear as two different values in P.

The domain P is defined more formally as the least solution of the following equation:

$$P = \{0,1\} + (P \times P)$$

We use the operations *cons*, *cons'*, *head* and *tail* to compose and decompose elements of *P*:

$cons(0,0) = 0$

$cons(x,y) = (x,y)$ $x{\neq}0$ or $y{\neq}0$

$cons'(1,1) = 1$

$cons'(x,y) = (x,y)$ $x{\neq}1$ or $y{\neq}1$

$head(0) = 0$

$head(1) = 1$

$head((x,y)) = x$

$tail(0) = 0$

$tail(1) = 1$

$tail((x,y)) = y$

The elements of *P* are ordered as follows:

$0 < (x,y) < 1$

$(x_1,y_1) \leq (x_2,y_2)$ iff $x_1 \leq x_2$ and $y_1 \leq y_2$

The following operators are useful for combining patterns:

"union" $1 \cup x = 1$ $x \cup 1 = 1$ $0 \cup x = x$ $x \cup 0 = x$

                     $(a,b) \cup (c,d) = (a \cup c, b \cup d)$

"intersection" $1 \cap x = x$ $x \cap 1 = x$ $0 \cap x = 0$ $x \cap 0 = 0$

                     $(a,b) \cap (c,d) = (a \cap c, b \cap d)$

It is convenient to use tuples of patterns to define the abstract interpretations; when combining tuples of patterns, the operators defined above are applied pairwise to the component patterns:

$(p_1,..., p_n) \cup (q_1,..., q_n) = (p_1 \cup q_1,..., p_n \cup q_n)$

$(p_1,..., p_n) \cap (q_1,..., q_n) = (p_1 \cap q_1,..., p_n \cap q_n)$

Greater patterns are those which characterize lists with more sharing, and are thus "safer" as assumptions about the degree of sharing present. It is easy to check that *P* is a complete lattice; the least upper bound of a subset is the union of its elements, the greatest lower bound is given by the intersection; 0 and 1 are respectively the least element and the greatest element.

The lattice may be pictured as follows (the dotted lines correspond to infinite collections of elements):

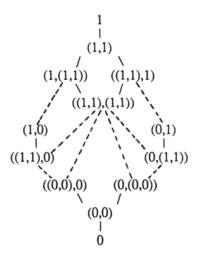

The abstract interpretation S associates with each function $f(x_1,...,x_n) = e$ a non-standard function $Sf(s_1,...,s_n)$; each s_i represents the sharing in argument x_i, and the result of Sf represents the sharing in the result of f. $Sf(s_1,...,s_n)$ is defined as the union of two sharing functions $Sf_c(s_1,...,s_n)$, which represents the sharing created by the evaluation of the function, and $Sf_t(s_1,...,s_n)$ corresponding to the transmission to the result of f of the sharing present in the arguments (represented by $s_1,...,s_n$).

For example: Let $f(l) = head(l)$. Then we will have:

$Sf_c(s_1) = 0$ "no sharing is created by the function"

$Sf_t(s_1) = head(s_1)$ "the sharing transmitted to the result is the sharing of the head"

$Sf(s_1) = head(s_1)$

and so:

$Sf(0) = head(0) = 0$ "if the argument of f is not shared then neither is its result"

$Sf((0,1)) = 0$ "even if the tail of the argument is shared, the result is not"

Let $g(l) = cons(l,l)$; we have:

$Sg_c(s_1) = (1,1)$ "the head and the tail of the result are shared by construction"

$Sg_t(s_1) = (s_1, s_1)$ "the sharing of the argument is transmitted to the head and the tail"

$Sg(s_1) = (1,1)$ "since $1 \cup s_1 = 1$"

The definition of S requires the introduction of another non-standard interpretation T (for "transmission"): in order to calculate the sharing in the result of, say $cons(e_1,e_2)$, we need to know which parts of the arguments $x_1,..., x_n$ (which might appear in e_1 and e_2) occur in the results of the evaluation of e_1 and e_2. This information is given by the interpretation T, in which functions return patterns describing the parts of the arguments of the standard interpretation of the function which appear at specified positions in the result of the standard interpretation of the function. T associates with each function $f(x_1,...,x_n) = e$ a non-standard function $Tf(r) = T[\![e]\!]\ r$; r is a pattern representing a part of the result of f, and the result of Tf is a tuple of patterns $(t_1,...,t_n)$ where t_i represents the part of x_i appearing into the part of the result of f specified by r. T is defined fully below. The abstraction T is defined on the domain P; here we understand the elements of P as transmission patterns. 0 denotes the absence of a part of the corresponding list in the result, and 1 denotes the (possible) presence of the corresponding part; a pair corresponds to a cell which is absent but may point towards a transmitted cell.

Continuing the example above, where $f(l) = head(l)$ and $g(l) = cons(l,l)$, we will have:

$$Tf(r) = (cons(r,0))$$
$$Tg(r) = (head(r) \cup tail(r))$$

and so:

$Tf(1) = ((1,0))$ "only the head of the argument appears in the result"

$Tf((0,1)) = (((0,1),0))$ "only the tail of the head of the argument appears in the tail of the result"

$Tg((1,0)) = (1)$ "the whole argument appears in the head of the result"

$Tg((0,1)) = (1)$ "the whole argument appears in the tail of the result"

We now give the formal definitions of S and T.

Definition: Sharing interpretation S

Each function $f(x_1,...,x_n) = e$ has two associated functions $Sf_c(s_1,...,s_n) = S_c[\![e]\!]$ and $Sf_t(s_1,...,s_n) = S_t[\![e]\!]\ [s_i/x_i]$. $Sf(s_1,...,s_n)$ is defined as $Sf_c(s_1,...,s_n) \cup Sf_t(s_1,...,s_n)$ and $S[\![e]\!]\ she = S_c[\![e]\!] \cup S_t[\![e]\!]\ she$. In the following she denotes a sharing environment ($she \in She = (Bv \rightarrow P)$).

$S_t: Exp \rightarrow She \rightarrow P$

$S_t[\![x]\!]\ she = she\ [\![x]\!]$ $\hspace{3cm}$ (S_{t1})

$S_t[\![k]\!]\ she = 0$ $\hspace{3cm}$ (S_{t2})

$S_t[\![if\ e_1\ then\ e_2\ else\ e_3]\!]\ she = (S_t[\![e_2]\!]\ she) \cup (S_t[\![e_3]\!]\ she)$ $\hspace{1cm}$ (S_{t3})

$S_t[\![cons(e_1,e_2)]\!]\ she = cons(S_t[\![e_1]\!]\ she, S_t[\![e_2]\!]\ she)$ $\hspace{1cm}$ (S_{t4})

$S_t[\![p(e_1,...,e_n)]\!]\ she = Sp_t(S_t[\![e_1]\!]\ she,..., S_t[\![e_n]\!]\ she)$ $\hspace{1cm}$ (S_{t5})

$S_t[\![f(e_1,...,e_n)]\!]\ she = Sf_t(S_t[\![e_1]\!]\ she,..., S_t[\![e_n]\!]\ she)$ $\hspace{1cm}$ (S_{t6})

$Shead_t(s) = head(s)$ $\hspace{3cm}$ (S_{t7})

$Stail_t(s) = tail(s)$ $\hspace{3cm}$ (S_{t8})

$S+_t(s_1,s_2) = 0$ $\hspace{3cm}$ (S_{t9})

$Seq_t(s_1,s_2) = 0$ $\hspace{3cm}$ (S_{t10})

$Snull_t(s_1,s_2) = 0$ $\hspace{3cm}$ (S_{t11})

Comments:

(S_{t1}) The sharing transmitted in the result of x is just the sharing in x.

(S_{t2}) There is no sharing in the value of a constant.

(S_{t3}) The result of a conditional expression may be the result of either branch, so the sharing in the result is the union of the sharings in the results of the two branches; this is where we lose information in the abstraction.

(S_{t4}) The sharing transmitted in the result of $cons(e_1,e_2)$ is the composition of the sharing present in e_1 and the sharing present in e_2.

(S_{t5}) (S_{t6}) are generalizations of (S_{t4}), and (S_{t7}), ..., (S_{t11}) are straightforward.

$S_c: Exp \rightarrow P$

$S_c[\![x]\!] = 0$ $\hspace{3cm}$ (S_{c1})

$S_c[\![k]\!] = 0$ $\hspace{3cm}$ (S_{c2})

$S_c[\![if\ e_1\ then\ e_2\ else\ e_3]\!] = (S_c[\![e_2]\!]) \cup (S_c[\![e_3]\!])$ $\hspace{1cm}$ (S_{c3})

$S_c[\![cons(e_1,e_2)]\!] = cons(S[\![e_1]\!]\ [(T[\![e_2]\!]\ [\![x]\!]\ 1)/x], S[\![e_2]\!]\ [(T[\![e_1]\!]\ [\![x]\!]\ 1)/x])$ $\hspace{0.5cm}$ (S_{c4})

$S_c[\![p(e_1,...,e_n)]\!] = Sp_t(S[\![e_1]\!]\ [((T[\![e_2]\!]\ [\![x]\!]\ 1) \cup ... (T[\![e_n]\!]\ [\![x]\!]\ 1))/x],$ $\hspace{0.5cm}$ (S_{c5})

$$...,$$

$$S[\![e_n]\!]\ [((T[\![e_1]\!]\ [\![x]\!]\ 1) \cup ... (T[\![e_{n-1}]\!]\ [\![x]\!]\ 1))/x])$$

$S_c[\![f(e_1,...,e_n)]\!] = Sf(S[\![e_1]\!]\ [((T[\![e_2]\!]\ [\![x]\!]\ 1) \cup ... (T[\![e_n]\!]\ [\![x]\!]\ 1))/x],$ $\hspace{0.5cm}$ (S_{c6})

$$...,$$

$$S[\![e_n]\!]\ [((T[\![e_1]\!]\ [\![x]\!]\ 1) \cup ... (T[\![e_{n-1}]\!]\ [\![x]\!]\ 1))/x])$$

Comments:

(S_{c1}) No sharing is created within the evaluation of a variable.

(S_{c2}) There is no sharing in the value of a constant.

(S_{c3}) The sharing of the result of a conditional expression is the union of the sharings of the two branches; again we lose information here.

(S_{c4}) *cons* may introduce sharing within its result if some parts of the variables appear in both subexpressions. The sharing is the composition of the sharings of the two expressions evaluated in a context where the parts of the variables appearing in the result of the other expression are considered as shared.

(S_{c5}) and (S_{c6}) are generalized forms of (S_{c4}); (S_{c6}) may also cause a loss of information, since f may ignore arguments which would otherwise give rise to sharing.

Definition: Transmission interpretation T

Each function $f(x_1,...,x_n)=e$ has an associated function $Tf(r)=(T[\![e]\!] [\![x_1]\!] r,...,T[\![e]\!] [\![x_n]\!] r)$. In the following r denotes a transmission pattern (element of P).

$$T: Exp \rightarrow Bv \rightarrow P \rightarrow P$$

$$T[\![x]\!] [\![x]\!] r = r \tag{T_1}$$

$$T[\![x]\!] [\![y]\!] r = 0 \quad (x \neq y) \tag{T_2}$$

$$T[\![k]\!] [\![x]\!] r = 0 \tag{T_3}$$

$$T[\![\text{if } e_1 \text{ then } e_2 \text{ else } e_3]\!] [\![x]\!] r = T[\![e_2]\!] [\![x]\!] r \cup T[\![e_3]\!] [\![x]\!] r \tag{T_4}$$

$$T[\![cons(e_1, e_2)]\!] [\![x]\!] r = T[\![e_1]\!] [\![x]\!] head(r) \cup T[\![e_2]\!] [\![x]\!] tail(r) \tag{T_5}$$

$$T[\![p(e_1,...,e_n)]\!] [\![x]\!] r = \text{let } (r'_1,...,r'_n) = Tp(r) \text{ in}$$
$$T[\![e_1]\!] [\![x]\!] r'_1 \cup...\cup T[\![e_n]\!] [\![x]\!] r'_n \tag{T_6}$$

$$T[\![f(e_1,...,e_n)]\!] [\![x]\!] r = \text{let } (r'_1,...,r'_n) = Tf(r) \text{ in}$$
$$T[\![e_1]\!] [\![x]\!] r'_1 \cup...\cup T[\![e_n]\!] [\![x]\!] r'_n \tag{T_7}$$

$$Thead(r) = (cons(r,0)) \tag{T_8}$$

$$Ttail(r) = (cons(0,r)) \tag{T_9}$$

$$Teq(r) = (0,0) \tag{T_{10}}$$

$$Tnull(r) = (0) \tag{T_{11}}$$

$$T+(r) = (0,0) \tag{T_{12}}$$

Comments:

(T_1) The part required of the variable is exactly the part required of the result.

(T_2) No part of a variable y appears in the result of x when $x \neq y$.

(T_3) Constants transmit no part of any variables.

(T_4) A conditional expression transmits those parts of variables transmitted by either of the branches.

(T$_5$) If we consider those parts specified by r of the result of $cons(e_1,e_2)$, then we transmit those parts of variables which occur in the parts of the value of e_1 specified by $head(r)$ plus those in the parts of the value of e_2 specified by $tail(r)$.

(T$_6$) and (T$_7$) are generalized forms of (T$_5$) in which we first calculate r', those parts of its arguments that the primitive or program function transmits given that we require the parts r of its result; r' is a tuple giving the required parts of each argument, and we determine the transmitted parts of a variable x by combining the parts transmitted by each argument.

(T$_8$), (T$_9$) If we require those parts r of the *head* of a structure, then we require the parts of the structure itself specified by $cons(r,0)$; similarly for *tail*.

(T$_{10}$), (T$_{11}$), (T$_{12}$) *eq*, *null* and + transmit no part of their arguments.

We introduce now a third interpretation $\mathcal{N}$ called necessity interpretation, which is used in the definition of the garbage collection method presented in the next section. $\mathcal{N}$ indicates the part of each argument of a function which may be necessary to evaluate a part of the result of the function. $\mathcal{N}$ is used in the garbage collection algorithm to detect the parts of a structure that will certainly not be used during the evaluation of an expression; it is this analysis that allows our garbage collection algorithm to collect certain structures earlier than traditional reference counting. $\mathcal{N}$ also operates on the domain P. 0 represents a part of the argument which is not necessary for the evaluation of the function and 1 a part of the argument which may be necessary; a pair corresponds to a necessary structure which may contain an unuseful substructure. In contrast with interpretations $\mathcal{S}$ and $\mathcal{T}$, patterns (0,0) and 0 have different meanings for $\mathcal{N}$: (0,0) specifies a cell that may be necessary whereas none of its substructures is necessary and 0 specifies a completely unuseful cell. On the other hand (1,1) and 1 represent the same piece of information (a structure all of whose substructures are potentially necessary); this explains the use of *cons'* instead of *cons* in the definition of $\mathcal{N}$. Apart from this fact, the formal definition of $\mathcal{N}$ is very close to the definition of $\mathcal{T}$; the only difference appears in the interpretation of primitives like *null*, *eq*, + because no part of their arguments occur in their result but the arguments are nevertheless necessary to evaluate the result; similarly the first argument of the conditional function is evaluated but does not appear in the result; *null* is an example of function which requires only the root cell of its argument.

Definition: Necessity interpretation $\mathcal{N}$

Each function $f(x_1,...,x_n)=e$ has an associated function $\mathcal{N}f(r)=(\mathcal{N}[\![e]\!]\,[\![x_1]\!]\,r,...,\mathcal{N}[\![e]\!]\,[\![x_n]\!]\,r)$. In the following r denotes a necessity pattern (element of P).

$\mathcal{N}: Exp \to Bv \to P \to P$

$\mathcal{N}[\![x]\!]\,[\![x]\!]\,r = r$

$\mathcal{N}[\![x]\!]\,[\![y]\!]\,r = 0 \quad (x \neq y)$

$\mathcal{N}[\![k]\!]\,[\![x]\!]\,r = 0$

$\mathcal{N}[\![\text{if } e_1 \text{ then } e_2 \text{ else } e_3]\!]\,[\![x]\!]\,r = \mathcal{N}[\![e_1]\!]\,[\![x]\!]\,1 \cup \mathcal{N}[\![e_2]\!]\,[\![x]\!]\,r \cup \mathcal{N}[\![e_3]\!]\,[\![x]\!]\,r$

$\mathcal{N}[\![cons(e_1, e_2)]\!]\,[\![x]\!]\,r = \mathcal{N}[\![e_1]\!]\,[\![x]\!]\,head(r) \cup \mathcal{N}[\![e_2]\!]\,[\![x]\!]\,tail(r)$

$\mathcal{N}[\![p(e_1,..., e_n)]\!]\,[\![x]\!]\,r = \text{let } r' = \mathcal{N}p(r) \text{ in } \mathcal{N}[\![e_1]\!]\,[\![x]\!]\,r'_1 \cup ... \cup \mathcal{N}[\![e_n]\!]\,[\![x]\!]\,r'_n$

$\mathcal{N}[\![f(e_1,..., e_n)]\!]\,[\![x]\!]\,r = \text{let } r' = \mathcal{N}f(r) \text{ in } \mathcal{N}[\![e_1]\!]\,[\![x]\!]\,r'_1 \cup ... \cup \mathcal{N}[\![e_n]\!]\,[\![x]\!]\,r'_n$

$\mathcal{N}head(r) = (cons'(r,0))$

$\mathcal{N}tail(r) = (cons'(0,r))$

$\mathcal{N}null(r) = ((0,0))$

$\mathcal{N}eq(r) = (1,1)$

$\mathcal{N}+(r) = (1,1)$

The reader may have noticed that this analysis is very reminiscent of the well-known concept of strictness analysis; actually strictness analysis indicates whether an argument will definitely be necessary to evaluate the result of a function whereas the $\mathcal{N}$ interpretation indicates whether an argument (or a part of it) will definitely be unnecessary to evaluate the result of a function. It is rather easy to define a strictness analyser from the definition of $\mathcal{N}$ above; the application of our method to strictness analysis on non-flat domains is described in [Jones et al. 89].

Let us now illustrate the interpretations introduced in this section with the example of the *reverse* function :

$reverse(l) = \text{if } l = nil \text{ then } nil \text{ else } append(reverse(tail(l)), cons(head(l), nil))$

$append(l_1,l_2) = \text{if } l_1 = nil \text{ then } l_2 \text{ else } cons(head(l_1), append(tail(l_1), l_2))$

S, T and $\mathcal{N}$ yield the following definitions:

$Sreverse(s) = Sappend(Sreverse\,(tail(s)), cons(head(s),0))$

$Sappend(s_1, s_2) = s_2 \cup cons(head(s_1), Sappend(tail(s_1), s_2))$

$Treverse(r) = \text{let } r'=Tappend(r) \text{ in } (\text{let } r''=Treverse(r'_1) \text{ in } (cons\,(head(r'_2), r''_1)))$

$Tappend(r) = \text{let } r' = Tappend(tail(r)) \text{ in } (cons(head(r),r'_1), r \cup r'_2)$

$\mathcal{N}reverse(r) = (1)$

$\mathcal{N}append(r) = \textbf{let } r' = \mathcal{N}append(tail(r)) \textbf{ in } (1, r \cup r'_2)$

The difference between $\mathcal{N}reverse$, $\mathcal{N}append$ and $\mathcal{T}reverse$, $\mathcal{T}append$ comes from the fact that the argument used in the test for equality with *nil* is necessary even if it does not appear in the result (that is, since $\mathcal{N}eq(r) = (1,1)$).

The functions produced are defined recursively on the infinite domain P. In order to be able to exploit this information at compile-time we have to map P onto a finite domain; this mapping is presented in section 4.6.

4.5 SHARING BASED GARBAGE COLLECTION

We show in this section how the interpretations presented above can be used to define a garbage collection algorithm. The method is based on the fact that a cell may safely be collected when it is dereferenced and it is not shared; in terms of reference counting it is equivalent to say that we can collect a cell when its reference count is decremented and reaches zero. In fact this strategy may be improved in the following way: a dereferenced cell may be collected even when it is shared in the case where the expressions sharing it *do not need it for their evaluation*. This information is provided by the $\mathcal{N}$ interpretation. The interpreter described in section 4.3 is enriched to integrate the sharing-based garbage collector; new arguments $sh_1,..., sh_n$ and $us_1,..., us_n$ are added to the semantics of functions $f(x_1,..., x_n)$; these arguments are patterns representing respectively the parts of $x_1,..., x_n$ that are shared and the parts of $x_1,..., x_n$ that may be used for the evaluation of another expression; these two pieces of information must be separated because they involve two different interpretations of the values of P (see section 4.4). They are propagated in the semantics of expressions through a sharing environment (*she* $\in$ *She* where *She* $= (Bv \rightarrow P)$) and a necessity environment (*use* $\in$ *Use* where *Use* $= (Bv \rightarrow P)$) associating each variable with a sharing pattern and a necessity pattern.

In order to make allocation (and in place updating) explicit, two arguments *free* and *allo* are added; they represent respectively a set of previously released locations, and a set of locations allocated but not yet released. Thus (*free - allo*) is a set of cells that may be used for further allocations without searching the store; note that, since previously released cells may be reallocated, cells may appear in both *free* and *allo*. We give now the complete definition of the new interpreter $\mathcal{R}p'$:

Rp' : $Prog{\rightarrow}Fve'$

$\mathcal{R}$: $Exp{\rightarrow}Fve'{\rightarrow}Bve{\rightarrow}She{\rightarrow}Use{\rightarrow}St{\rightarrow}\{Loc\}{\rightarrow}\{Loc\}{\rightarrow}(E \times St \times \{Loc\} \times \{Loc\})$

$Fve' = Fv{\rightarrow}E^*{\rightarrow}St{\rightarrow}P^*{\rightarrow}P^*{\rightarrow}\{Loc\}{\rightarrow}\{Loc\}{\rightarrow}(E \times St \times \{Loc\} \times \{Loc\})$

Rp' $[\![\{f_i(x_1, ..., x_n) = e_i\}]\!] =$

$\quad$ **letrec** $fve = [strict(\lambda v_1 ... v_n \, st \, sh_1 ... sh_n \, us_1 ... us_n \, free \, allo.$

$\qquad\qquad$ **let** $free' = dealloc (\{(v_j, sh_j, us_j) \mid x_j \notin e_i\}, st)$

$\qquad\qquad$ **in** $\mathcal{R} [\![e_i]\!] \, fve \, [v_j/x_j] \, [sh_j/x_j] \, [us_j/x_j] \, st \, (free \cup free') \, (allo\text{-}free') \, / f_i]$

$\mathcal{R} [\![x]\!] \, fve \, bve \, she \, use \, st \, free \, allo = (bve \, [\![x]\!], st, free, allo)$

$\mathcal{R} [\![k]\!] \, fve \, bve \, she \, use \, st \, free \, allo = (\mathcal{K}\beta [\![k]\!], st, free, allo)$

$\mathcal{R} [\![\textbf{if} \, e_1 \, \textbf{then} \, e_2 \, \textbf{else} \, e_3]\!] \, fve \, bve \, she \, use \, st \, free \, allo =$

$\quad$ **let** $use_1 = [((use \, [\![x]\!]) \cup \mathcal{N} [\![e_2]\!] \, [\![x]\!] \, 1 \cup \mathcal{N} [\![e_3]\!] \, [\![x]\!] \, 1)/x]$

$\qquad (v_1, st_1, free_1, allo_1) = \mathcal{R} [\![e_1]\!] \, fve \, bve \, she \, use_1 \, st \, free \, allo$

$\quad$ **in** **if** v_1 **then**

$\qquad$ **let** $free'_1 = dealloc (\{(bve \, [\![x]\!], she \, [\![x]\!], use \, [\![x]\!]) \mid [\![x]\!] \in e_3 \, \textbf{and} \, [\![x]\!] \notin e_2\}, st_1)$

$\qquad$ **in** $\mathcal{R} [\![e_2]\!] \, fve \, bve \, she \, use \, st_1 \, (free_1 \cup free'_1) \, (allo_1 - free'_1)$

$\qquad$ **else**

$\qquad$ **let** $free'_1 = dealloc (\{(bve \, [\![x]\!], she \, [\![x]\!], use \, [\![x]\!]) \mid [\![x]\!] \in e_2 \, \textbf{and} \, [\![x]\!] \notin e_3\}, st_1)$

$\qquad$ **in** $\mathcal{R} [\![e_3]\!] \, fve \, bve \, she \, use \, st_1 \, (free_1 \cup free'_1) \, (allo_1 - free'_1)$

$\mathcal{R} [\![cons \, (e_1, e_2)]\!] \, fve \, bve \, she \, use \, st \, free \, allo =$

$\quad$ **let** $use_1 = [((use \, [\![x]\!]) \cup \mathcal{N} [\![e_2]\!] \, [\![x]\!] \, 1)/x]$

$\qquad (v_1, st_1, free_1, allo_1) = \mathcal{R} [\![e_1]\!] \, fve \, bve \, she \, use_1 \, st \, free \, allo$

$\qquad she_2 = [((she \, [\![x]\!]) \cup \mathcal{T} [\![e_1]\!] \, [\![x]\!] \, 1)/x]$

$\qquad (v_2, st_2, free_2, allo_2) = \mathcal{R} [\![e_2]\!] \, fve \, bve \, she_2 \, use \, st_1 \, free_1 \, allo_1$

$\qquad loc = \textbf{if} \, (free_2 - allo_2) = \emptyset \, \textbf{then} \, newloc \, (allo_2) \, \textbf{else} \, oneof \, (free_2 - allo_2)$

$\quad$ **in** $(loc, st_2[(v_1, v_2)/loc], free_2, allo_2 \cup \{loc\})$

$\mathcal{R} [\![head \, (e)]\!] \, fve \, bve \, she \, use \, st \, free \, allo =$

$\quad$ **let** $(loc, st_1, free_1, allo_1) = \mathcal{R} [\![e]\!] \, fve \, bve \, she \, use \, st \, free \, allo$

$\qquad free'_1 = dealloc (\{(loc, S [\![e]\!] \, she \cup (1,0), S_t [\![e]\!] \, use)\}, st_1)$

$\quad$ **in** $(head(st_1 \, loc), st_1, (free_1 \cup free'_1), (allo_1 - free'_1))$

$\mathcal{R} [\![tail \, (e)]\!] \, fve \, bve \, she \, use \, st \, free \, allo =$

$\quad$ **let** $(loc, st_1, free_1, allo_1) = \mathcal{R} [\![e]\!] \, fve \, bve \, she \, use \, st \, free \, allo$

$\qquad free'_1 = dealloc (\{(loc, S [\![e]\!] \, she \cup (0,1), S_t [\![e]\!] \, use)\}, st_1)$

$\quad$ **in** $(tail(st_1 \, loc), st_1, (free_1 \cup free'_1), (allo_1 - free'_1))$

$\mathcal{R} [\![null \, (e)]\!] \, fve \, bve \, she \, use \, st \, free \, allo =$

$\quad$ **let** $(loc, st_1, free_1, allo_1) = \mathcal{R} [\![e]\!] \, fve \, bve \, she \, use \, st \, free \, allo$

$\qquad ree'_1 = dealloc (\{(loc, S [\![e]\!] \, she, S_t [\![e]\!] \, use)\}, st_1)$

$\quad$ **in** $(loc=nil, st_1, (free_1 \cup free'_1), (allo_1 - free'_1))$

$\mathcal{R}[\![eq\ (e_1, e_2)]\!]$ *fve bve she use st free allo* $=$

> **let** $use_1 = [(((use\ [\![x]\!])\cup \mathcal{N}[\![e_2]\!]\ [\![x]\!]\ 1)/x]$
>
> $(v_1, st_1, free_1, allo_1) = \mathcal{R}[\![e_1]\!]$ *fve bve she use_1 st free allo*
>
> $she_2 = [(((she\ [\![x]\!])\cup \mathcal{T}[\![e_1]\!]\ [\![x]\!]\ 1)/x]$
>
> $(v_2, st_2, free_2, allo_2) = \mathcal{R}[\![e_2]\!]$ *fve bve she_2 use st_1 $free_1$ $allo_1$*
>
> $free'_2 = dealloc\ (\{\ (loc_1, S[\![e_1]\!]\ she, S_t[\![e_1]\!]\ use),$
>
> $\qquad\qquad\qquad\quad (loc_2, S[\![e_2]\!]\ she, S_t[\![e_2]\!]\ use)\},\ st_2)$
>
> **in** $(v_1 = v_2, st_2, (free_2 \cup free'_2), (allo_2 - free'_2))$

$\mathcal{R}[\![+\ (e_1, e_2)]\!]$ *fve bve she use st free allo* $=$

> **let** $use_1 = [(((use\ [\![x]\!])\cup \mathcal{N}[\![e_2]\!]\ [\![x]\!]\ 1)/x]$
>
> $(v_1, st_1, free_1, allo_1) = \mathcal{R}[\![e_1]\!]$ *fve bve she use_1 st free allo*
>
> $she_2 = [(((she\ [\![x]\!])\cup \mathcal{T}[\![e_1]\!]\ [\![x]\!]\ 1)/x]$
>
> $(v_2, st_2, free_2, allo_2) = \mathcal{R}[\![e_2]\!]$ *fve bve she_2 use st_1 $free_1$ $allo_1$*
>
> **in** $(v_1 + v_2, st_2, free_2, allo_2)$

$\mathcal{R}[\![f(e_1, ..., e_n)]\!]$ *fve bve she use st free allo* $=$

> **let** $use_1 = [(((use\ [\![x]\!])\cup_{i\in[2,n]}\mathcal{N}[\![e_i]\!]\ [\![x]\!]\ 1)/x]$ **for all** $x\in dom(use)$
>
> $(v_1, st_1, free_1, allo_1) = \mathcal{R}[\![e_1]\!]$ *fve bve she use_1 st free allo*
>
> $she_2 = [(((she\ [\![x]\!])\cup \mathcal{T}[\![e_1]\!]\ [\![x]\!]\ 1)/x]$ **for all** $x\in dom(she)$
>
> $use_2 = [(((use\ [\![x]\!])\cup_{i\in[3,n]}\mathcal{N}[\![e_i]\!]\ [\![x]\!]\ 1)/x]$ **for all** $x\in dom(use)$
>
> $(v_2, st_2, free_2, allo_2) = \mathcal{R}[\![e_2]\!]$ *fve bve she_2 use_2 st_1 $free_1$ $allo_1$*
>
> $\qquad\qquad ...$
>
> $she_n = [(((she\ [\![x]\!])\cup_{i\in[1,..,n-1]}\mathcal{T}[\![e_i]\!]\ [\![x]\!]\ 1)/x]$ **for all** $x\in dom(she)$
>
> $(v_n, st_n, free_n, allo_n) = \mathcal{R}[\![e_n]\!]$ *fve bve she_n use st_{n-1} $free_{n-1}$ $allo_{n-1}$*
>
> **in** $(fve\ [\![f]\!])\ v_1\ ...\ v_n\ st_n\ (S[\![e_1]\!]\ [(((she\ [\![x]\!])\cup_{i\in[2,..,n]}\mathcal{T}[\![e_i]\!]\ [\![x]\!]\ 1)/x])$
>
> $\qquad\qquad\qquad\qquad ...$
>
> $\qquad\qquad (S[\![e_n]\!]\ [(((she\ [\![x]\!])\cup_{i\in[1,..,n-1]}\mathcal{T}[\![e_i]\!]\ [\![x]\!]\ 1)/x])$
>
> $\qquad\qquad (S_t[\![e_1]\!]\ use)$
>
> $\qquad\qquad\qquad ...$
>
> $\qquad\qquad (S_t[\![e_n]\!]\ use)$
>
> $\qquad\qquad free_n\ allo_n$

$dealloc(\emptyset, st) = \emptyset$

$dealloc(\{(loc,sh,us)\} \cup S, st) = dealloc_1(loc, sh, us, st) \cup dealloc(S, st)$

$dealloc_1(loc, sh, us, st) =$

        if $(loc = nil)$ **or** $(sh = 1)$ **or** $(us = 1)$

        then $\emptyset$

        else   **if** $us \neq 0$

                    then $dealloc_1(head(st\ loc), head(sh), head(us), st) \cup$

                            $dealloc_1(tail(st\ loc), tail(sh), tail(us), st)$

                else $dealloc_1(head(st\ loc), head(sh), 0, st) \cup$

                            $dealloc_1(tail(st\ loc), tail(sh), 0, st) \cup \{loc\}$

Let us make a few remarks about this semantics:

(1) *dealloc* is a function taking two arguments: a set of triples representing dereferenced locations with their associated sharing and necessity pattern and a state; it yields a set of locations of the state that can be collected according to the sharing and necessity indicated; notice that non-atomic patterns correspond to non-shared cells when they occur as sharing patterns and to necessary cells when they occur as necessity patterns; this explains why these two kinds of information must be managed separately; *newloc* takes a set of locations and yields a location that is not an element of this set; *oneof* yields one element of its set argument.

(2) allocations only occur in the evaluation of *cons*; if a deallocated cell is available (*free-allo* $\neq \emptyset$), it is used, otherwise a new cell is provided by *newloc*.

(3) the collection of cells that are still accessible must be done carefully in order to avoid any attempt to collect these cells again when they become inaccessible (which could entail the collection of cells which are once again in use). The technique for avoiding this is not described here for the sake of brevity (it roughly consists in modifying the pointer to the unuseful cell in order to make it inaccessible).

We present now the application of this definition to the functions *reverse* and *append*. We do not give the details of the derivation of these results for space considerations: they are obtained by the systematic application of the rules above and some straightforward simplifications. For the sake of clarity, we do not present the result of the application of $\mathcal{R}p'$ as a function environment containing a function corresponding to *reverse* and a function corresponding to *append*; we just give the definitions of these two functions and call them $\mathcal{R}reverse$ and $\mathcal{R}append$.

$\mathcal{R}reverse\ loc\ st\ sh\ us\ free\ allo =$

    if $loc = nil$

    then $(nil, st, free, allo)$

    else **let** $us' = us \cup \mathcal{N}[\![cons(head(l), nil)]\!]\ [\![l]\!]\ 1$

                $(loc_1, st_1, free_1, allo_1) = \mathcal{R}reverse\ (tail(st\ loc))\ st\ tail(sh)\ tail(us')\ free\ allo$

                $free'_1 = dealloc(\{(loc, sh \cup \mathcal{T}[\![reverse(tail(l))]\!]\ [\![l]\!]\ 1 \cup (1,0), us)\}, st_1)$

                $free''_1 = (free_1 \cup free'_1)$

                $allo''_1 = (allo_1 - free'_1)$

                $loc_2 =$ **if** $(free''_1 - allo''_1) = \varnothing$

                    then $newloc\ (allo''_1)$

                    else $oneof\ (free''_1 - allo''_1)$

      in $\mathcal{R}append\ loc_1\ loc_2\ (st_1[(head(st_1\ loc),nil)/loc_2])$

           $\mathcal{S}[\![reverse(tail(l))]\!]\ [sh \cup (\mathcal{T}[\![cons(head(l),nil)]\!]\ [\![l]\!]\ 1)\ /\ l]$

           $\mathcal{S}[\![cons(head(l),nil)]\!]\ [sh \cup (\mathcal{T}[\![reverse(tail(l))]\!]\ [\![l]\!]\ 1)\ /\ l]$

           $\mathcal{S}_t[\![reverse(tail(l))]\!]\ [us\ /\ l]$

           $\mathcal{S}_t[\![cons(head(l),nil)]\!]\ [us\ /\ l]$

           $free''_1$

           $(allo''_1 \cup \{loc_2\})$

$\mathcal{R}append\ loc_1\ loc_2\ st\ sh_1\ sh_2\ us_1\ us_2\ free\ allo =$

    if $loc_1 = nil$

    then $(loc_2, st, free, allo)$

    else **let** $free' = dealloc(\{(loc_1, sh_1 \cup \mathcal{T}[\![head(l_1)]\!]\ [\![l_1]\!]\ 1 \cup (0,1), us_1)\}, st)$

               $free_1 = (free \cup free')$

               $allo_1 = (allo - free')$

               $(loc'', st'', free'', allo'') =$

                  $\mathcal{R}append\ (tail(st\ loc_1))\ loc_2\ st$

                  $\mathcal{S}[\![tail(l_1)]\!]\ [sh_i \cup (\mathcal{T}[\![head(l_1)]\!]\ [\![l_i]\!]\ 1) \cup (\mathcal{T}[\![l_2]\!]\ [\![l_i]\!]\ 1)\ /\ l_i]_{i=1,2}$

                  $\mathcal{S}[\![l_2]\!]\ [sh_i \cup (\mathcal{T}[\![head(l_1)]\!]\ [\![l_i]\!]\ 1) \cup (\mathcal{T}[\![tail(l_1)]\!]\ [\![l_i]\!]\ 1)\ /\ l_i]_{i=1,2}$

                  $\mathcal{S}_t[\![tail(l_1)]\!]\ [us_i\ /\ l_i]_{i=1,2}$

                  $\mathcal{S}_t[\![l_2]\!]\ [us_i\ /l_i]_{i=1,2}$

                  $free_1\ allo_1$

               $loc =$ **if** $(free'' - allo'') = \varnothing$

                   then $newloc\ (allo'')$

                   else $oneof\ (free'' - allo'')$

      in $(loc, st''[(head(st\ loc_1),loc'')/loc]), free'', allo'' \cup \{loc\})$

The general method for the evaluation of expressions of the form $T[\![exp]\!]$ and $S[\![exp]\!]$ is presented in the next section; however these expressions can be evaluated directly when they do not involve recursive functions. Applying the rules in the definitions of T and S we obtain:

$N[\![cons(head(l),nil)]\!]\ [\![l]\!]\ 1 = (1,0)$

$T[\![cons(head(l),nil)]\!]\ [\![l]\!]\ 1 = (1,0)$

$T[\![head(l_1)]\!]\ [\![l_1]\!]\ 1 = (1,0)$

$S[\![tail(l_1)]\!]\ [sh_i \cup (T[\![head(l_1)]\!]\ [\![l_i]\!]\ 1) \cup (T[\![l_2]\!]\ [\![l_i]\!]\ 1)\ /\ l_i]_{i=1,2} = tail(sh_1)$

$S[\![l_2]\!]\ [sh_i \cup (T[\![head(l_1)]\!]\ [\![l_i]\!]\ 1) \cup (T[\![tail(l_1)]\!]\ [\![l_i]\!]\ 1)\ /\ l_i]_{i=1,2} = sh_2$

$S_t[\![tail(l_1)]\!]\ [us_i\ /\ l_i]_{i=1,2} = tail(us_1)$

$S_t[\![l_2]\!]\ [us_i\ /\ l_i]_{i=1,2} = us_2$

We can now use these results to simplify the definitions of $Rreverse$ and $Rappend$:

$Rreverse\ loc\ st\ sh\ us\ free\ allo =$
    if $loc = nil$
    then $(nil, st, free, allo)$
    else   **let** $us' = us \cup (1,0)$
                $(loc_1, st_1, free_1, allo_1) = Rreverse\ (tail(st\ loc))\ st\ tail(sh)\ tail(us')\ free\ allo$
                $free'_1 = dealloc(\{(loc, sh \cup T[\![reverse(tail(l))]\!]\ [\![l]\!]\ 1 \cup (1,0), us)\}, st_1)$
                $free''_1 = (free_1 \cup free'_1)$
                $allo''_1 = (allo_1 - free'_1)$
                $loc_2 = $ **if** $(free''_1 - allo''_1) = \emptyset$
                      then $newloc\ (allo''_1)$
                      else $oneof\ (free''_1 - allo''_1)$
        in $Rappend\ loc_1\ loc_2\ (st_1[(head(st_1\ loc),nil)/loc_2])$
                $S[\![reverse(tail(l))]\!]\ [sh \cup (1,0)\ /\ l]$
                $S[\![cons(head(l),nil)]\!]\ [sh \cup (T[\![reverse(tail(l))]\!]\ [\![l]\!]\ 1)\ /\ l]$
                $S_t[\![reverse(tail(l))]\!]\ [us\ /\ l]$
                $S_t[\![cons(head(l),nil)]\!]\ [us\ /\ l]$
                $free''_1$
                $(allo''_1 \cup \{loc_2\})$

$\mathcal{R}append\, loc_1\, loc_2\, st\, sh_1\, sh_2\, us_1\, us_2\, free\, allo =$

    if $loc_1 = nil$

    then $(loc_2, st, free, allo)$

    else **let** $free' = dealloc(\{(loc_1, sh_1 \cup (1,1), us_1)\}, st)$

                 $free_1 = (free \cup free')$

                 $allo_1 = (allo - free')$

                 $(loc'', st'', free'', allo'') =$

                        $\mathcal{R}append\, (tail(st\, loc_1))\, loc_2\, st$

                                    $tail(sh_1)\, sh_2\, tail(us_1)\, us_2\, free_1\, allo_1$

               $loc =$ **if** $(free'' - allo'') = \emptyset$

                     then $newloc\, (allo'')$

                     else $oneof\, (free'' - allo'')$

       in $(loc, st''[(head(st\, loc_1), loc'') / loc]), free'', allo'' \cup \{loc\})$

$\mathcal{R}reverse$ and $\mathcal{R}append$ can be seen as partially compiled versions of *reverse* and *append* where the garbage collection operations are made explicit; these versions could be used directly as specifications of the actions to be compiled into the object code; however the dynamic garbage collection involved would not be very effective for several reasons: first of all the evaluation of the sharing patterns would be quite expensive at run-time; furthermore the collection would not be complete because sharing patterns are basically approximations of the actual sharings. The other side of this abstraction property (and the justification of the whole approach) is that sharing is a better basis for static analysis. We justify this claim in the next section by showing how sharing and necessity information can be evaluated and exploited at compile-time.

4.6 FINITE DOMAINS AND COMPILE-TIME GARBAGE COLLECTION

Functions Sf, Tf and Nf defined by interpretations S, T and N are recursive if the original function $f = E(f)$ is recursive. These functions are defined on the infinite domain of patterns P which is a complete lattice; the least solution of a recursive definition can therefore be defined in the usual way by successive applications of the transformation E starting with the least function $(f_0(p_1, ..., p_n) = 0$ here). However this evaluation can be achieved statically only if the domain is finite. For this reason we define now a collection of finite domains P_n included in P:

$$P_0 = \{0, 1\}$$
$$P_{n+1} = P_n + (P_n \times P_n)$$

For example:

$$P_1 = \{0, 1, (0,0), (0,1), (1,0), (1,1)\}$$

It is easy to show that these domains are also complete lattices. Corresponding mappings M_i may be defined in the following way:

$M_i: P \rightarrow P_i$
$M_i \; p$ = the least element of P_i greater than p
               (this element exists since p is an element of P)

$(M_i \; p)$ is greater than p to ensure correctness (remember that greater patterns are safer patterns) and we take the least of these elements to be as accurate as possible. For example:

$M_0 \, (0,1) = 1$
$M_1((1,0),(1,1)) = (1,1)$

All primitive functions pf defined on P (for example $cons$, $head$, ...) are also defined on P_i as $pf_i \, (x) = M_i(pf(x))$. For example in the domain P_1, $cons \, ((0,1),1) = (1,1)$.

The analysis of each particular program may require a domain of a particular size. In practice P_1 is most often enough and a sufficient criterion to choose the right size is the possibility of deducing that all allocations of the program can be implemented as in place updatings. Let us now come back to the example of *reverse* and *append* to show how their recursive sharing and transmission definitions can be solved and exploited to compile the garbage collection completely.

We recall the recursive definitions produced at the end of section 4.4:

$Sreverse(s) = Sappend \, (Sreverse \, (tail(s)), cons(head(s), 0))$
$Sappend(s_1, s_2) = s_2 \cup cons(head(s_1), Sappend(tail(s_1), s_2))$
$Treverse(r) = $ **let** $r' = Tappend(r)$ **in** (**let** $r'' = Treverse(r'_1)$ **in** $(cons(head(r'_2), r''_1)))$
$Tappend(r) = $ **let** $r' = Tappend(tail(r))$ **in** $(cons(head(r),r'_1), r \cup r'_2)$

We consider here the finite domain P_1; we evaluate for example the application of the least fixed point of the definition of $Tappend$ to 1:

$Tappend_0(1) = (0,0)$

$Tappend_1(1) = \textbf{let } r' = Tappend_0(1) \textbf{ in } (cons(1, r'_1), 1)$

$\qquad\qquad\quad = ((1,0),1)$

$Tappend_2(1) = \textbf{let } r' = Tappend_1(1) \textbf{ in } (cons(1, r'_1), 1)$

$\qquad\qquad\quad = ((1,1),1)$

$Tappend_3(1) = ((1,1),1)$

So we have:

$Tappend(1) = ((1,1),1)$

We find the following results in the same way:

$Treverse(1) = ((1,1))$

$Treverse((1,1)) = ((1,1))$

$Sreverse(0) = 0 \qquad ...$

Let us now see how this technique can be used to simplify the semantics of *reverse* and *append* given at the end of section 4.5; we assume that *reverse* is the top-level function, so its arguments contain no sharing and we try to simplify ($\mathcal{R}reverse\ loc\ st\ 0\ 0\ free\ allo$); looking at the definition of $\mathcal{R}reverse$ we have to evaluate the following expressions:

$\mathcal{N}[\![cons(head(l), nil)]\!]\ [\![l]\!]\ 1 = (1,0)$

$\mathcal{T}[\![reverse(tail(l))]\!]\ [\![l]\!]\ 1 = (0,1)$

$\mathcal{S}[\![reverse(tail(l))]\!]\ [(\mathcal{T}[\![cons(head(l), nil)]\!]\ [\![l]\!]\ 1) / l] = 0$

$\mathcal{S}[\![cons(head(l), nil)]\!]\ [(\mathcal{T}[\![reverse(tail(l))]\!]\ [\![l]\!]\ 1) / l] = 0$

$\mathcal{S}_t[\![reverse(tail(l))]\!]\ [0 / l] = 0$

$\mathcal{S}_t[\![cons(head(l), nil)]\!]\ [0 / l] = 0$

So ($\mathcal{R}reverse\ loc\ st\ 0\ 0\ free\ allo$) can be simplified in the following way:

$\mathcal{R}reverse\ loc\ st\ 0\ 0\ free\ allo=$

$\qquad\textbf{if } loc = nil$

$\qquad\textbf{then } (nil, st, free, allo)$

$\qquad\textbf{else}\quad \textbf{let } (loc_1, st_1, free_1, allo_1) = \mathcal{R}reverse\ (tail(st\ loc))\ st\ 0\ 0\ free\ allo$

$\qquad\qquad\quad \textbf{in } \mathcal{R}append\ loc_1\ loc\ (st_1[(head(st_1\ loc), nil)/loc])\ 0\ 0\ 0\ 0\ free_1\ allo_1$

Similarly for *append* we have:

$$T[\![head(l_1)]\!]\ [\![l_1]\!]\ 1 = (1,0)$$
$$S[\![tail(l_1)]\!]\ [((T[\![head(l_1)]\!]\ [\![l_i]\!]\ 1) \cup (T[\![l_2]\!]\ [\![l_i]\!]\ 1) / l_i]_{i=1,2} = 0$$
$$S[\![l_2]\!]\ [((T[\![head(l_1)]\!]\ [\![l_i]\!]\ 1) \cup (T[\![tail(l_1)]\!]\ [\![l_i]\!]\ 1) / l_i]_{i=1,2} = 0$$
$$S_t[\![tail(l_1)]\!]\ [0 / l_i]_{i=1,2} = 0$$
$$S_t[\![l_2]\!]\ [0 / l_i]_{i=1,2} = 0$$

and:

$\mathcal{R}append\ loc_1\ loc_2\ st\ 0\ 0\ 0\ 0\ free\ allo =$
    if $loc_1 = nil$
    then $(loc_2, st, free, allo)$
    else let $(loc'', st'', free'', allo'') = \mathcal{R}append\ (tail(st\ loc_1))\ loc_2\ st\ 0\ 0\ 0\ 0\ free\ allo$
        in $(loc_1, (st''[(head(st\ loc_1),loc'')/loc_1], free'', allo'')$

The key transformation to obtain these results is the replacement of **let**-expressions of the form:

    let $free' = (free \cup \{loc\})$
        $allo' = (allo - \{loc\})$
        $\cdots$
        $loc' = $ **if** $(free'' - allo'') = \emptyset$ **then** $newloc(allo'')$ **else** $oneof(free'' - allo'')$
    in E

by:

    let $free' = free$
        $allo' = allo$
        $\cdots$
        $loc' = loc$
    in E

So, after simplification, functions $\mathcal{R}reverse$ and $\mathcal{R}append$ do not make use of *newloc*, which means that all allocations have been implemented as in place updatings. In $\mathcal{R}reverse$ the cell *loc* is reused at each recursive call and in $\mathcal{R}append$ the cell loc_1 is reused.

4.7 COMPARISON WITH PREVIOUS WORK

Concern about the storage efficiency of functional languages is widespread. Much work in the area is directed at improving the design of the run-time environment of functional programs. We consider here only research directed at analysis of programs or transformation of programs to improve their efficiency. The analysis described in this chapter is complementary to program transformations techniques like [Burstall et al. 77] or [Wadler 88] which may entail a reduction of the number of allocations required by the execution of a program. Our technique does not affect the number of allocations required by a program but may allow us to implement them as in place updatings and to avoid all the traditional overhead incurred by dynamic garbage collection algorithms.

The pioneer in this area is J.M. Barth [Barth 77] who proposed a method to avoid redundant operations in a transaction-based collection algorithm: for example pairs of cancelling transactions are detected, transactions are grouped into larger batches ...

[Schwarz 78] describes a method to detect when destructive operations can be used without altering the meaning of an applicative expression. Programs are represented by graphs labelled by isolation classes which correspond to our sharing patterns. The purpose of this system is to check the declarations of sharing supplied by the user. This contrasts with our method which provides a way to derive and exploit the sharing information from the usual functional definition.

The objective of the work described in [Inoue et al. 88] is close to ours; the goal is to detect the places in a program where a cell can safely be collected but there is no attempt to perform in place updating. The strategy consists in collecting after the execution of a function the cells that have been created during the evaluation of its arguments and which do not appear in its result; this is clearly a safe deallocation policy; however it seems that it may entail a possibly long time between the point where a cell is no longer useful and the point where it is collected; the extreme consequence could be that a program compiled using this technique may run out of memory because many collectable cells are temporarily ignored; in contrast, a program whose garbage collection has been completely compiled using our technique can be safely executed without any background dynamic garbage collector.

[Hudak 87] analyses functional programs by abstract interpretation of reference counts. It is concerned with determining the loss of the last reference to aggregate data structures, such as arrays, in order to avoid performing a new allocation. It is shown how a functional encoding of Hoare's quicksort algorithm can be optimized to have space complexity equal to that of the imperative version. The technique described here tackles the general problem of non-flat lists and is able to optimize a standard functional encoding of quicksort, based on lists.

The work reported in [Meira 84] analyses execution paths in functional programs to be executed by a combinator graph reducer. It performs a form of sharing analysis, but with the intention of deciding at what point run-time sharing flags are to be set; many opportunities for compile-time optimization are lost, since sharing flags are never unset.

The analysis technique described in this chapter also appears to be closely related to the techniques reported in [Hughes 87] and [Wadler et al. 87]. The $\mathcal{T}$ and $\mathcal{N}$ interpretations perform a kind of backwards analysis since they yield information about the arguments of a function from information about its result. It seems that our pattern domain may be seen as generalization of the contexts and projections proposed by Hughes and Wadler: starting with an infinite pattern domain P, we provide a systematic way to map this domain onto a finite domain. We believe that our pattern domain P is interesting in its own right; we show in [Jones et al. 89] how it can be used for strictness analysis on non-flat domains.

The analysis method described here has been implemented. As far as efficiency is concerned, the crucial point is clearly the evaluation of the least fixpoints which depend on the size of the pattern domain required. Hand analysis suggests that P_0 and P_1 are often sufficient but experiments are necessary to assess the practicability of the method.

There are several directions in which the work described in this chapter should be extended:

- the opportunities to perform in place updating depend on the computation rule chosen for the implementation of the language. Further work has to be done to adapt our analysis to call-by-need;

- we have assumed binary *cons* cells; a first attempt to handle variable-sized cells would be to complement our analyser with a type system allowing us to deduce information about the relative sizes of a collected cell and a requested cell.

REFERENCES

[Abramsky et al. 87] S. Abramsky, C. Hankin. Abstract interpretation of declarative languages. Ellis Horwood, 1987.

[Barth 77] J. M. Barth. Shifting garbage collection overhead to compile time. CACM, Vol. 20, No 7, pp. 513-518, July 1977.

[Burstall et al. 77] R. M. Burstall, J. Darlington. A transformation system for developing recursive programs. JACM, Vol. 24, No. 1, pp. 44-67, January 1977.

[Hudak 87] P. Hudak. A semantic model of reference counting and its abstraction. In [Abramsky et al. 87], pp. 45-62.

[Hughes 87] J. Hughes. Backwards analysis of functional programs. University of Glasgow, Dept of Computing Science, Research Report CSC/87/R3, March 1987.

[Inoue et al. 88] K. Inoue, H. Seki, H. Yagi. Analysis of functional programs to detect run-time garbage cells. ACM TOPLAS, Vol. 10, No. 4, pp. 555-578, October 1988.

[Jones et al. 89] S. B. Jones, D. Le Métayer. A new method for strictness analysis on non-flat domains. Proc. of IEEE TENCON 89, Session on Functional Programming Languages: Theories and Applications, November 1989.

[Meira 84] S. L. Meira. Optimized combinatoric code for applicative language implementation. Proceedings of 6th International Symposium on Programming, LNCS 167, pp. 206-216, 1984.

[Schwarz 78] J. Schwarz. Verifying the safe use of destructive operations in applicative programs. Proc. of 3rd International Symposium on Programming, Dunod informatique, pp. 395-411, 1978.

[Stoye et al. 84] W. R. Stoye, T. J. W. Clarke, A. C. Norman. Some practical methods for rapid combinator reduction. Proc. of ACM Symposium on Lisp and Functional Programming, pp. 159-166, 1984.

[Wadler et al. 87] P. L. Wadler, R. J. M. Hughes. Projections for strictness analysis. Proc. of 3rd Int. Conference on Functional Programming and Computer Architecture, pp. 385-407, September 1987.

[Wadler 88] P. L. Wadler. Deforestation: Transforming programs to eliminate trees. Proc . of European Symposium on Programming, March 1988.

CHAPTER 5

ANALYSIS OF FUNCTIONAL PROGRAMS
BY PROGRAM TRANSFORMATION

Daniel Le Métayer

5.1 INTRODUCTION

In chapter 3 we presented a technique for program analysis called abstract interpretation; this technique was applied in chapter 4 to the detection of sharing in order to optimize the implementation of memory management of functional languages. We propose now a different method for the analysis of functional programs based on program transformation. We first make a quick survey of the motivations and the techniques for program transformation in section 5.2; the general method for program analysis by program transformation is introduced in section 5.3; it is then applied to the analysis of time complexity in a strict first-order language (section 5.4) and in a higher-order language (section 5.5); then we describe the application of the method to two other kinds of analyses: the potential level of parallelism (section 5.6) and the memory complexity of programs (section 5.7). Section 5.8 is devoted to the presentation of the system ACE (Automatic Complexity Evaluator) which is an implementation of the method described in this chapter. In section 5.9 we review the approach and make a comparison with the abstract interpretation technique.

5.2 SURVEY OF PROGRAM TRANSFORMATION TECHNIQUES

There is a growing interest in program transformation and various systems have been built to (partially) mechanize program transformation methods. We shall not give many details on the existing systems here (the interested reader may refer to [Partsch et al. 83] and [Feather 87] for surveys and rich bibliographies); we shall rather focus on the transformation techniques and on their applicability for various purposes. We consider *program transformation* as the derivation from an original program P_L in a language L of a program P'_L *in the same language* such that a certain *correctness* property $C(P_L, P'_L)$ holds. Ideally a second relation $E(P_L, P'_L)$ should be associated with the transformation which would represent its *effectiveness*: since the transformation is carried out to reach a certain goal, the transformed program should be satisfactory in this respect. We impose the requirement that programs are expressed within the same language; if this is not the case, we prefer to use the word *translation* rather than transformation; translation conveys the idea of change of world whereas transformation is a change of the "form" in the same world. The correctness and the effectiveness properties depend on the goal of the transformation.

The main techniques used to achieve program transformations may be summarized as follows [Burstall et al. 77]:

(1) *application of pre-defined rules*: examples of pre-defined rules may be:

T_1 $(f$ (if p then a else b)) $=$ if p then $T_1(f(a))$ else $T_1(f(b))$
T_2 $(length(cons(a,b))) = 1 + T_2$ $(length(b))$
T_3(if p then a else b) $= T_3(p) +$ (if p then $T_3(a)$ else $T_3(b)$)

The correctness property of the two first rules (which correspond to laws of the primitives of the language) is equivalence, but this is not the case for the third one.

(2) *Unfolding*: unfolding consists in replacing a function call by the appropriately instantiated body of the function.

(3) *Folding*: the inverse of unfolding, which consists in replacing the instantiated body of a function by the corresponding call.

(4) *Introduction of new definitions*: this technique is generally used to provide a more general definition of the original program.

(5) *Abstraction*: it consists in replacing an expression E containing subexpressions $E_1,..., E_n$ by:

$E[U_1/E_1,..., U_n/E_n]$ **where** $U_1 = E_1 ... U_n = E_n$

The notation $E[U_1/E_1,..., U_n/E_n]$ represents the expression E where E_i are replaced by U_i.

This technique may be useful to factorize some expressions in order to avoid their reevaluation.

(6) *recursion induction*: the recursion induction principle can be stated as follows [McCarthy 63]: "two functions which satisfy the same recursive equation are equivalent over the domain of the function defined by this equation". For example let f be a function satisfying the following equation:

$$f(x) = \textbf{if } x = 0 \textbf{ then } 0 \textbf{ else } 1 + f(x\text{-}1)$$

Since the identity function on positive integers satisfies this equation too, we may conclude:

$$x \geq 0 \ \Rightarrow f(x) = id(x) = x$$

Let us now review the main areas of application of program transformation.

5.2.1 Program optimization

The program construction philosophy behind functional languages is to separate as much as possible correctness issues and efficiency issues; basically the programmer should provide a possibly inefficient but correct program and the system is responsible for deriving an equivalent and efficient version of it. It turns out that most of these optimizations can be carried out within the functional language itself by program transformation. Among the well-known optimizing transformation techniques let us mention:
- the transformation of recursive programs into iterative (left-recursive) ones: [Burstall et al. 77, Wand 80, Arsac et al. 82],
- the transformation of programs to combine list traversals (or loops): [Burstall et al. 77, Wadler 81],
- the transformation of programs to avoid redundant computations: [Burstall et al. 77].

Let us take a few examples to illustrate these techniques; we first start with the traditional recursive definition of factorial:

$$fact\ (n) = \textbf{if } n = 0 \textbf{ then } 1 \textbf{ else } n \times fact(n\text{-}1)$$

We introduce a new definition (which is a generalization of *fact* because $fact(n) = g(n,1)$):

$$g\ (n, m) = m \times fact(n)$$

Unfolding the definition of g, we get:

$$g(n, m) = m \times (\text{ if } n = 0 \text{ then } 1 \text{ else } n \times fact(n\text{-}1))$$

Using a law of the conditional primitive we get:

$$g(n, m) = \text{if } n = 0 \text{ then } m \times 1 \text{ else } m \times (n \times fact(n\text{-}1))$$

Using the associativity of multiplication and the fact that 1 is its neutral element we have:

$$g(n, m) = \text{if } n = 0 \text{ then } m \text{ else } (m \times n) \times fact(n\text{-}1)$$

Now $(m \times n) \times fact(n\text{-}1)$ is an instantiation of the body of g; so we can fold it:

$$g(n,m) = \text{if } n = 0 \text{ then } m \text{ else } g(m \times n, n\text{-}1)$$

Since $fact(n) = g(n,1)$, we have derived an iterative version of the factorial function; in the functional framework, a function is said to be iterative if it is left-recursive (or tail recursive) because it can be implemented in an iterative way. More details about tail recursion and its implementation are provided in chapter 6.

Let us now consider the function $conc_3$, defined in terms of $conc_2$, which concatenates three lists:

$$conc_3(x,y,z) = conc_2(conc_2(x,y),z)$$
$$conc_2(x,y) = \text{if } null(x) \text{ then } y \text{ else } cons(head(x), conc_2(tail(x), y))$$

Function $conc_3$ involves two traversals of the list x and constructs an intermediate list; let us now see how it can be improved by program transformation; unfolding the inner call of $conc_2$ in the definition of $conc_3$, we get:

$$conc_3(x,y,z) = conc_2(\text{ if } null(x) \text{ then } y \text{ else } cons(head(x), conc_2(tail(x), y)), z)$$

Distributing $conc_2$ over the conditional expression we have:

$$conc_3(x,y,z) = \text{if } null(x) \text{ then } conc_2(y,z) \text{ else } conc_2(cons(head(x), conc_2(tail(x), y)), z)$$

Unfolding again the body of $conc_2$ and simplifying the conditional expression we get:

$conc_3(x,y,z) = $ **if** $null(x)$ **then** $conc_2(y,z)$ **else** $cons(head(x), conc_2(conc_2(tail(x), y), z))$

We can now fold the body of the definition of $conc_3$ and we have:

$conc_3(x,y,z) = $ **if** $null(x)$ **then** $conc_2(y,z)$ **else** $cons(head(x), conc_3(tail(x), y, z))$

This new version involves only one traversal of the list x and does not build any intermediate structure.

Let us now take an example of transformation to avoid redundant computations; the Fibonacci function is usually defined in the following way:

$fib(n) = $ **if** $n \le 1$ **then** 1 **else** $fib(n-1) + fib(n-2)$

Its complexity is clearly exponential but the function may be improved because this initial version involves many redundant computations; we introduce a new definition:

$g(n) = cons\ (fib(n),\ fib(n-1))$

fib can be expressed in terms of g in the following way:

$fib(n) = $ **if** $n \le 1$ **then** 1 **else** $head(gn) + tail(gn)$ **where** $gn = g(n-1)$ \hfill (1)

Unfolding the body of fib in the definition of g, and simplifying we get:

$g(n) = cons(\ $ **if** $n \le 1$ **then** 1 **else** $fib(n-1) + fib(n-2), fib(n-1))$

Applying a law of the conditional, we get:

$g(n) = $ **if** $n \le 1$ **then** $cons(1, fib(n-1))$ **else** $cons(fib(n-1) + fib(n-2), fib(n-1))$

Which can be simplified into (by unfolding and using a law of the conditional):

$g(n) = $ **if** $n \le 1$ **then** $cons(1,1)$ **else** $cons(fib(n-1) + fib(n-2), fib(n-1))$

Since the expression $fib(n-1)$ is duplicated we can apply the abstraction rule and we obtain:

$g(n) = $ **if** $n \le 1$ **then** $cons(1,1)$ **else** $cons(head(gn) + tail(gn), head(gn))$
$$\textbf{where } gn = cons\ (fib(n-1),\ fib(n-2))$$

Now we can fold the body of g and we get:

$$g(n) = \textbf{if } n \leq 1 \textbf{ then } cons(1,1) \textbf{ else } cons(head(gn) + tail(gn), head(gn))$$
$$\textbf{where } gn = g(n\text{-}1)$$

and, if we take this together with definition (1) of *fib*, we have obtained a linear version of the Fibonacci function.

The correctness property of optimizing transformations is obviously equivalence (the initial program and the transformed program must return the same result) and the effectiveness property is the time (or space) complexity (the transformed program must be more efficient than the original one). The former property is generally well formalized and it is ensured by the system but the second one is more difficult to express and is treated in an informal way. One conclusion of [Burstall et al. 77] for example is that further work has to be done to provide sufficient conditions that guarantee that the transformations produce an improvement. This remark provides a further motivation for the design of complexity analysis tools.

5.2.2 Program synthesis

The basic idea is to extend a functional language in order to be able to express non-executable specifications (expressions "*x suchthat P(x)*" for example) [Clark et al. 80]. Programs are transformed in order to replace these specifications by equivalent expressions. Another solution, avoiding the need to extend the functional language, is to consider specifications as executable (even if possibly very expensive) programs of the "generate and test" form; for example a sort specification would be *sort(l) = ordered(perm(l))* where *perm(l)* generates all the permutations of a list *l* and *ordered* is a filter selecting only the ordered ones. So the motivations and the techniques involved are very close to the program optimization case. Chapter 1 presents an example of program development by program transformation.

5.2.3 Program compilation

It has been known for a long time that a functional expression with variables can be transformed into an equivalent functional expression without variables (with the introduction of special basic functions called combinators); this transformation is called *abstraction*. Turner [Turner 79] showed that this technique could be applied to the implementation of functional languages because the reduction of combinatoric expressions is simpler than the reduction of expressions with variables; in some sense, combinators can be seen as machine instructions for a reduction machine. Abstraction is clearly a program transformation according to the definition given at the beginning of this section; however it is very different from the two previous ones with respect to the techniques involved. Abstraction and compilation by program transformation are explained in detail in chapter 6. The correctness property of abstraction is usually equivalence (however we present in chapter 6 a particular abstraction algorithm with a more elaborate correctness property) and its effectiveness property is a syntactic criterion (namely, that the expressions produced should not involve any variables).

5.2.4 Proof of properties of programs

The method consists in deriving from the definition of the program an expression of the property within the functional language. For example, one may try to prove that the function $conc_2$ defined above satisfies the following property:

$$length(conc_2(x,y)) = length(x) + length(y)$$

To this aim, we introduce a new definition:

$$llength(x, y) = length(x) + length(y)$$

where *length* is defined in the usual way:

$$length(l) = \textbf{if } null(l) \textbf{ then } 0 \textbf{ else } 1 + length(tail(l))$$

Unfolding the definition of *length* in the body of *llength* we get:

$$llength(x, y) = \textbf{if } null(x) \textbf{ then } length(y) \textbf{ else } 1 + length(tail(x)) + length(y)$$

Folding the body of *llength* we have:

$$llength(x, y) = \textbf{if } null(x) \textbf{ then } length(y) \textbf{ else } 1 + llength(tail(x), y)$$

Now we want to transform the definition $f(x,y) = length(conc_2(x,y))$; unfolding the body of $conc_2$ we get:

$$f(x,y) = length(conc_2(x,y))$$
$$= length(\textbf{if } null(x) \textbf{ then } y \textbf{ else } cons(head(x), conc_2(tail(x), y)))$$

Distributing *length* over the conditional expression we have:

$f(x,y) =$ **if** *null*(x) **then** *length*(y) **else** *length*$(cons(head(x), conc_2(tail(x), y)))$

Unfolding the definition of *length* and simplifying the conditional expression, we get:

$f(x,y) =$ **if** *null*(x) **then** *length*(y) **else** $1 + length(conc_2(tail(x), y))$

The body of f can be folded:

$f(x,y) =$ **if** *null*(x) **then** *length*(y) **else** $1 + f(tail(x), y)$

Now, we see that this recursive equation is exactly the definition of *llength* and, according to the recursion induction principle, we conclude:

$f(x,y) = llength(x,y)$

That is to say:

$length(conc_2(x,y)) = length(x) + length(y)$

The complexity analysis described below makes a pervasive use of this technique and chapter 8 presents another example of the proof of a property by program transformation. The correctness property of the transformation is again equivalence and its effectiveness is the property of the program to be found (the transformation is effective if it establishes the desired property).

The analysis technique presented in the following sections of this chapter is another kind of transformation whose correctness property is not equivalence; in rough terms the correctness property of the transformation T described in section 5.3 will be:

$C(f,T(f)) = (T(f)$ *is the complexity of the function* $f)$

and its effectiveness property will be:

$E(f,T(f)) = (T(f)$ *is a non recursive expression defined only in terms of primitive functions such as id, length, size, +, log, square, ...)*

5.3 PROGRAM ANALYSIS BY PROGRAM TRANSFORMATION

Most program analysis methods are based on abstract interpretation [Cousot 77, Mycroft 80, Abramsky 85, Burn 87] which is presented in chapter 3. The crucial part of the analysis by abstract interpretation consists in finding a non-recursive expression of the property $P(F)$. In order to achieve this it is necessary that the domain D_P on which the property is defined is finite. The least fixpoint of equations can then be found by symbolic evaluation because the sequence of approximations of a recursive function is finite. However this is a rather strong limitation since it precludes the use of the technique to derive information, such as complexity, that cannot be encoded within a finite domain.

The approach we take is to consider program analysis as a special case of program transformation. Let us consider the analysis of a program F to find a property $P(F)$; F is expressed in a language L whose semantics is S; instead of keeping the text of F and considering a new interpretation S_P, we use program transformation techniques to deduce $P(F)$ from F. So $P(F)$ is also expressed in the language L. The transformation is generally carried out in two phases; the first one is the syntax-directed derivation of $P(F)$ from F and the second one is an equivalence-preserving transformation to get a simpler expression of the property. So the whole analysis is achieved within the same framework, which is the source language L, by program transformation.

We give in this chapter several examples of analysis illustrating this principle; most of them cannot be achieved by a traditional (with finite domains) abstract interpretation. We do not prove the correctness of, nor consider the mechanization of, the transformations here since our goal is mainly to show the relevance of the method for various kinds of analysis. Further details on these points can be found in [Le Métayer 88]. We start with the first order part of our functional language. Section 5.4 applies the technique to the definition of a time complexity analyser. Section 5.5 extends the results to a higher order language. Sections 5.6 and 5.7 show how program transformation can be used to find a measure of the potential parallelism and of the space complexity of programs. Section 5.8 is a presentation of the system ACE which is based on the technique described in this chapter. In conclusion we review the approach and possible extensions.

Before getting into the details of program analysis, we describe some particular program transformation techniques that will be used in the remainder of the chapter. Most of these techniques are well known; we just recall their principle and illustrate them with a small example.

(1) Simplifications

We first list some very useful properties of primitive functions which are used to simplify expressions:

$$0 + e => e$$
$$head(cons(e_1, e_2)) => e_1$$
$$eq0(length(l)) => null(l)$$
$$length(cons(e_1, e_2)) => 1 + length(e_2)$$
$$length(tail(e)) => length(e) - 1$$
$$f(\text{if } e_1 \text{ then } e_2 \text{ else } e_3) => \text{if } e_1 \text{ then } f(e_2) \text{ else } f(e_3)$$

Some of these simplifications are only partially correct in a strict semantics, which means that the result may be more defined than the original expression; total correctness is ensured when the original expression cannot be undefined.

(2) Argument removal

When an argument x_k does not occur in the body of a definition of a function f, then f can be simplified by the introduction of the new function g such that:

$$f(x_1, ..., x_n) = g(x_1, ..., x_{k-1}, x_{k+1}, ..., x_n)$$

This transformation can also be achieved when x_k is only used in expressions occurring in the kth argument of recursive calls of f. For example the function:

$$f(x, y) = \text{if } null(x) \text{ then } 0 \text{ else } 1 + f(tail(x), y+1)$$

can be simplified in the following way:

$$f(x, y) = g(x)$$
$$g(x) = \text{if } null(x) \text{ then } 0 \text{ else } 1 + g(tail(x))$$

This transformation is again partially correct.

(3) Factorization

We may also add to a function a new argument representing an expression occurring in its body. This operation may be seen as a factorization: when the corresponding expression appears several times in the definition of the function, it will be evaluated only once when it is passed by value. For example, let the definition of $f(l_1, l_2)$ be:

$$f(l_1, l_2) = \textbf{if } length(l_1) = length(l_2) \textbf{ then } length(l_1) \textbf{ else } f(tail(l_1), cons(head(l_1), l_2))$$

We can transform f in the following way:

$$f(l_1, l_2) = f'(l_1, l_2, length(l_1))$$
$$f'(l_1,l_2,ll_1) = \textbf{if } ll_1 = length(l_2)$$
$$\textbf{then } ll_1$$
$$\textbf{else } f'(tail(l_1),cons(head(l_1), l_2), length(tail \; (l_1)))$$

Using the rules: "$length(tail(l)) \Rightarrow length(l) - 1$" and "$length(l_1) \Rightarrow ll_1$", we have:

$$f'(l_1,l_2,ll_1) = \textbf{if } ll_1 = length(l_2) \textbf{ then } ll_1 \textbf{ else } f'(tail(l_1), cons(head(l_1), l_2), ll_1\text{-}1)$$

This transformation is totally correct if the expression which is added as a parameter cannot diverge or is necessary for the evaluation of the function. It can be generalized to non-function expressions in the following way: an expression e containing a subexpression e' can be transformed into $((\lambda x.e[x/e']) \; e')$ if x is not a variable of e and if all the variables free in e' are not bound in e. This transformation is called beta expansion in lambda calculus.

(4) Specialization

When constant values occur as arguments of recursive calls, a new function is defined which is a specialization of the original one. For example, let $f(x, y, z)$ be defined by:

$$f(x, y, z) = \textbf{if } x = 0 \textbf{ then } y + z \textbf{ else } f(x\text{-}1, y+1, 0)$$

f can be simplified into:

$$f(x, y, z) = \textbf{if } x = 0 \textbf{ then } y + z \textbf{ else } f'(x\text{-}1, y+1)$$
$$f'(x, y) = \textbf{if } x = 0 \textbf{ then } y \textbf{ else } f'(x\text{-}1, y+1)$$

A similar technique can be applied when one argument of a function is not changed through the recursive calls; the transformation in this case involves the introduction of a **where** expression. For example, the first argument of the function
$$g(x,l) = \textbf{if } head(l) = x \textbf{ then } 0 \textbf{ else } 1 + g(x,tail(l))$$

is not changed through the recursive calls; so g can be transformed into:

$g(x,l) = g'(l)$ **where** $g'(l) = $ **if** $head(l) = x$ **then** 0 **else** $1 + g'(tail(l))$

5.4 TIME COMPLEXITY ANALYSIS IN A FIRST ORDER LANGUAGE

There has been a great deal of research done on the evaluation of the complexity of particular algorithms [Aho et al. 74]. Little effort however has been applied to the mechanization of this evaluation. Such a tool will be of great importance in the future especially in automatic program synthesis and program transformation systems in order to assess the efficiency of the produced program. We present in this section a method for the evaluation of the order of magnitude of the worst case time-complexity of programs. Our method consists in deriving from the original recursive function f, a recursive function Cf. Cf takes the same argument as f, but its result is an integer value which represents the number of function applications necessary for evaluating f applied to its argument. We obtain Cf by a transformation of the original program. The rules associated with the first-order version of the language introduced in section 2.6 are the following:

$$C(x) = 0 \tag{1}$$
$$C(k) = 0 \tag{2}$$
$$C(\text{if } e_1 \text{ then } e_2 \text{ else } e_3)) = C(e_1) + (\text{if } e_1 \text{ then } C(e_2) \text{ else } C(e_3)) \tag{3}$$
$$C(op^k(e_1, ..., e_k)) = C(e_1) + ... + C(e_k) \tag{4}$$
$$C(f(e_1, ..., e_k)) = C(e_1) + ... + C(e_k) + 1 + Cf (e_1, ..., e_k) \tag{5}$$

The complexity of a function f defined by:

$$f(x_1, ..., x_n) = e$$

is equal to:

$$Cf(x_1, ..., x_n) = C(e)$$

These rules are deduced from the call-by-value operational semantics of the language. For example, rule (3) means that e_1 is always evaluated whereas the evaluation of e_2 or e_3 depends on the result of e_1. Rules (4) and (5) come from the fact that the arguments are evaluated before a function call. In rule (5), 1 stands for the recursive call and $Cf(e_1, ..., e_k)$ is the number of recursive calls generated by the application of f to $(e_1, ..., e_k)$. This step is only partially correct because the original function may stop earlier (so its time complexity may be smaller) when it is applied to arguments outside its domain [Le Métayer 88].

This syntax-directed transformation is not sufficient as it generally yields a recursive function which may be difficult to exploit. We would like to produce results in the form "the complexity of the selection-sort function is the square of the length of the argument" for example. So the remaining task is basically a program transformation problem to find a non-recursive expression of the complexity function. This goal is achieved by the use of the transformation techniques described in section 5.3. Let us now take two simple examples to illustrate the method.

Example 5.1
We are interested in evaluating the complexity of the factorial function defined by:

$$fact\ (n) = \textbf{if } n = 0 \ \textbf{ then } \ 1 \textbf{ else } n \times fact\ (n - 1)$$

Applying the transformation rules defined above, we get:

$$Cfact\ (n) = (0 + 0) + (\textbf{if } n = 0 \textbf{ then } \ 0 \textbf{ else } 0 + (0 + 1 + Cfact\ (n - 1)))$$

After simplification by "$e + 0 => e$" and "$0 + e => e$", we get:

$$Cfact\ (n) = \textbf{if } n = 0 \ \textbf{ then } \ 0 \textbf{ else } 1 + Cfact\ (n - 1)$$

As stated above, this is a recursive definition of the identity function over the domain of positive integers. So the result is $Cfact(n) = n$, that is to say: the complexity of the factorial function is linear in its argument.

We describe now the analysis of two definitions of *reverse* to show that the system can be used to compare different versions of the same program.

Example 5.2
A simple but inefficient definition of reverse is the following:

$$reverse(l) = \textbf{if } null(l) \textbf{ then } nil \textbf{ else } append(reverse(tail(l)), head(l))$$
$$append(l, x) = \textbf{if } null(l) \textbf{ then } cons(x, nil) \textbf{ else } cons(head(l), append(tail(l), x))$$

The syntax-directed transformation of these definitions gives (after simplification):

$$Creverse(l) = \quad \textbf{if } null(l)$$
$$\textbf{then } 0$$
$$\textbf{else } 1 + Cappend(reverse(tail(l)), head(l)) + 1 + Creverse(tail(l))$$

$Cappend(l, x) = $ **if** $null(l)$ **then** 0 **else** $1 + Cappend(tail(l), x)$

The second argument of *Cappend* appears only in the second argument of the recursive call; so it can be discarded and:

$Cappend(l, x) = Cappend'(l)$
$Cappend'(l) = $ **if** $null(l)$ **then** 0 **else** $1 + Cappend'(tail(l))$

and $Cappend'(l) = length(l)$ by recursion induction.
So $Cappend(l, x) = length(l)$ and:

$Creverse(l) = $ **if** $null(l)$ **then** 0 **else** $2 + length(reverse(tail(l))) + Creverse(tail(l))$

$length(reverse(tail(l)))$ has to be simplified.
To this aim, the function $lengthr(l) = length(reverse(l))$ is defined and simplified:

$lengthr(l) = length$ (**if** $null(l)$ **then** nil **else** $append(reverse(tail(l)), head(l))$)
$\quad = $ **if** $null(l)$ **then** $length(nil)$ **else** $length(append(reverse(tail(l)), head(l)))$
$\quad = $ **if** $null(l)$ **then** 0 **else** $length(append(reverse(tail(l)), head(l)))$

The same operation is applied to simplify $length(append(reverse(tail(l)), head(l)))$; the function $lengtha(l, x) = length(append(l, x))$ is transformed in the following way:

$lengtha(l, x) = length($**if** $null(l)$ **then** $cons(x, nil)$ **else** $cons(head(l),append(tail(l), x)))$
$\quad = $ **if** $null(l)$ **then** $length$ $(cons(x, nil))$ **else** $length(cons(head(l),append(tail(l), x)))$

Applying the rules "$length(cons(e_1, e_2)) => 1 + length(e_2)$" and "$length(nil) => 0$", we get :

$lengtha(l, x) = $ **if** $null(l)$ **then** 1 **else** $1 + length(append(tail(l), x))$
$\quad = $ **if** $null(l)$ **then** 1 **else** $1 + lengtha(tail(l), x)$

by folding, and we can discard the second argument:

$lengtha(l, x) = lengtha'(l)$
$lengtha'(l) = $ **if** $null(l)$ **then** 1 **else** $1 + lengtha'(tail(l))$

and:
$lengtha'(l) = length(l) + 1$

by recursion induction; so: $lengtha(l, x) = length(l) + 1$ and:

$lengthr(l) = $ **if** $null(l)$ **then** 0 **else** $length(reverse(tail(l))) + 1$
$= $ **if** $null(l)$ **then** 0 **else** $lengthr(tail(l)) + 1$

So: $lengthr(l) = length(l)$ by recursion induction.
We come back to $Creverse(l)$:

$Creverse(l) = $ **if** $null(l)$ **then** 0 **else** $2 + length(tail(l)) + Creverse(tail(l))$
$= $ **if** $null(l)$ **then** 0 **else** $1 + length(l) + Creverse(tail(l))$

because $length(tail(l)) = length(l) - 1$.
As the expression $length(l)$ appears in the definition of $Creverse$, we add a new argument to $Creverse$ such that :

$Creverse(l) = Creverse'(l, length(l))$
$Creverse'(l, n) = $ **if** $null(l)$ **then** 0 **else** $1 + n + Creverse'(tail(l), length(tail(l)))$
$= $ **if** $null(l)$ **then** 0 **else** $1 + n + Creverse'(tail(l), length(l) - 1)$
$= $ **if** $null(l)$ **then** 0 **else** $1 + n + Creverse'(tail(l), n - 1)$
$= $ **if** $n = 0$ **then** 0 **else** $1 + n + Creverse'(tail(l), n - 1)$

As "$null(l) => (length(l) = 0)$" and "$length(l) => n$".
The first argument is no longer used and we have:

$Creverse'(l, n) = Creverse''(n)$
$Creverse''(n) = $ **if** $n = 0$ **then** 0 **else** $1 + n + Creverse''(n - 1)$

By recursion induction, $Creverse''(n) \sim n^2$, $Creverse'(l, n) \sim n^2$ and $Creverse(l) \sim length(l)^2$, with symbol $\sim$ denoting asymptotic equality.
So the complexity of this reverse function is the square of the length of its argument.
A second well-known definition of *reverse* is the following:

$reverse'(l) = reverse''(l, nil)$
$reverse''(l_1, l_2) = $ **if** $null(l_1)$ **then** l_2 **else** $reverse''(tail(l_1), cons(head(l_1), l_2))$

Applying the transformation rules defined above, we get:

$Creverse'(l) = 1 + Creverse''(l, nil)$

$Creverse''(l_1, l_2) =$ **if** $null(l_1)$ **then** 0 **else** $1 + Creverse''(tail(l_1), cons(head(l_1), l_2))$

The second argument can be discarded and we get:

$Creverse''(l_1, l_2) = Creverse'''(l_1)$

$Creverse'''(l_1) =$ **if** $null(l_1)$ **then** 0 **else** $1 + Creverse'''(tail(l_1))$

So:

$Creverse'''(l_1) = length(l_1)$

and

$Creverse''(l_1, l_2) = length(l_1)$

So: $Creverse'(l_1) \sim length(l_1)$

This second version of reverse is more efficient since its complexity is linear in terms of the length of the argument whereas the first was quadratic. The interested reader will find in [Le Métayer 88] the application of this method to the evaluation of the complexity of a sorting program.

5.5 EXTENSION OF THE ANALYSIS TO HIGHER ORDER LANGUAGES

We describe in this section how the previous results can be extended to higher-order languages. In higher-order languages, functions are first-class objects: they can be passed as arguments or returned as results of other functions.

The complexity of an expression $e(e_1, ..., e_k)$ is the sum of:
- the complexity of the evaluation of e (which yields a function),
- the complexity of the evaluation of $e_1, ..., e_k$,
- the complexity of the application of the result of e to the results of $e_1, ..., e_k$.

We can notice that there are at least two kinds of complexities for a functional expression like e above: the complexity of its evaluation and the complexity of the evaluation of the function it yields. The first order language is a particular case where e is always a symbol (primitive function or user-defined function) whose evaluation cost is zero. In general, an expression may have even more kinds of complexities; in the expression $e_1 e_2 ... e_k$ for example, we have to evaluate:
- the complexity of the evaluation of e_1,
- the complexity of the application of the result of e_1 to e_2,

   ...

- the complexity of the application of the result of $(e_1 ... e_{k-1})$ to e_k.

These complexities are respectively given by $C_0(e_1), C_1(e_1) \, e_2, ..., \quad C_{k-1}(e_1) \, e_2 ... e_k.$. So $C(e)$ and Cf in section 5.3 correspond respectively to $C_0(e)$ and $C_1(f)$ here. We give now the rules for the evaluation of $C_i(e)$. We assume in the following $j>0$.

$$C_0(x) = 0 \tag{1}$$
$$C_j(x) = C_j(x) \tag{2}$$
$$C_0(k) = 0 \tag{3}$$
$$C_0(\text{if } e_1 \text{ then } e_2 \text{ else } e_3) = C_0(e_1) + (\text{if } e_1 \text{ then } C_0(e_2) \text{ else } C_0(e_3)) \tag{4}$$
$$C_j(\text{if } e_1 \text{ then } e_2 \text{ else } e_3) = \text{if } e_1 \text{ then } C_j(e_2) \text{ else } C_j(e_3) \tag{5}$$
$$C_0(op^k \, (e_1, ..., e_k)) = C_0(e_1) + ... + C_0(e_k) \tag{6}$$
$$C_1(op^k) = 0 \tag{7}$$
$$C_0(f(e_1, ..., e_k)) = C_0(e_1) + ... + C_0(e_k) + 1 + C_1(f) \, (e_1, ..., e_k) \tag{8}$$
$$C_j(f(e_1, ..., e_k)) = C_{j+1}(f) \, (e_1, ..., e_k) \tag{9}$$
$$C_0(e \, (e_1, ..., e_k)) = C_0(e) + C_0(e_1) + ... + C_0(e_k) + 1 + C_1(e) \, (e_1, ..., e_k) \tag{10}$$
$$C_j(e \, (e_1, ..., e_k)) = C_{j+1}(e) \, (e_1, ..., e_k) \tag{11}$$
$$C_0(\lambda(x_1, ..., x_k). \, e) = 0 \tag{12}$$
$$C_j(\lambda(x_1, ..., x_k). \, e) = \lambda(x_1, ..., x_k). \, C_{j-1}(e) \tag{13}$$

The rules for the evaluation of C_0 correspond to the rules for the evaluation of C in section 5.3. Rule (12) is explained by the fact that the evaluation of a lambda expression is just the construction of a closure. $C_j(e)$ can be defined as:

$$C_j(e) = \lambda \, x_1 \, ... \, x_j. \text{ complexity of the application of } (e \, x_1 \, ... \, x_{j-1}) \text{ to } x_j$$

which justifies rules (9), (11) and (13). Rule (2) is used when functional arguments occur in the definition of a function; as the complexity of such functions is not known statically, it remains in the definition in a symbolic form. Following rule (13), the complexity $C_j(f)$ of a function defined by the equation:

$$f(x_1, ..., x_n) = e$$

is given by:

$$C_j(f) \, (x_1, ..., x_n) = C_{j-1}(e)$$

and $C_0(f) = 0$.

Let us now illustrate these rules with a small example.

Example 5.3

We define the *map* function in the following way:

$$map(f) = \lambda l. \text{ if } null(l) \text{ then } nil \text{ else } cons(f(head(l)), map(f)\ (tail(l)))$$

The complexity of *map*, that is $C_1(map)$, can be derived:

$$C_1(map)(f) = C_0(\lambda l. \text{ if } null(l) \text{ then } nil \text{ else } cons(f(head(l)), map(f)\ (tail(l)))) = 0$$

This result is natural as the evaluation of *map(f)* is just a closure construction.
The complexity of *map(f)*, that is $C_1(map\ (f)) = C_2(map)(f)$ can be derived:

$$
\begin{aligned}
C_2(map)(f) &= C_1(\lambda l. \text{ if } null(l) \text{ then } nil \text{ else } cons(f(head(l)), map(f)\ (tail(l)))) \\
&= \lambda l.\ C_0(\text{if } null(l) \text{ then } nil \text{ else } cons(f(head(l)), map(f)\ (tail(l)))) \\
&= \lambda l. \text{ if } null(l) \text{ then } 0 \text{ else } 1 + C_1(f)\ (head(l)) + 1 + C_1(map(f))\ (tail(l)) + 1 \\
&= \lambda l. \text{ if } null(l) \text{ then } 0 \text{ else } 3 + C_1(f)\ (head(l)) + C_2(map)(f)\ (tail(l))
\end{aligned}
$$

This function cannot be further simplified.
Let us now apply this result to the analysis of the complexity of a function using *map*.

$$
\begin{aligned}
allzero\ (l) &= map(eq0)\ (l) \\
C_1(allzero)\ (l) &= C_0(map(eq0)\ (l)) \\
&= 1 + C_1(map(eq0))\ (l) \\
&= 1 + C_2(map)\ (eq0)\ (l) \\
C_2(map)\ (eq0)\ l &= \text{if } null(l) \text{ then } 0 \text{ else } 3 + C_1(eq0)\ (head(l)) + C_2(map)(eq0)\ (tail(l)) \\
&= \text{if } null(l) \text{ then } 0 \text{ else } 3 + C_2(map)(eq0)\ (tail(l))
\end{aligned}
$$

As the recursive call to $C_2(map)$ is applied to the constant *eq0*, we can define a specialization $Cmap0(l) = C_2(map)\ (eq0)\ (l)$:

$$Cmap0(l) = \text{if } null(l) \text{ then } 0 \text{ else } 3 + Cmap0\ (tail(l))$$

and we have by recursion induction:

$$Cmap0(l) = 3 \times length(l)$$

So:

$$C_1(allzero)\ (l) \quad = 1 + 3 \times length(l)$$
$$\sim length(l)$$

We describe in [Le Métayer 87] how the extension to higher order languages can be used for the analysis of a non-strict language.

5.6 A MEASURE OF THE POTENTIAL PARALLELISM OF PROGRAMS

It has been claimed for a long time that functional programs are attractive candidates for execution on parallel architectures and much work has been done in this area [Vegdahl 84]. However it is obvious that, even in a functional language, certain programs are better suited than others to a parallel evaluation. So it would be interesting to have a tool providing information about the potential level of parallelism of programs in order to help the user to choose between several equivalent programs. We describe in this section a method for the evaluation of one measure of the potential parallelism of programs that we call the *maximum speedup*; we first present a set of rules for the evaluation of the *parallel complexity* of programs. The parallel complexity of a function is defined as the maximum number of reduction steps for its evaluation by *parallel call-by-value*. Parallel call-by-value consists in reducing simultaneously all the arguments before a function call (and all reductions carried out simultaneously count as one reduction step). In practice, this entails that an unbounded number of computing elements is assumed and communication delays are not taken into account; so all redexes can always be evaluated simultaneously and instantaneously. These are of course very optimistic assumptions and the result of the analysis is a rough *underestimation* of the real parallel complexity. We define the *maximum speedup* as the ratio of *sequential complexity* (as defined in section 5.4) to *parallel complexity*. So this ratio gives an *overestimation* of the speedup one can expect from a parallel evaluation of the program.

We give now the rules for the evaluation of the parallel complexity of programs:

$$P(x) = 0 \tag{1}$$
$$P(k) = 0 \tag{2}$$
$$P(\text{if } e_1 \text{ then } e_2 \text{ else } e_3) = P(e_1) + (\text{if } e_1 \text{ then } P(e_2) \text{ else } P(e_3)) \tag{3}$$
$$P(op^k\ (e_1, ..., e_k)) = max(P(e_1),\ ... ,\ P(e_k)) \tag{4}$$
$$P(f(e_1, ..., e_k)) = max\ (P(e_1), ..., P(e_k)) + 1 + Pf(e_1,..., e_k) \tag{5}$$

The parallel complexity of a function f defined by:

$$f(x_1, ..., x_n) = e$$

is equal to:

$$Pf(x_1, ..., x_n) = P(e)$$

Rule (3) means that e_1 is always evaluated whereas the evaluation of e_2 or e_3 depends on the result of e_1. The parallel evaluation appears in rules (4) and (5) which indicate that the arguments of op^k and f are evaluated simultaneously; the time for the evaluation of all the arguments is the maximum of their individual execution times.

The evaluation of the parallel complexity of the function *fact* defined in section 5.4 is very similar to the evaluation of its sequential complexity and yields the same result:

$$Pfact(n) = Cfact(n)$$

So we have:

$$maximum\_speedup(fact)\ (n) = 1$$

which corresponds to our intuition that this definition of *fact* is sequential and that no efficiency would be gained by executing this function in parallel.

Let us now analyse an alternative definition of factorial:

$$fact'(n) = fact''(n,1)$$
$$fact''(n,m) = \text{if } n = m \text{ then } n \text{ else } fact''(n, E((n+m)/2)+1) \times fact''(E((n+m)/2), m)$$

where $E(k)$ returns the greatest integer smaller than or equal to k. The sequential complexity of *fact'* is the same as the sequential complexity of *fact* ($Cfact'(n) = n$) but the parallel complexity of *fact'* is $Pfact'(n) \sim log(n)$; so the maximum speedup of *fact'* is:

$$maximum\_speedup(fact')(n) \sim n/log(n)$$

Even if rough approximations have been used to obtain these results, the difference in the order of magnitude of the two values clearly shows that the second program is better suited to a parallel evaluation than the first one.

5.7 EVALUATION OF THE SPACE COMPLEXITY OF PROGRAMS

Another interesting measure of program performance is the space complexity. We show in this section how the method described for the evaluation of the time complexity of programs can be applied to the evaluation of the space complexity. We assume a string reduction evaluation and our measure of the space complexity of programs is the maximum of the size (that is to say the number of symbols) of the string representing the expression during the evaluation. As in the previous sections, we define a set of rules for the derivation of the memory complexity function. These rules use the primitive *size* giving the number of atoms of a list. Furthermore a second transformation, called *sizexp*, is needed to obtain the size of an expression. Let us call $M(E)$ the space complexity of an expression E. A function definition $f(x_1, ..., x_n) = e$ is transformed into:

$$Mf(x_1, ..., x_n) = M(e)$$

where $M(e)$ is defined by:

$$M(x) = size(x) \tag{1}$$
$$M(k) = size(k) \tag{2}$$
$$M(\text{if } e_1 \text{ then } e_2 \text{ else } e_3) = max(M(e_1) + sizexp(e_2) + sizexp(e_3) + 1, \tag{3}$$
$$(\text{if } e_1 \text{ then } M(e_2) \text{ else } M(e_3)))$$
$$M(op^k (e_1, ..., e_k)) = max(M(e_1) + sizexp(e_2) + ... + sizexp(e_k) + 1, \tag{4}$$
$$...$$
$$size(e_1) + ... + size(e_{k-1}) + M(e_k) + 1,$$
$$Mop^k (e_1, ..., e_k))$$
$$M(f(e_1, ..., e_k)) = max(M(e_1) + sizexp(e_2) + ... + sizexp(e_k) + 1, \tag{5}$$
$$...$$
$$size(e_1) + ... + size(e_{k-1}) + M(e_k) + 1,$$
$$Mf(e_1, ..., e_k))$$

These rules are deduced from a leftmost innermost operational semantics of the language; the transformation *sizexp* is used to take into account the unevaluated parts of the expression; for example rule (3) indicates that the sizes of expressions e_2 and e_3 have to be added to the memory complexity of e_1 because these expressions are kept by the evaluator during the computation of e_1. The constant 1 stands for the memory complexity of function symbols. The space complexity Mop^k of primitive functions is the maximum of the size of their arguments and the size of their result; for example $M+(n, m) = 2$, $M=(n, m) = 2$, $Mlength(l) = size(l)$ ... We give now the definition of the *sizexp* transformation:

$$sizexp(x) = size(x) \tag{1}$$
$$sizexp(k) = size(k) \tag{2}$$
$$sizexp(\text{if } e_1 \text{ then } e_2 \text{ else } e_3) = 1 + sizexp(e_1) + sizexp(e_2) + sizexp(e_3) \tag{3}$$
$$sizexp(op^k (e_1, ..., e_k)) = 1 + sizexp(e_1) + sizexp(e_2) + ... + sizexp(e_k) \tag{4}$$
$$sizexp(f(e_1, ..., e_k)) = 1 + sizexp(e_1) + sizexp(e_2) + ... + sizexp(e_k) \tag{5}$$

Let us now illustrate these transformations by the analysis of two versions of the factorial function.

<u>Example 5.4</u>

We start with the traditional recursive definition of factorial:

$$fact\ (n) = \text{if } n = 0 \text{ then } 1 \text{ else } n \times fact\ (n - 1)$$

Applying the above rules we get:

$$Mfact(n) = max(M(n = 0) + sizexp(1) + sizexp(n \times fact\ (n - 1)) + 1,$$
$$(\text{if } n = 0 \text{ then } M(1) \text{ else } M(n \times fact\ (n - 1))))$$

$$M(n = 0) = max(M(n) + sizexp(0) + 1,\ \ size(n) + M(0) + 1,\ \ M=(n,0))$$
$$= max(size(n) + 2,\ size(n) + 2, 2)$$
$$= size(n) + 2$$
$$sizexp(1) = 1$$
$$sizexp(n \times fact\ (n - 1)) = 4 + 2 \times size(n)$$
$$M(1) = size(1) = 1$$
$$M(n \times fact\ (n - 1)) = max(M(n) + sizexp(fact(n - 1)) + 1,$$
$$size(n) + M(fact(n - 1)) + 1,$$
$$M \times (n, fact(n - 1)))$$
$$= max(2 \times size(n) + 4,$$
$$size(n) + max(M(n - 1) + 1, Mfact(n - 1)) + 1,$$
$$2)$$
$$= max(2 \times size(n) + 4,$$
$$size(n) + max(size(n) + 3, Mfact(n - 1)) + 1)$$
$$= size(n) + 1 + max(size(n) + 3, Mfact(n - 1))$$

Putting all these results together we get:

$Mfact(n) = max(3 \times size(n)+8,$

$\qquad$ (if $n = 0$ then 1 else $size(n)+1+max(size(n)+3, Mfact(n-1))))$

$\quad$ = if $n = 0$ then $3 \times size(n) + 8$ else $size(n) + 1 + max(2 \times size(n) + 7, Mfact(n - 1))$

The property "$size(n) = 1$" can be deduced from the type information implicit in the definition of *fact*. So:

$Mfact(n) =$ if $n = 0$ then 11 else $2 + max(9, Mfact(n - 1))$

$\qquad$ = if $n = 0$ then 11 else $2 + Mfact(n - 1)$

by unfolding and folding and:

$Mfact(n) = 2 \times n + 11$

by recursion induction. This means that the space complexity of this factorial function is linear. Let us now analyse an iterative version of factorial:

$fact'(n) = fact''(n,1)$

$fact''(n, m) =$ if $n = 0$ then m else $fact''(n - 1, n \times m)$

Applying the above transformation rules we get:

$Mfact'(n) = max(size(n) + 2, size(n) + 2, Mfact''(n, 1))$

$\quad = max(3, Mfact''(n, 1))$

$Mfact''(n, m) = max(M(n = 0) + sizexp(m) + sizexp(fact''(n - 1, n \times m)) + 1,$

$\qquad$ (if $n = 0$ then $M(m)$ else $M(fact''(n - 1, n \times m))))$

$\quad = max(size(n) + 2 + size(m) + 4 + 2 \times size(n) + size(m) + 1,$

$\qquad$ (if $n = 0$ then $size(m)$ else $max(size(n) + 2 + size(m) + size(m) + 1 + 1,$

$\qquad\qquad\qquad size(n - 1) + size(n) + size(m) + 1 + 1,$

$\qquad\qquad\qquad Mfact''(n - 1, n \times m)))$

· Since $size(n) = 1$ and $size(m) = 1$, we have:

$Mfact''(n, m) = max(12,$ (if $n = 0$ then 1 else $max(7, 5, Mfact''(n - 1, n \times m))))$

$\quad =$ if $n = 0$ then 12 else $max(11, Mfact''(n - 1, n \times m))$

And:

$\quad Mfact''(n,m) = 11$

$\quad Mfact'(n) = 11$

So we obtain the expected result: the second version of *factorial* has a constant space complexity whereas the first version has a linear complexity.

For the sake of brevity, we do not give here the details of the treatment of graph reduction. The transformation rules given above are still relevant, but they do not apply to the original program. In order to reuse these rules, we first have to transform the original program to make the sharing explicit. The argument of the new program is a pair of lists: the first corresponds to the original arguments and the second represents the sublists which are shared by the arguments. Of course primitive functions are also transformed to take this new representation into account. This transformation can be used to show that the space complexity of some programs is dramatically decreased by a graph-reduction evaluation.

The method for extending the analysis to a higher order language is basically the same as the one described in section 5.4 for the complexity evaluation. Instead of one transformation M, we need transformations M_i such that $M_0(e)$ is the space complexity for the evaluation of e (equivalent to $M(e)$ above), $M_1(e)$ is the space complexity of the application of e to one argument (corresponding to Mf above) and so on. The transformation rules associated with the higher order version of our language (defined in chapter 2) are the following (we assume $j > 0$ and *sizexp* is extended to lambda expressions):

$$M_0(x) = size(x) \tag{1}$$
$$M_j(x) = M_j(x) \tag{2}$$
$$M_0(k) = size(k) \tag{3}$$
$$M_0(\text{if } e_1 \text{ then } e_2 \text{ else } e_3) = max(M_0(e_1) + sizexp(e_2) + sizexp(e_3)+1, \tag{4}$$
$$\text{if } e_1 \text{ then } M_0(e_2) \text{ else } M_0(e_3))$$
$$M_j(\text{if } e_1 \text{ then } e_2 \text{ else } e_3) = \text{ if } e_1 \text{ then } M_j(e_2) \text{ else } M_j(e_3) \tag{5}$$
$$M_1(op^k) = Mop^k \tag{6}$$
$$M_0(op^k\,(e_1, ..., e_k)) = max(M_0(e_1) + sizexp(e_2) + ... + sizexp(e_k)+1, \tag{7}$$
$$\cdots$$
$$size(e_1) + ... + size(e_{k-1}) + M_0(e_k) + 1,$$
$$M_1(op^k)(e_1, ..., e_k))$$
$$M_0(f(e_1, ..., e_k)) = max(M_0(e_1) + sizexp(e_2) + ... + sizexp(e_k)+1, \tag{8}$$
$$\cdots$$
$$size(e_1) + ... + size(e_{k-1}) + M_0(e_k) + 1,$$
$$M_1(f)(e_1, ..., e_k))$$
$$M_j(f(e_1, ..., e_k)) = M_{j+1}(f)\,(e_1, ..., e_k) \tag{9}$$

$$M_0(e(e_1, ..., e_k)) = max(M_0(e) + sizexp(e_1) + ... + sizexp(e_k), \qquad (10)$$
$$size(e) + M_0(e_1) + sizexp(e_2) + ... + sizexp(e_k) +$$
$$\cdots$$
$$size(e) + size(e_1) + ... + size(e_{k-1}) + M_0(e_k) +$$
$$M_1(e)(e_1, ..., e_k))$$
$$M_j(e(e_1, ..., e_k)) = M_{j+1}(e) (e_1, ..., e_k) \qquad (11)$$
$$M_0(\lambda(x_1, ..., x_k).e) = sizexp(e) + k + 1 \qquad (12)$$
$$M_j(\lambda(x_1, ..., x_k).e) = \lambda(x_1, ..., x_k). M_{j-1}(e) \qquad (13)$$

5.8 ACE: AN AUTOMATIC COMPLEXITY EVALUATOR

The system ACE was produced as a deliverable of ESPRIT Project 302. One of the goals of the project was to evaluate the method described in this chapter as a software engineering tool. ACE is a very general tool for performing analysis by program transformation. It is driven using files of rules which can be enhanced or overriden by the user, which makes it very flexible. The current system contains built-in rules for the analysis of:

(1) the worst-case time complexity of a program,

(2) the order of magnitude of the worst-case time complexity of a program,

(3) the average parallelism of a program.

The only difference between (1) and (2) is that the latter is evaluated using approximate patterns whereas the former provides the accurate value of the complexity. For example the worst-case time complexity of the function

$$f(n) = \textbf{if } n \geq 1 \textbf{ then } 1 \textbf{ else } n \times f(n-1)$$

is $Cf(n) = n-1$ and the order of magnitude of the complexity is $Cf(n) \sim n$. The choice between (1) and (2) is a trade-off between accuracy and conciseness.

We present in the following subsections the organization of ACE, examples of its use and an assessment of the system with respect to its original goals.

5.8.1 Organization of the system

The internal language used by the system is a version of FP [Backus 78]. FP programs are well suited to formal manipulation techniques because they do not involve variables: they are composed only of functions and combinators. Since very few FP programs are available, ACE integrates a tool for the translation of LISPKIT (a purely functional version of LISP

[Henderson 80]) into FP. The transformation rules of the system are classified according to a rule type which may be "*transformation*" (for the original syntactic transformation), "*sim_i*" (for simplification rules of type *i*) or "*pattern*" (for a recursive pattern). For correctness and efficiency reasons, only a part of the transformation rules library is accessible in a particular phase of the system. In the following we use the expression "solving a function" in the sense of "finding a non recursive expression of the function"; the non recursive expression of the function is referred to as "the solution of the function".

The system always starts analysing the top-level function, even if it refers to other user defined functions. This order is important and the reason for doing this is twofold:

- First, when the outermost function is expressed non recursively the references to other functions may disappear during the analysis. Thus there is no need to analyse them.
- Second, the solution to a function may be a large complex expression. If this is substituted in the original function, it is possible that ACE may fail to solve it, even if it could have solved it in its original form.

Conversely, it is possible that the function may be simplified when the solution of a used function is substituted in its body. So if it fails to solve a function but solves some of the functions it uses, it makes another attempt at solving the original function.

To solve a function, ACE applies techniques in the following order (simplification is not mentioned explicitly in what follows, generally speaking simplification is performed every time a function is changed):

(1) The original function is transformed into the complexity function; to this aim the system uses the set of rules corresponding to the required complexity measure.

(2) The function is matched against the recursive patterns available. If this succeeds the matching may produce an expression of the original function in terms of simpler recursive functions. If this happens, the system is recursively called to solve them.

(3) If the matching fails, the system tries various techniques such as factorization, argument removal (presented in section 5.3), or splitting (described in [Le Métayer 86]). If one of these attempts succeeds, the system goes back to step (2) to try to find a pattern corresponding to the new function.

5.8.2 Using ACE

When ACE is invoked, it prompts the user for commands. The major commands are as follows:

data ... enddata

introduces the definition of functions and rules.

find analysis-type function$_1$ function$_2$ ... function$_n$

provokes the evaluation of the appropriate analysis of the given functions. The types of analysis
ACE performs are given at the beginning of section 5.8. The functions must already have been defined using the *data* command above.

use filename$_1$ filename$_2$ ... filename$_n$

The next commands will be read from the given files. *use* commands may be nested in command files.

Even if it fails to analyse the whole program, ACE tries to solve all the intermediate functions and it prints out all the partial results and the functions it has failed to solve. The user may see that if another recursive pattern is supplied then ACE could make progress. He can then type in the pattern and analyse the program again.

ACE provides some flexibility in allowing the user to make different assumptions. For instance, if the user supplies a program containing some undefined functions, ACE will try to find a solution in terms of those functions. The user can also override a result produced by the system. For example it is possible to impose the assumption that a function has a certain complexity; this allows the user to investigate the effects of changing a component of a program. It also provides a convenient way of speeding up the analysis, or yielding a more concise expression than the one ACE would find by itself.

5.8.3 Some results of analysis

We present now some results produced by the system. As stated above, the internal language of the system is FP and the results of the analysis are expressed in FP. However we shall keep in this section the notation adopted in the rest of the book; we give now the definition in this notation of the combinators and primitive functions we will use in the following:

$ata(f) = \lambda\ l.$ **if** *null(l)* **then** *nil* **else** *cons(f(head(l)), ata(f)(tail(l)))*
$reduce(f,c) = \lambda\ l.$ **if** *null(l)* **then** *c* **else** *f(head(l), reduce(f,c)(tail(l)))*
$apndr(l,x) =$ **if** *null(l)* **then** *cons(x,nil)* **else** *cons(head(l), apndr(tail(l),x))*
$distl(x,l) =$ **if** *null(l)* **then** *nil* **else** *cons(cons(x,cons(head(l),nil)), distl(x, tail(l)))*
$distl'(l) = distl(head(l),tail(l))$

$distr(l,x) =$ **if** $null(l)$ **then** nil **else** $cons(cons(head(l),cons(x,nil)), distr(tail(l),x))$
$trans(l) =$ **if** $head(l) = nil$ **then** nil **else** $cons(ata(head)(l), trans(ata(tail)(l)))$
$sublists(l) =$ **if** $null(l)$ **then** nil **else** $cons(l, sublists(tail(l)))$

ata and $reduce$ correspond to the usual α and $/$ combinators of FP. Since ACE performs only a first order analysis, it introduces automatically a new definition for each application of these combinators to a particular function. For instance if the expression $reduce(f,0)$ (l) appears in the body of the function to analyse, with $f(x,y) = y + 1$, then the system generates the function $reduce\_f$ defined in the following way:

$reduce\_f(l) =$ **if** $null(l)$ **then** 0 **else** $1 + reduce\_f(tail(l))$

This function is solved as any ordinary intermediate function and ACE finds that

$reduce(f,0)$ $(l) = length(l)$

The functions $apndr$, $distl$, $distl'$, $distr$ and $trans$ and $sublists$ defined above are considered as primitive functions; so they are assumed to take a unit time to execute and to contain no parallelism. As stated in section 5.8.2 the user is free to make different assumptions if necessary.

We first consider the matrix multiplication program defined in [Backus 78]; a matrix is represented in the usual way as a list of sublists corresponding to its rows.

$mm(m_1,m_2) = ata\ (ata\ (ip))\ (ata\ (distl')\ (distr\ (m_1,\ trans(m_2))))$
$ip(l) = reduce(+,\ 0)\ (ata\ (\times)\ (trans\ (l)))$

ACE yields the following result for the order of magnitude of the sequential complexity of mm:

$Cmm(m_1,m_2) =$
$\quad length(m_1) \times length(head(m_2)) +$
$\quad length(head(m_2)) \times (reduce(+,0)\ (ata(length)\ (m_1))) + length(m_1)$

Since the order of magnitude of $length(m_1) \times length(head(m_2)) + length(m_1)$ is the order of magnitude of $length(m_1) \times length(head(m_2))$, Cmm can be simplified into:

$Cmm(m_1,m_2) =$
$\quad length(m_1) \times length(head(m_2)) +$
$\quad length(head(m_2)) \times (reduce(+,0)\ (ata(length)\ (m_1)))$

The result is complicated by the fact that ACE cannot use the implicit assumption that all the sublists of m_1 have equal lengths. Using this property, one may simplify the result further:

$$Cmm(m_1,m_2) \sim length(m_1) \times length(head(m_1)) \times length(head(m_2))$$

This is the expected result since the number of operations required to perform the multiplication of a $n \times m$ matrix by a $m \times p$ matrix is proportional to $n \times m \times p$.
The average parallelism analysis of *mm* yields the following result:

$Apmm(m_1,m_2) = 1 +$
  $(8+10 \times length(m_1) \times length(head(m_1))$
  $+ 11 \times length(head(m_2)) \times reduce(+,0)(ata(length)(m_1))$
  $+ 11 \times length(m_1))$
  $/$
  $(5 + reduce(a_1,2) (ata(a_2) (distr(m_1, trans(m_2)))) + 3 \times length(m_1)))$
where
$a_1(x,y) = 3 + max(x,y)$
$a_2(l) = 4 + 7 \times length(head(l)) + 3 \times length(tail(l))$

Using the assumption that the sublists have equal length and simplifying the result we obtain:

$Apmm(m_1,m_2) = 1 +$
  $((8 + 11 \times n \times m \times p + 10 \times n \times m + 11 \times n) / (9 + 6 \times n + 7 \times m + 3 \times p))$
where
$n = length(m_1)$
$m = length(head(m_1))$
$p = length(head(m_2))$

We give now the results returned by ACE for a small library of Me-too support functions. Me-too is a set-based executable specification language [Henderson et al. 85] implemented by embedding it in Lisp. The functions considered here are mainly set manipulation functions:

$appendall(l) = reduce(append, \emptyset) (l)$
$buildset(l) = reduce(addifnot, \emptyset) (l)$
$unionall(l) = reduce(union, \emptyset) (l)$
$intersection(l_1,l_2) = filter(ata(itis) (distr(l_1,l_2)))$

$append(l_1,l_2) = reduce(cons, l_2) (l_1)$

$union(l_1,l_2) = append(difference(l_1,l_2),l_2)$

$difference(l_1,l_2) = filter(ata(itisnot) (distr(l_1,l_2)))$

$member(x,l) = reduce(or, false) (ata(eqlist) (distl(x,l)))$

$eqlist(l) = equals (head(l), head(tail(l)))$

$filter(l) = $ **if** $null(l)$ **then** nil **else**

$\qquad$ **if** $head(head(l))$ **then** $cons(head(tail(head(l))), filter(tail(l)))$ **else** $filter(tail(l))$

$addifnot(x,l) = $ **if** $member(x,l)$ **then** l **else** $cons(x,l)$

$itis(l) = cons(member(head(l),head(tail(l))), head(l))$

$itisnot(l) = cons(not(member(head(l),head(tail(l)))), head(l))$

The top-level functions are *appendall*, *buildset*, *unionall* and *intersection*. *appendall* concatenates a list of lists into one list; *buildset* builds a set from a list of elements; *unionall* returns the union of a list of sets and *intersection* is the usual set intersection. ACE yields the following results for the order of magnitude of the time complexity of the top level functions:

$Cappendall(l) = length(l) + reduce(+, 0) (ata (length) (l))$

$Cbuildset(l) = length(l) + reduce(+, 0) (ata (length) (sublists(l)))$

$Cunionall(l) = length(l) + (reduce(+, 0) (ata (length) (l)) +$

$\qquad reduce(+, 0) (ata (multlength) (sublists(l))))$

$\quad$ **where** $multlength(l) = length(head(l)) \times reduce(+, 0) (ata (length) (tail(l)))$

$Cintersection(l_1,l_2) = length(l_1) + (length(l_1) \times length(l_2))$

Actually ACE does not perform much simplification of the result and these complexities may be simplified a lot. Using the property

$reduce(+, 0) (ata (length) (sublists(l))) = square(length)$

and the fact that the result is an order of magnitude of the complexity, we obtain:

$Cappendall(l) = reduce(+, 0) (ata (length) (l))$

$Cbuildset(l) = square(length(l))$

$Cunionall(l) = reduce(+, 0) (ata (multlength) (sublists(l)))$

$\quad$ **where** $multlength(l) = length(head(l)) \times reduce(+, 0) (ata (length) (tail(l)))$

$Cintersection(l_1,l_2) = length(l_1) \times length(l_2)$

The complexity of *appendall(l)* is the sum of the lengths of the sublists of *l*; the complexity of *buildset* is the square of the length of *l*; the complexity of *unionall(l)* is:

$$l_1 \times (l_2 + ... + l_n) +$$
$$l_2 \times (l_3 + ... + l_n) +$$
$$... \quad +$$
$$l_{n-1} \times l_n$$

where l_i stands for the length of the ith sublist of l; the complexity of intersection (l_1,l_2) is the product of the lengths of l_1 and l_2.

5.8.4 Discussion

As stated in the previous section, ACE has been used to tackle a wide variety of problems using program transformation. However there are functions arising in the programs we have analysed which do not appear to be solvable by ACE. In some cases we can see enhancements which could be made to allow some progress. In other cases however it is not clear how we could proceed. We should notice however that the analysis of a large program by ACE never fails completely; even if the whole result cannot be expressed in a non recursive form, the system returns all intermediate results and the recursive form of the complexity. This may help the user to understand his program better and also suggest to him the addition of some rules to enhance the system. Experience shows that the introduction of new transformations is a very error prone activity (especially when the user wants to define the most general possible patterns); so in a real environment the right to introduce new transformations would be reserved to special *super-users*.

The examples of section 5.8.3 have revealed another drawback concerning the practical use of ACE: the result produced by the system is sometimes a large expression that may be difficult to understand (and the result examples of section 5.8.3 are very straightforward in comparison with the results produced by the system for certain programs). There are several reasons for this: first, the use of FP does not increase the readability of expressions (this reason does not apply to the examples presented here since we have adopted a different notational convention); a straightforward enhancement would be to translate the result into a more usual language of arithmetic expressions. The second reason is that the result sometimes involves complicated expressions corresponding to common functions of the considered data type that the system does not know (for example the number-of-rows and number-of-columns of a matrix, the depth of a tree). One way to alleviate these problems would be to extend the source language to allow the user to define new data types with associated measures that the system can use in the analysis of functions on these types. This extension is described in detail in [Jones et al. 87].

Finally, let us mention that the result produced by ACE is sometimes complicated just because the complexity function is inherently complicated (see the complexity of function *unionall* in section 5.8.3 for example). Another enhancement could be to provide approximation rules to derive a lower bound and an upper bound of the order of magnitude of the complexity. The choice here is again a trade-off between accuracy and readability.

5.9 CONCLUSION

We have tried to show in this chapter the relevance of the program transformation approach in analysing functional programs. Using a small set of transformation rules, we have described the evaluation of time and space complexities.

The program transformation approach has one main advantage over abstract interpretation: it can be used to infer information which cannot be encoded within a finite domain (for example complexity properties or data-dependent strictness information). We should notice however that when abstract interpretation is well suited to the analysis, it is more straightforward and efficient than program transformation. Furthermore, abstract interpretation is complete for properties which can be encoded within finite domains, whereas the power of the program transformation analysis depends on the transformation techniques.

REFERENCES

[Abramsky 85] S. Abramsky. Strictness analysis and polymorphic invariance. Workshop on Programs as data objects, LNCS 217, Springer-Verlag, pp. 1-23, October 1985.

[Aho et al. 74] A. V. Aho, J. E. Hopcroft, J. D. Ullman. The design and analysis of computer algorithms. Addison-Wesley, 1974.

[Arsac et al. 82] J. Arsac, Y. Kodratoff. Some techniques for recursion removal from recursive functions. ACM TOPLAS, Vol. 4, No. 2, pp. 295-322, April 1982.

[Backus 78] J. Backus. Can programming be liberated from the von Neumann style? A functional style and its algebra of programs. CACM, Vol. 21, No. 8, pp.613-641, August 1978.

[Burn 87] G. L. Burn. Abstract interpretation and the parallel evaluation of functional languages. Ph. D. Thesis, Imperial College, London, 1987.

[Burstall et al. 77] R. M. Burstall and J. Darlington. A transformation system for developing recursive programs. JACM, Vol. 24, No. 1, pp. 44-67, January 1977.

[Clark et al. 80] K. L. Clark, J. Darlington. Algorithm classification through synthesis. The Computer Journal, Vol. 23, No. 1, pp. 61-65, 1980.

[Cousot 77] P. Cousot, R. Cousot. Abstract interpretation: a unified lattice model for static analysis of programs by construction of approximation of fixpoints. Proc. of 4th ACM Symp. on Principles of Programming Languages, pp. 238-252, 1977.

[Feather 87] M. S. Feather, A survey and classification of some program transformation approaches and techniques. In Program specification and transformation. L.G.L.T. Meertens (ed.), North-Holland, pp. 165-195, 1987.

[Henderson 80] P. Henderson. Functional Programming: application and implementation. Prentice-Hall International, Series in Computer Science, 1980.

[Henderson et al. 85] P. Henderson and C. Minkowitz. The Me-too method of software design. Research Report FPN/10, University of Stirling, 1985.

[Jones et al. 87] S. B. Jones, D. Le Métayer. Desired language characteristics with respect to the computation of complexity and degree of parallelism: the potential contribution of an abstract data type discipline. ESPRIT Document E302/WP 1.4/2.4, March 1987.

[Le Métayer 87] D. Le Métayer. Analysis of functional programs by program transformation. Proc. of 2nd France-Japan Artificial Intelligence and Computer Science Symposium, K. Fuchi, L. Kott (eds.), North-Holland, pp. 203-231, 1987.

[Le Métayer 88] D. Le Métayer. ACE: an Automatic Complexity Evaluator. ACM TOPLAS, Vol. 10, No. 2, pp. 248-266, April 1988.

[McCarthy 63] J. McCarthy. A basis for a mathematical theory of computation. In Computer programming and formal systems. Braffort, P., and Hirsberg, D. (eds.), North-Holland, 1963.

[Mycroft 80] A. Mycroft. The theory and practice of transforming call-by-need into call-by-value. Proc. of Int. Symp. on Programming, LNCS 83, Springer-Verlag, pp. 269-281, 1980.

[Partsch et al. 83] H. Partsch, R. Steinbrüggen. Program transformation systems. Computing Surveys, Vol. 15, No. 3, pp. 199-236, 1983.

[Turner 79] D. A. Turner. A new implementation technique for applicative languages. Software-Practice and Experience, Vol. 9, pp. 31-49, 1979.

[Vegdahl 84] S. R. Vegdahl. A survey of proposed architectures for the execution of functional languages. IEEE Trans. on Computers, Vol. C-33, No. 12, pp. 1050-1071, 1984.

[Wadler 81] P. Wadler. Applicative style programming, program transformation and list operators. Proc. 1981 ACM Conference on Functional Programming Languages and Computer Architecture, pp. 25-32, October 1981.

[Wand 80] M. Wand. Continuation based program transformation strategies. JACM, Vol. 27, No. 1, pp. 164-180, 1980.

CHAPTER 6

FROM LAMBDA CALCULUS TO MACHINE CODE
BY
PROGRAM TRANSFORMATION

Pascal Fradet

Daniel Le Métayer

6.1 INTRODUCTION

The implementation of functional languages is generally described in terms of an abstract machine [Landin 64, Burge 75, Johnsson 84, Cousineau et al. 87] reducing either the source functional program or a compiled version of this program. The abstract machine itself is implemented on a traditional von Neumann computer. So a complete correctness proof of the implementation should involve three steps:

(1) proof of the compilation process,
(2) proof that the reduction of a compiled expression by a specific computation rule and its execution on the abstract machine yield the same result,
(3) proof that the implementation of the abstract machine is correct.

Part (1) is generally easy because the compilation produces a functional expression. Part (2) however involves the operational description of a specific machine which is much more difficult to tackle. Part (3) is generally omitted because the abstract machine is supposed to be close to the real one. This step would probably deserve more attention if the implementation of the abstract machine on the real one involves a non trivial translation process.

Since correctness proofs are much easier in the functional framework, we believe that the whole implementation process should be described in a purely functional way. We present a method for transforming lambda expressions into simpler functional expressions whose reduction can be seen as an execution on a traditional machine with two components: the code and the stack. The important point is that we do not have to introduce a machine with an operational description indicating how the state evolves during the computation. The functional expressions produced are of the form $f\ g\ s_1...\ s_n$ where f is a basic function which behaves like a machine instruction operating on the stack $(s_1\ ...\ s_n)$ and g is an expression representing the rest of the code.

The execution of a functional program involves two main tasks:

(1) searching for the next expression to reduce according to a specific computation rule,

(2) the management of the environment.

We achieve the compilation of these two tasks in the functional framework. Section 6.2 describes the compilation of the computation rule. The resulting expressions can be evaluated from left to right by successively reducing the head operator. The compilation of environment management, presented in section 6.3, is done by an abstraction algorithm in the same spirit as [Turner 79, Lemaître et al. 86]. This abstraction uses a set of combinators acting like traditional machine instructions (*move, push,...*). In conclusion we show that the produced code is very efficient and we compare the approach with related work.

6.2 COMPILATION OF THE COMPUTATION RULE

The source language we use in this chapter is the higher-order version of the language defined in chapter 2. In addition, we consider only functions with one argument: a function with several arguments can be emulated as a higher-order function (a curried function). The syntax may be summarized as follows:

$$e ::= x \mid k \mid cond\ e_1\ e_2\ e_3 \mid op^k\ e_1\ ...\ e_k \mid e_1\ e_2 \mid \lambda x.e \mid \textbf{letrec}\ f = \lambda x.e$$

where e_i are expressions, x is a variable, k is a basic constant, and op^k is a strict primitive operator of arity k ; the primitive *cond* is the only non strict operator.

We consider in this chapter that the language is strict, so it can be evaluated by call-by-value. The method has also been applied to compile a call-by-name version of the language [Fradet 88]. The definition of factorial in this language is:

$$\textbf{letrec}\ fact = \lambda x.\ cond\ (eq\ 0\ x)\ 1\ (mult\ x\ (fact\ (sub\ x\ 1)))$$

Evaluation of the application of this expression to some argument by call-by-value involves a repeated search for the next redex: the first operation to execute is *eq*, then *cond*, then either 1 or *sub*, and so on.... The compilation of the computation rule should produce an expression which can be evaluated by systematic application of the first operator (from left to right).

Basically we have to invert the order of subexpressions in a composition: the evaluation of a composition $(e_1\ e_2)$ by value entails the evaluation of e_2, then the evaluation of e_1, and finally the application of the result of e_1 to the result of e_2 (we take here the rightmost innermost interpretation of call-by-value: the leftmost innermost strategy could have been chosen as well). But replacing $(e_1\ e_2)$ by $(e_2\ e_1)$ is not correct ; we have to provide a mechanism for putting the result of e_2 back in its place after its evaluation. This effect is achieved via the use of *continuations*. Continuations were introduced in section 2.2.4.5. They have been primarily used in the context of denotational semantics [Schmidt 86] as a convenient way to describe functionally the control involved in imperative languages. For example the direct (without continuations) semantics of an expression like $e_1 + e_2$ in an imperative language could be expressed as follows:

$$E[\![e_1 + e_2]\!]\ s\ =\ (E\ [\![e_1]\!]\ s\ )\ plus\ (E[\![e_2]\!]\ s)$$

E is the semantic function which takes an expression and a state and yields a value; this semantic definition is sufficient if expressions cannot produce side-effects (modifications of the state); if it is not the case, the semantics must express the ordering between the execution of e_1 and the execution of e_2; this effect is achieved via the introduction of a new argument, called the continuation, which is a function representing the "remainder of the program"; this function takes a value (the intermediate value of the partially evaluated expression), and a state, and yields a state; the continuation semantics of the expression $e_1 + e_2$ would be:

$$E\ [\![e_1 + e_2]\!]\ s\ c\ =\ E\ [\![e_1]\!]\ s\ (\lambda n_1.\ E[\![e_2]\!]\ s\ (\lambda n_2.\ c(n_1 + n_2)))$$

This semantics expresses the fact that e_1 is evaluated before e_2 and expressions producing side-effects could be formalized by introducing a new component (representing the modified state) in the result of the evaluation of an expression.

We use a very similar technique to compile the computation rule of our functional language; we transform each expression e into an expression $\Psi(e)$ taking a continuation as argument and applying it to the result of evaluating e. In the same way, we define a new operator $op^k{}_c$ for each operator op^k such that:

$$op^k{}_c\ c\ e_1\ ...e_k = c\ (op^k\ e_1\ ...\ e_k)\quad \text{and}\quad cond_c\ e_2\ e_3\ e_1 = cond\ e_1\ e_2\ e_3$$

$cond_c$ is a particular function which takes two continuations (e_2 and e_3).
The following describes the transformation rules of the first compilation step:

$$\Psi(x) = \lambda c.\, c\, x \qquad\qquad (\Psi 1)$$

$$\Psi(k) = \lambda c.\, c\, k \qquad\qquad (\Psi 2)$$

$$\Psi(cond\ e_1\ e_2\ e_3) = \lambda c.\ \Psi(e_1)\ (cond_c\ (\Psi(e_2)\ c)\ (\Psi(e_3)\ c)\,) \qquad\qquad (\Psi 3)$$

$$\Psi(op^k\ e_1\ ...\ e_k) = \lambda c.\ \Psi(e_k)\ (\Psi(e_{k-1})\ (...(\Psi(e_1)\ (op^k_c\ c))...)\,) \qquad\qquad (\Psi 4)$$

$$\Psi(e_1\ e_2) = \lambda c.\ \Psi(e_2)\ (\Psi(e_1)\ \mathbf{id}\ c) \qquad\qquad (\Psi 5)$$

$$\Psi(\lambda x.e) = \lambda c.\, c\ (\lambda c.\lambda x.\ \Psi(e)\ c) \qquad\qquad (\Psi 6)$$

$$\Psi(\mathbf{letrec}\ f = \lambda x.e) = \lambda c.\, c\ (\mathbf{letrec}\ f = \lambda c.\lambda x.\ \Psi(e)\ c) \qquad\qquad (\Psi 7)$$

id denotes the identity function $\lambda c.c$. Rules ($\Psi 1$) and ($\Psi 2$) follow from the convention described above that expressions take a continuation and apply it to their result. ($\Psi 4$) makes explicit the call-by-value evaluation of a composition $(...(op^k\ e_1)...\ e_k)$: e_k is evaluated first, then $e_{m-1},..., e_1$, and op^k_c can finally be applied with continuation c. Let us note that $\Psi(e_m)$ takes $(\Psi(e_{m-1})...(\Psi(e_1)(op^k_c\ c))...)$ as a continuation which means that its result will be put in the right place after its evaluation. ($\Psi 3$) can be explained in the same way. Rule ($\Psi 5$) applies when e_1 is not a primitive function: the first continuation **id** is necessary to get the functional value of e_1 (look for example at ($\Psi 6$) to see how a lambda expression is transformed) and the second continuation c will be the continuation taken by this function. In rules ($\Psi 6$) and ($\Psi 7$), the continuation is applied to the whole expression because a lambda expression is not evaluated by call-by-value; it is returned unchanged.

Remark: For call-by-name, rules ($\Psi 1$) and ($\Psi 5$) become:

$$\Psi'(x) = x \qquad\qquad (\Psi'1)$$

$$\Psi'(e_1\ e_2) = \lambda c.\ \Psi'(e_1)\ \mathbf{id}\ c\ \Psi'(e_2) \qquad\qquad (\Psi'5)$$

We take the convention that the top-level expression is always applied to the continuation **id**. For example, a top level application of a function f defined by ($\mathbf{letrec}\ f = \lambda x.e$) to a constant n would be:

$$\Psi(f\ n)\ \mathbf{id}$$
$$= (\lambda c.\ \Psi(n)\ (\Psi(f)\ \mathbf{id}\ c))\ \mathbf{id}$$
$$= (\lambda c.c\ n)\ (\Psi(f)\ \mathbf{id}\ \mathbf{id})$$
$$= \Psi(f)\ \mathbf{id}\ \mathbf{id}\ n$$
$$= (\lambda c.c\ (\mathbf{letrec}\ f = \lambda c.\lambda x.\Psi(e)\ c))\ \mathbf{id}\ \mathbf{id}\ n$$
$$= (\mathbf{letrec}\ f = \lambda c.\lambda x.\Psi(e)\ c)\ \mathbf{id}\ n$$

The property that the top-level continuation is always **id** can sometimes be exploited to achieve drastic improvements of the code: if f does not appear in e, we can replace

$(\textbf{letrec } f = \lambda c.\lambda x. \Psi(e) \, c) \textbf{ id}$

by:

$\textbf{letrec } g = \lambda x. \; \Psi(e) \textbf{ id}$

and carry out further simplifications if $\Psi(e)$ **id** can be reduced.

If f is recursive and $\Psi(e)$ **id** can be simplified, by beta-reduction, into an expression e' where f occurs only in the context $(f \textbf{ id})$ then we can replace $(\textbf{letrec } f = \lambda c.\lambda x. \Psi(e) \, c) \textbf{ id}$ by:

$\textbf{letrec } g = \lambda x. \; e' \; [g/(f \textbf{ id})]$

This situation, which can easily be detected, occurs when the continuation of f is always **id**. This optimization corresponds to an improvement of the compiler to preserve tail recursion; an important payoff of the functional approach is that most well-known compilator optimization techniques can be expressed (and formally justified) by simple program transformation rules. We give now the result of the compilation of the factorial function according to these rules:

$$
\begin{aligned}
\textbf{letrec } fact &= \lambda c.\lambda x. \; \Psi(cond \; (eq \; 0 \; x) \; 1 \; (mult \; x \; (fact \; (sub \; x \; 1)))) \, c \\
&= \lambda c.\lambda x. \; (\lambda c.(\Psi \; (eq \; 0 \; x) \; (cond_c \; (\Psi(1) \, c) \; (\Psi(mult \; x \; (fact \; (sub \; x \; 1))) \, c)))) \, c \qquad (\Psi 4) \\
&= \lambda c.\lambda x_{\scriptscriptstyle\downarrow} \; (\lambda c.(\; (\lambda c. \; \Psi(x) \; (\Psi(0) \; (eq_c \; c))) \\
&\qquad (cond_c \; ((\lambda c. \; c \; 1) \, c) \; (\Psi(mult \; x \; (fact \; (sub \; x \; 1))) \, c)))) \, c \qquad\qquad (\Psi 3),(\Psi 2) \\
&= \lambda c.\lambda x. \; (\lambda c.(\; (\lambda c. \; (\lambda c. \; c \; x) \; (\; (\lambda c. \; c \; 0) \; (eq_c \; c))) \\
&\qquad (cond_c \; ((\lambda c. \; c \; 1) \, c) \; (\Psi(mult \; x \; (fact \; (sub \; x \; 1))) \, c)))) \, c \qquad\qquad (\Psi 1),(\Psi 2) \\
&= \; \ldots\ldots
\end{aligned}
$$

After simplification by beta-reduction, we get

$$\textbf{letrec } fact = \lambda c. \; \lambda x. \; eq_c \; (cond_c \; (c \; 1) \; (sub_c \; (fact \; (mult_c \; c \; x)) \; x \; 1) \,) \; 0 \; x$$

In order to convince the reader that the function can really be evaluated by reducing systematically the first operator of the current expression, we describe now the evaluation of $(fact \textbf{ id } 1)$. The operator applied at each step is underlined.

(**letrec** *fact* = λc. λx. eq_c (*cond$_c$* (c 1) (*sub$_c$* (*fact* (*mult$_c$* c x)) x 1)) 0 x) **id** 1

$\quad$ = $\underline{eq_c}$ (*cond$_c$* (**id** 1) (*sub$_c$* (*fact* (*mult$_c$* **id** 1)) 1 1)) 0 1

$\quad$ = $\underline{cond_c}$ (**id** 1) (*sub$_c$* (*fact* (*mult$_c$* **id** 1)) 1 1) *false*

$\quad$ = $\underline{sub_c}$ (*fact* (*mult$_c$* **id** 1)) 1 1

$\quad$ = (**letrec** *fact* = λc. λx. eq_c (*cond$_c$* (c 1) (*sub$_c$* (*fact* (*mult$_c$* c x)) x 1)) 0 x) (*mult$_c$* **id** 1) 0

$\quad$ = $\underline{eq_c}$ (*cond$_c$* (*mult$_c$* **id** 1 1) (*sub$_c$* (*fact* (*mult$_c$* (*mult$_c$* **id** 1) 0)) 0 1)) 0 0

$\quad$ = $\underline{cond_c}$ (*mult$_c$* **id** 1 1) (*sub$_c$* (*fact* (*mult$_c$* (*mult$_c$* **id** 1) 0)) 0 1) *true*

$\quad$ = $\underline{mult_c}$ **id** 1 1

$\quad$ = $\underline{\textbf{id}}$ 1

$\quad$ = 1

In order to prove the correctness of the transformation Ψ, we have to show that evaluating the transformed expression by systematic reduction of the first symbol amounts to evaluating the original expression by call-by-value. Let $CR(e)$ denote the result of the evaluation of e by the computation rule CR ; CBV denotes call-by-value and $FIRST$ is our new computation rule. We must prove the following properties:

Property 1: if the evaluation of an expression e by CBV does not terminate, then for any c the evaluation of $(\Psi(e)\ c)$ by $FIRST$ does not terminate.

Property 2: if the evaluation of an expression e by CBV terminates then:
$\quad$ ($\forall c$) $\ FIRST\ (\Psi(e)\ c) \equiv FIRST\ (\Psi(CBV(e))\ c)$ $\ where\ "\equiv"\ denotes\ the\ syntactic\ equality$

Corollary: ($\forall e$) $\ $ if $CBV(e) \equiv k$ then $FIRST\ (\Psi(e)\ \textbf{id}) \equiv k$

$\quad$ Property 1 is shown by proving that the termination by $FIRST$ implies the termination by CBV. This is done by induction on the length of the reduction sequence by $FIRST$. Property 2 is shown by induction on the length of the reduction sequence by CBV and structural induction. These proofs are not complicated but involve a tedious inspection of the different cases [Fradet 88, Fradet et al. 89].

6.3 COMPILATION OF ENVIRONMENT MANAGEMENT

Let us come back to the evaluation of (*fact* **id** 1) described in the previous section to make a comparison with machine code execution. Throughout the reduction of (*fact* **id** 1) the expression under evaluation is always of the form:

$$exp_1 \, exp_2 \, exp_3 \, \ldots \, exp_m \, \ldots \, exp_n$$

where exp_1 is the next function to apply, exp_2 its continuation and exp_3 to exp_m are the arguments of exp_1. When exp_1 is evaluated and returns the value e_1, the expression becomes $exp_2 \, e_1 \, exp_{m+1} \, \ldots \, exp_n$. Let us now look at these expressions as machine states. Clearly exp_1 would be the next instruction to execute, exp_2 would be the rest of the code and $(exp_3 \, \ldots \, exp_n)$ would play the role of a stack. However these expressions are still far from machine code; the basic reason is the occurrence of lambda expressions whose reduction involves some kind of environment management. We use a well-known technique for the compilation of environment management within the functional framework, which is called abstraction [Curry 68, Turner 79]. The abstraction process consists in translating a functional expression into an equivalent one which contains no variables via the use of combinators. We take as an illustration the well-known set of combinators **S**, **K** and **I** [Curry 68] defined in the following way:

$$\mathbf{S} \, x \, y \, z = x \, z \, (y \, z)$$
$$\mathbf{K} \, x \, y = x$$
$$\mathbf{I} \, x = x$$

Expressions with variables may be transformed into equivalent combinatoric expressions by repeated application (for each free variable x of the expression) of the following abstraction algorithm:

$$[x] \, x = \mathbf{I}$$
$$[x] \, y = \mathbf{K} \, y \quad \text{where } y \text{ is a variable different from } x$$
$$[x] \, k = \mathbf{K} \, k \quad \text{where } k \text{ is a constant}$$
$$[x] \, e_1 \, e_2 = \mathbf{S} \, ([x] \, e_1) \, ([x] \, e_2)$$

It can easily be shown that

$$([x] \, e) \, x = e$$

or, in other words:

$$[x] \, e = \lambda x. \, e$$

So the abstraction $[x]$ is in some sense equivalent to the lambda abstraction λx; however it should be clear that $[x]$ describes a compile-time transformation of expressions whereas λx is part of the language and is treated dynamically (beta-reduction). This explains why we consider abstraction as a compilation of the environment management.

Instead of considering "high-level" combinators such as **S**, **K** and **I**, we choose here a set of indexed combinators which act on their arguments as machine instructions on a stack:

$$\textbf{id } x = x$$

$$\textbf{push } x\, f = f\, x$$

$$\textbf{dupl}_n\, f\, s_1 \ldots s_n = f\, s_n\, s_1 \ldots s_n$$

$$\textbf{move}_{m,n}\, f\, s_1 \ldots s_n \ldots s_{m-1}\, s_m = f\, s_1 \ldots s_n \ldots s_{m-1}\, s_n \qquad \{\text{if } n < m\}$$

$$\textbf{move}_{m,n}\, f\, s_1 \ldots s_{m-1}\, s_m\, s_{m+1} \ldots s_n = f\, s_1 \ldots s_{m-1}\, s_n\, s_{m+1} \ldots s_n \qquad \{\text{if } n \geq m\}$$

$$\textbf{flsh}_n\, f\, s_1 \ldots s_n = f$$

$$\textbf{ldcl}_n\, f\, g\, s_1 \ldots s_n = f\, (g\, s_n)\, s_1 \ldots s_n$$

These combinators can be seen as machine instructions operating in the following way:
- **id** corresponds to a return instruction: if the stack contains a single element then **id** returns it ; otherwise it causes a jump to the address given by the top of the stack,
- **push** is the traditional push instruction with an immediate argument,
- **dupl**$_n$ pushes the nth element of the stack,
- **move**$_{m,n}$ replaces the mth element of the stack by the nth element,
- **flsh**$_n$ pops the first n elements off the stack: it amounts to a modification of the stack pointer,
- **ldcl**$_n$ is used to build a closure on the top of the stack. In a real machine, the top of the stack would contain a pointer to the currently built closure and **ldcl**$_n$ would involve the allocation of a new memory cell to the new value. The expression of this operation within the functional framework amounts to adding to the terms new elements representing the memory cells [Fradet 88].

In order to make the description of the abstraction algorithm clearer, we introduce more powerful combinators which can be defined in terms of the previous ones:

$$\textbf{exed}_{m,n,i}\, s_1 \ldots s_m\, x_1 \ldots x_n = x_i\, s_1 \ldots s_m$$

$$\textbf{mkcl}_{m,n}\, f\, g\, s_1 \ldots s_m\, x_1 \ldots x_n = f\, (g\, x_1 \ldots x_n)\, s_1 \ldots s_m\, x_1 \ldots x_n$$

$$\textbf{delt}_{m,n}\, f\, s_1 \ldots s_m\, x_1 \ldots x_n = f\, s_1 \ldots s_m$$

In operational terms, **exed**$_{m,n,i}$ is a jump to the address contained in the $i+m^{\text{th}}$ element of the stack, after having removed from the stack the n elements corrresponding to the current "environment" (i.e. arguments of the function under evaluation). The first m elements correspond to the arguments of the called function. The combinator **mkcl**$_{m,n}$ builds in one step a closure on the top of the stack and **delt**$_{m,n}$ removes n elements from the stack. The following properties can be easily checked:

$$\mathbf{exed}_{m,n,i} = \mathbf{dupl}_{m+i} \, (\mathbf{move}_{m+n+1,m+1} \, (...(\mathbf{move}_{n+1,1} \, (\mathbf{flsh}_n \, id))...))$$
$$\mathbf{mkcl}_{m,n} \, f = \mathbf{ldcl}_{m+1} \, (...(\mathbf{ldcl}_{m+n} \, f)...)$$
$$\mathbf{delt}_{m,n} \, f = \mathbf{move}_{m+n,m} \, (...(\mathbf{move}_{n+1,1} \, (\mathbf{flsh}_n \, f))...)$$

We can now present our abstraction algorithm; the abstraction of variables $x_1, ..., x_n$ from M is denoted by $[x_1, ..., x_n]_0 \, M$. In other words, $[x_1, ..., x_n]_0 \, M$ is an expression, containing no variables, such that $([x_1, ..., x_n]_0 \, M) \, x_1 ... x_n = M$. Actually we give a more general definition of the abstraction $[x_1, ..., x_n]_p \, M$ such that:

$$([x_1, ..., x_n]_p \, M) \, s_1 \, ... \, s_p \, x_1 ... x_n = M \, s_1 \, ... \, s_p$$

We take the convention that when a function is called its arguments are on the top of the stack. The function execution may involve the installation of new elements on the top of the stack: index p in the abstraction algorithm denotes the number of values pushed on the stack over the arguments of the function at a particular execution step. So the ith argument of a function can always be found at the $p+i^{th}$ position in the stack.

The global expression is first normalized: nested lambda expressions are transformed into combinators in the following way:

$$\lambda x_1. \, ... \, \lambda \, x_n. \, exp \quad --> \quad (\lambda y_1. \, ... \, \lambda y_k. \, \lambda x_1. \, ... \, \lambda \, x_n. \, exp) \, y_1 \, ... \, y_k$$

where $y_1, ..., y_k$ are the free variables of the original lambda expression.

This normalization, which is very much in the spirit of supercombinators [Hughes 82] (but does not exhibit full laziness), allows us to apply the abstraction algorithm to the innermost lambda expressions in a bottom-up fashion.

Abstraction algorithm

(A1)	$[x_1, ..., x_n]_p \, M$	$= \mathbf{delt}_{p,n} \, []_p \, M$	if $x_1, ..., x_n \notin M$, $n \neq 0$
(A2)	$[x_1, ..., x_n]_p \, M \, x_i$	$= \mathbf{dupl}_{p+1} \, ([x_1, ..., x_n]_{p+1} \, M)$	if $x_i \in \{x_1, ..., x_n\}$
(A3)	$[x_1, ..., x_n]_p \, M \, y$	$= ([x_1, ..., x_n]_{p+1} \, M) \, y$	if $y \notin \{x_1, ..., x_n\}$
(A4)	$[x_1, ..., x_n]_p \, M \, k$	$= \mathbf{push} \, k \, ([x_1, ..., x_n]_{p+1} \, M)$	
(A5)	$[x_1, ..., x_n]_p \, op^k_c \, M$	$= op^k_c \, ([x_1, ..., x_n]_{p-k+1} \, M)$	
(A6)	$[x_1, ..., x_n]_p \, cond_c \, M \, N$	$= cond_c \, ([x_1, ..., x_n]_{p-1} \, M) \, ([x_1, ..., x_n]_{p-1} \, N)$	
(A7)	$[x_1, ..., x_n]_p \, x_i$	$= \mathbf{exed}_{p,n,i}$	if $x_i \in \{x_1, ..., x_n\}$
(A8)	$[x_1, ..., x_n]_p \, y$	$= y$	if $y \notin \{x_1, ..., x_n\}$
(A9)	$[x_1, ..., x_n]_p \, M \, N$	$= \mathbf{push} \, ([x_1, ..., x_n]_0 \, N) \, (\mathbf{mkcl}_{p,n} \, ([x_1, ..., x_n]_{p+1} \, M))$	
			if M is not a basic operator

(A1) means that the arguments of the function can be discarded from the stack as soon as they are no longer referenced in the remaining code.

(A2) indicates that a composition $(M\ x_i)$ is evaluated by first pushing the value of x_i and then evaluating M with one more element on the stack.

(A4) achieves the same effect with a constant argument k.

(A3) and (A8) are applied in the abstraction of a nested expression containing free variables (i.e. function names) which are left unchanged.

(A5) describes the treatment of operators: an operator of arity m consumes m elements and produces one.

(A6) expresses the fact that $cond_c$ consumes one (boolean) element and then transfers the control to one of its two alternatives.

(A7) is applied when the remaining expression is an argument which means that all other arguments can be discarded. This effect is achieved by the **exed** combinator.

(A9) deals with the evaluation of a non-basic expression M with a non basic continuation N. A representation of the continuation N must be pushed on the stack with its environment so that the expression M can call it after its own evaluation (this is achieved by **push** and **mkcl**).

Let us note that rule (A9) can be optimized in the following way:

$$(A9')\quad [x_1,\ldots,\ x_n]_p\, f_i\, N = \textbf{push}\ ([x_1,\ldots,\ x_n]_1\, N)\, f_i$$

where f_i denotes a user-defined function of $p+1$ arguments whose definition does not contain $x_1,\ldots,\ x_n$ as free variables. This implies that the execution of f_i will not destroy the environment, so there is no need to save it. This rule is an optimization of (A9) because it avoids the stack manipulations involved in the construction and execution of a closure.

Let us now come back to the factorial function to illustrate this abstraction algorithm. The function produced by the first transformation Ψ is (section 6.2):

letrec $fact = \lambda c.\ \lambda x.\ eq_c\ (cond_c\ (c\ 1)\ (sub_c\ (fact\ (mult_c\ c\ x))\ x\ 1)\ )\ 0\ x$

Applying the abstraction rules defined above we get:

letrec $fact = [c, x]_0\ (eq_c\ (cond_c\ (c\ 1)\ (sub_c\ (fact\ (mult_c\ c\ x))\ x\ 1)\ )\ 0\ x)$

$\qquad = \textbf{dupl}_2\ ([c, x]_1\ (eq_c\ (cond_c\ (c\ 1)\ (sub_c\ (fact\ (mult_c\ c\ x))\ x\ 1)\ )\ 0))$ (A2)

$\qquad = \textbf{dupl}_2\ (\textbf{push}\ 0\ ([c, x]_2\ (eq_c\ (cond_c\ (c\ 1)\ (sub_c\ (fact\ (mult_c\ c\ x))\ x\ 1)\ )))$ (A4)

$\qquad = \textbf{dupl}_2\ (\textbf{push}\ 0\ (eq_c\ ([c, x]_1\ (cond_c\ (c\ 1)\ (sub_c\ (fact\ (mult_c\ c\ x))\ x\ 1)\ ))))$ (A5)

$\qquad = \textbf{dupl}_2\ (\textbf{push}\ 0\ (eq_c\ (cond_c\ ([c, x]_0\ (c\ 1))\ ([c, x]_0\ (sub_c\ (fact\ (mult_c\ c\ x))\ x\ 1))))$

$$(A6)$$

$$=........$$ $\{using \ (A9') \ instead \ of \ (A9)\}$

$= \textbf{dupl}_2 \ (\textbf{push} \ 0 \ (eq_c \ (cond_c$
$(\textbf{push} \ 1 \ \textbf{exed}_{1,2,1})$
$(\textbf{push} \ 1 \ (\textbf{dupl}_3 \ (sub_c \ (\textbf{push} \ (\textbf{dupl}_3 \ (mult_c \ \textbf{exed}_{1,2,1})) \ fact)))))))$

$\textbf{exed}_{1,2,1} = \ \textbf{dupl}_2 \ (\textbf{move}_{4,2} \ (\textbf{move}_{3,1} \ (\textbf{flsh}_2 \ \textbf{id})))$

The following rules allow us to perform peephole optimizations:

$\textbf{dupl}_i \ (\textbf{move}_{j,k} \ exp) = \ \textbf{move}_{j-1,k-1} \ (\textbf{dupl}_i \ exp)$ with $j, k \neq 1, j{-}1 \neq i$
$\textbf{dupl}_i \ (\textbf{flsh}_j \ exp) = \textbf{flsh}_{j-1} \ exp$

We get: $\textbf{exed}_{1,2,1} = \ \textbf{move}_{3,1} \ (\textbf{flsh}_1 \ \textbf{id})$,   and:

$\textbf{letrec} \ fact = \ \textbf{dupl}_2 \ (\textbf{push} \ 0 \ (eq_c \ (cond_c$
$(\textbf{push} \ 1 \ (\textbf{move}_{3,1} \ (\textbf{flsh}_1 \ \textbf{id})))$
$(\textbf{push} \ 1 \ (\textbf{dupl}_3 \ (sub_c \ (\textbf{push} \ (\textbf{dupl}_3 \ (mult_c \ (\textbf{move}_{3,1} \ (\textbf{flsh}_1 \ \textbf{id}))))$
$fact \ )))))))$

The correctness property of the abstraction algorithm can be stated in the following way:

Property 3: $(\forall \ s_1 \ ...s_p) \ \ ([x_1,..., \ x_n]_p \ M) \ s_1 \ ... \ s_p \ x_1... \ x_n = M \ s_1 \ ... \ s_p$

The proof is a routine inspection of the different cases of the algorithm [Fradet 88].

The expressions yielded by the abstraction algorithm look very much like machine code. The only remaining difference is the fact that these expressions are still binary trees whereas machine code is sequences of instructions. The linearization is achieved by the introduction of names denoting embedded composed expressions. In operational terms, these names correspond to code addresses. The last remark concerns function names in recursive definitions. These names remain unchanged by the abstraction process since they are free variables. If we assume that names represent code addresses we must translate the occurrences of function names into **jump** instructions. In functional terms, (**jump** f) is defined by **jump** $f = f$. The application of this last transformation to the expression of factorial produced by the previous step yields:

letrec $fact = $ **dupl$_2$** (**push** 0 (eq_c ($cond_c$ $f_0 f_1$)))

let $f_0 = $ **push** 1 (**move$_{3,1}$** (**flsh$_1$** **id**))

let $f_1 = $ **push** 1 (**dupl$_3$** (sub_c (**push** f_2 (**jump** $fact$))))

let $f_2 = $ **dupl$_3$** ($mult_c$ (**move$_{3,1}$** (**flsh$_1$** **id**)))

We have now several linearized trees which can be written as sequences of instructions in the following way:

fact	dupl	2		f_1	push	1
	push	0			dupl	3
	eq_c				sub_c	
	$cond_c$	f_0, f_1			push	f_2
					jump	fact
f_0	push	1				
	move	3,1		f_2	dupl	3
	flsh	1			$mult_c$	
	id				move	3,1
					flsh	1
					id	

We describe now the evolution of the stack during the execution of (*fact* **id** 1) in order to illustrate the duality (functional expression/machine code) of the result of the compilation. We show in parallel the evaluation as the execution of code on a stack machine and as the call-by-name reduction of a functional expression. In the central part of the figure we represent the state of the stack (the top being the leftmost element) before the execution of the corresponding instruction.

	Machine Code		**Functional Expression**
fact	dupl 2	id:1	**dupl$_2$** (**push** 0 (eq_c ($cond_c$ f_0 f_1))) **id** 1
	push 0	1: id:1	**push** 0 (eq_c ($cond_c$ f_0 f_1)) 1 **id** 1
	eq$_c$	0:1: id:1	eq_c ($cond_c$ f_0 f_1) 0 1 **id** 1
	cond$_c$ f$_0$, f$_1$	false: id:1	$cond_c$ f_0 f_1 *false* **id** 1
f$_1$	push 1	id:1	**push** 1 (**dupl$_3$** (sub_c (**push** f_2 (**jump** *fact*)))) **id** 1
	dupl 3	1:id:1	**dupl$_3$** (sub_c (**push** f_2 (**jump** *fact*))) 1 **id** 1
	sub$_c$	1:1:id:1	sub_c (**push** f_2 (**jump** *fact*)) 1 1 **id** 1
	push f$_2$	0:id:1	**push** f_2 (**jump** *fact*) 0 **id** 1
	jump fact	f$_2$:0:id:1	**jump** *fact* f_2 0 **id** 1
fact	dupl 2	f$_2$:0:id:1	**dupl$_2$** (**push** 0 (eq_c ($cond_c$ f_0 f_1))) f_2 0 **id** 1
	push 0	0: f$_2$:0:id:1	**push** 0 (eq_c ($cond_c$ f_0 f_1)) 0 f_2 0 **id** 1
	eq$_c$	0:0: f$_2$:0:id:1	eq_c ($cond_c$ f_0 f_1) 0 0 f_2 0 **id** 1
	cond$_c$ f$_0$, f$_1$	true: f$_2$:0:id:1	$cond_c$ f_0 f_1 *true* f_2 0 **id** 1
f$_0$	push 1	f$_2$:0:id:1	**push** 1 (**move$_{3,1}$** (**flsh$_1$** **id**)) f_2 0 **id** 1
	move 3,1	1: f$_2$:0:id:1	**move$_{3,1}$** (**flsh$_1$** **id**) 1 f_2 0 **id** 1
	flsh 1	1: f$_2$:1:id:1	**flsh$_1$** **id** 1 f_2 1 **id** 1
	id	f$_2$:1:id:1	**id** f_2 1 **id** 1
f$_2$	dupl 3	1:id:1	**dupl$_3$** ($mult_c$ (**move$_{3,1}$** (**flsh$_1$** **id**))) 1 **id** 1
	mult$_c$	1: 1:id:1	$mult_c$ (**move$_{3,1}$** (**flsh$_1$** **id**)) 1 1 **id** 1
	move 3,1	1:id:1	**move$_{3,1}$** (**flsh$_1$** **id**) 1 **id** 1
	flsh 1	1: id:1	**flsh$_1$** **id** 1 **id** 1
	id	id:1	**id** **id** 1
	id	1	**id** 1
	result = 1		1

6.4 CONCLUSION

We have described a transformation of functions defined in a lambda calculus with constants into "equivalent" functions defined in terms of combinators acting on their arguments like machine instructions on a stack. The major originality of this approach as compared to the SECD machine [Landin 64, Burge 75] and the CAM [Cousineau et al. 87] is that we do not have to introduce a machine and describe it in terms of state transitions. In other words, we can say that the state of the machine is the expression itself and its evolution is specified by the definition of the combinators. For example, the evaluation of the result of the compilation of the factorial function can be described as the reduction of a functional expression or as the execution of code on a stack machine. This approach has interesting payoffs as far as correctness proofs are concerned. We do not have to prove that the operational definition of the machine is coherent with the operational semantics of the language as in [Plotkin 75, Cousineau et al. 87, Lester 87] since they are identical. The only operational argument in our proof appears in section 6.2 where we have to show that reduction of the transformed expression by FIRST amounts to the reduction of the original expression by call-by-value (for instance). However this proof does not involve reasoning on machine states.

The formalization of the implementation process has also been studied by Reynolds [Reynolds 72], followed by Wand [Wand 82]; they proceed by successive transformations of a semantics of the source language to derive an interpreter or a compiler and an abstract machine. [Wand 82] presents some heuristics for analysing the compilation process. This method also involves continuations and combinators, but in a quite different way: it takes a continuation-based semantics as input whereas in our work continuations appear in the compilation process as a formalization of the computation rule. Furthermore, Wand translates the semantics of the program into a sequence representing the code and a program (or "machine") to execute it; in our approach, semantics and machines do not appear explicitly. We believe that staying in the functional framework and proceeding exclusively by program transformation (instead of interpreter transformation) makes formal proofs easier. Let us remark however that Wand's goal is a bit different since he deals in the same way with any language (imperative or functional) which can be described by a continuation semantics.

The benefits of the use of continuations to compiler design have already been illustrated by previous work on Orbit [Kranz 86]. They integrate continuation conversion as a preliminary "standardization" step but the compilation (code generation in particular) is not entirely described by program transformation.

Even if performance considerations are not the main topic of the work described here, we have to say a few words about the produced code. First, we should mention that the transformation described in section 6.2 does not depend on the chosen implementation and could as well be applied in the context of graph reduction (it would lead to a simpler graph evaluator reducing systematically the first term of the expression). We have chosen the environment-based approach rather than graph reduction [Turner 79, Johnsson 84, Johnsson 86] because it is closer to traditional von Neumann machines. The code produced by our transformation rules is rather close to the code of [Burge 75] for the SECD machine and [Cousineau et al. 87] for the CAM. The main difference with the SECD machine is the place where environment savings are achieved: as in the CAM we achieve the savings when encountering intermediate subexpressions rather than at function call. We depart from the CAM as far as environment representation is concerned; in the CAM, environments are represented as trees which entails less expensive closure building but costly access time.

Another possible choice is to keep a pointer to the global environment and to distinguish access to local identifiers and to global identifiers [Cardelli 84]; this makes function calls more efficient because context switching amounts to a pointer movement.

A prototype compiler based on this approach has been implemented on a SUN workstation. Let us point out that the implementation of a compiler based on our transformation rules in a language with pattern matching such as ML is quite straightforward. The following table shows the execution times of the code produced by our compiler for the traditional *fib* 20 with call-by-value, call-by-name and call-by-need.

	c. b. value	c. b. name	c. b. need
time	80 ms	2.2 s	0.55 s
call/sec	274 000	10 000	40 000

These results show that the code produced by our compiler is realistic (the efficiency of the code produced by the C compiler for the same function is 263,000 calls/sec). We believe that this performance is made possible by the program transformation approach which allows the systematic application of optimization rules. Actually, most well-known compiler optimization techniques can be described in a functional way; each technique should be applied at the appropriate transformation level: for example common subexpression elimination, and tail recursion optimization should be carried out after the first transformation step whereas peephole optimizations must be applied on the resulting code [Fradet et al. 89]. However we should mention that only the simple language described in section 6.2 has been implemented so far and the performance has to be confirmed for a more realistic language including lists, user-defined data types and pattern matching.

REFERENCES

[Burge 75] W.H. Burge. Recursive Programming Techniques. Addison-Wesley, 1975.

[Cardelli 84] L. Cardelli. Compiling a Functional Language. Proc. of ACM Symp. on Lisp and Functional Programming, pp. 208-226, 1984.

[Cousineau et al. 87] G. Cousineau, P.-L. Curien, M. Mauny. The Categorical Abstract Machine. Science of Computer Programming, Vol. 8, pp. 173-202, 1987.

[Curry et al. 68] H. B. Curry, R. Feys, W. Craig. Combinatory Logic. Vol. 1, North-Holland, 1958, Second printing 1968.

[Fradet 88] P. Fradet. Compilation des langages fonctionnels par transformation de programmes. Thèse, Université de Rennes, November 1988.

[Fradet et al. 89] P. Fradet, D. Le Métayer. Compilation of functional languages by program transformation. INRIA Research Report, No. 1040, May 1989.

[Hughes 82] R. J. M. Hughes. Supercombinators: a new implementation method for applicative languages. Proc. of ACM Symp. on Lisp and Functional Programming, pp. 208-226, 1982.

[Johnsson 84] T. Johnsson. Efficient compilation of lazy Evaluation. Proc. of ACM SIGPLAN Symp. on Compiler Construction, SIGPLAN Notices, Vol. 19, No. 6, pp. 58-69, 1984.

[Johnsson 86] T. Johnsson. Target Code Generation from G-Machine Code. Proc. of Workshop on Graph Reduction, LNCS 279, Springer Verlag, pp. 119-159, 1986.

[Kranz et al. 86] D. Kranz, R. Kelsey, J. Rees, P. Hudak, J. Philbin, N. Adams. Orbit: an Optimizing compiler for Scheme. Proc. of the ACM SIGPLAN Symp. on Compiler Construction, pp. 219-233, 1986.

[Landin 64] P. J. Landin. The Mechanical Evaluation of Expressions. Computer Journal, Vol. 6, pp. 308-320, 1964.

[Lemaître et al. 86] M. Lemaître, M. Castan, M.-H. Durand, G. Durrieu, B. Lecussan. Mechanisms for Efficient Multiprocessor Combinator Reduction. Proc. of ACM Symposium on Lisp and Functional Programming, pp. 113-121, 1986.

[Lester 87] D. Lester. The G-Machine as a Representation of Stack Semantics. Proc. of Conference on Functional Programming Languages and Computer Architecture, LNCS 274, Springer Verlag, pp. 46-59, 1987.

[Plotkin 75] G.D. Plotkin. Call-by-name, Call-by-value and the λ-Calculus. Theoretical Computer Science, Vol. 1, pp. 125-159, 1975.

[Reynolds 72] J. C. Reynolds. Definitional interpreters for higher-order programming languages. Proc. of ACM annual conference, Vol. 2, pp. 717-740, 1972.

[Schmidt 86] D. A. Schmidt. Denotational semantics. Allyn and Bacon, 1986.

[Turner 79] D. A. Turner. A New Implementation Technique for Applicative Languages. Software-Practice and Experience, Vol. 9, pp. 31-49, 1979.

[Wand 82] M. Wand. Deriving target code as a representation of continuation semantics. ACM TOPLAS, Vol. 4, No. 3, pp. 496-517, 1982.

CHAPTER 7

ON INPUT AND OUTPUT IN FUNCTIONAL LANGUAGES

Simon B. Jones
Andrew F. Sinclair

7.1 INTRODUCTION

If we wish to exploit the simple formal properties of functional programming languages discussed in the previous chapters we must adopt a *purely* functional style. This does not permit input and output in the traditional way via read and write commands. In this chapter, we examine the problem in more detail, and indicate how a solution may be found within the purely functional framework.

7.1.1 Why is there a problem?

A casual examination of a simple session with one of the many functional programming systems available would generally reveal the following pattern of usage:

> The user enters definitions of functions, definitions of variables, and expressions to be evaluated. Each expression to be evaluated may involve previously defined functions, previously defined variables, and explicit data. Evaluation proceeds until some result is obtained, at which point the result is bound to a variable and/or displayed for the user.

Since all data to be acted upon must, apparently, be included in the expression entered, and the result must be computed before it is displayed, it is not immediately clear how a function representing an *interactive computation* could be expressed, nor how an expression invoking that function could be evaluated in an interactive fashion. Neither is it clear how such a function could access or update external data, such as that held in a database or file store. A straightforward example of such a problematical application is that of a function which could allow interactive access to a database; this is clearly an interactive problem, since we may only be able to formulate queries once we have seen the responses to earlier ones.

In fact a number of functional language systems, for example Miranda[*] [Turner 87] and Lazy ML (LML [Johnsson 87]), do provide facilities for terminal and file input and output, although the facilities for input are not so consistent with purely functional semantics as might be desired.

Thus, there is a large, and obviously important, class of programming problems to which functional programming does not, at first sight, seem suited. These problems can, perhaps, be characterized as those in which a desired *external behaviour* is to be implemented; interactive programs in particular fall into this class, as do operating systems.

How may we approach these problems in a purely functional style?

We shall show how the apparent inability of functional programs to express interactive computations may be overcome. It arises from the rather naïve view of the mechanism for evaluating expressions that we hinted at above, namely the *eager mode of evaluation*; it and its variants are also known as *strict evaluation, applicative order evaluation, data driven evaluation*, and *call-by-value*. Functions may be regarded as representing interactive computations if we adopt an alternative mechanism for evaluation, namely *lazy evaluation* [Henderson et al. 76]; this and its variants are also known as *non-strict evaluation, normal order evaluation, demand driven evaluation* and *call-by-need*. In section 7.2 we shall show how lazily evaluated lists, *streams*, can be exploited to fulfil the role of interactive communication channels between program subsystems and external devices, and between the subsystems themselves. The approach extends quite naturally to a software design paradigm in which systems comprise a collection of autonomous processes communicating via a network of streams; this style of design is already encouraged by design methods such as MASCOT [MASCOT]. Operating systems constructed within this paradigm are essentially distributed in nature, and may be mapped more or less easily (depending on low level details) onto a network of processors in order to exploit their potential for concurrent execution.

A complete text editor will be presented to illustrate the exploitation of streams (section 7.3). The style of functional programming used will be examined critically; an improved style will be suggested which depends on higher order functions and continuations (section 7.4), and an improved design for the editor will be developed.

In section 7.5 we look at how networks, parallelism and nondeterminism can be dealt with in functional programming. This is followed, in section 7.6, by a demonstration of how these

---

[*] Miranda is a trademark of Research Software Ltd

ideas may be exploited in the functional implementation of an operating system.

In section 7.7 we conclude that the streams approach to input/output is very workable, although the programming style engendered may become palatable only when the full potential of functional programming is brought to bear, and appropriate higher order functions and combining forms have been designed so as to hide much of the low level detail.

7.1.2 A historical perspective

First let us look at the development of the ideas on which this chapter is based. McCarthy's original proposal for Lisp [McCarthy 60] described a purely functional programming language with a call-by-value evaluation rule; although the "program feature" is mentioned briefly ("to allow programming in the style of Algol60"), there is no reference to input and output facilities in the language. However, by the publication of the Lisp 1.5 Programmer's Manual in 1962 [McCarthy et al. 62], the program feature, together with assignments, gotos and many pseudo-functions for input and output had become a firm part of Lisp. The parameterless pseudo-function *read* had as its result the next s-expression from the input device, and the pseudo-function *print* had the effect of printing its argument as well as returning that value as its result. These pseudo-functions operate by side effects and are thus outside the purely functional paradigm: functions which use them have results which depend on data other than their arguments and free variables, and have results which are produced in addition to their normal return value. The results, both printed and returned, also depend on the exact sequencing of evaluations within the function, which must therefore be taken into account by the programmer; purely functional programmers do not need to know about this sequencing, as it does not affect the correctness of programs.

It is clear why practical Lisp systems needed these non-functional facilities in the early days: they enabled efficient implementations using known technology (eager evaluation was the order of the day, and not lazy evaluation). Thus, there was a constructive compromise between the expressive power of the purely functional parts of Lisp and the need to be useable. These principles have been maintained to the present time in Lisp systems. Similar, though not identical, pragmatic principles of input and output have been adopted more recently in functional programming systems such as Standard ML [Harper et al. 86].

In the mid 1970s there was a revival of interest in purely functional programming. This was due partly to improvements in hardware performance, but mainly to the convergence of three areas of research:

(i) Software engineering had provided the motivation to find programming languages which were more tractable for both informal and formal reasoning;

(ii) Important developments were being made in the transformation and optimization of functional programs;

(iii) It was thought that functional languages would be a good means of exploiting the developments in parallel machine architecture.

These three avenues converged on functional languages – but the respective technologies are applicable with great effect only to *purely* functional languages: if there is any form of side-effect, then proof rules become less manageable, transformation and optimization techniques lose their potency or may fail to preserve correctness, and parallel execution may produce unpredictable results. Thus, there was, and still is, a great pressure to remain within the purely functional context. This has, perhaps, had the effect of slowing the spread of functional languages for serious programming, since, as we have suggested, it was not clear how to integrate input and output into purely functional programming.

The mid to late 1970s saw research homing in on what we now know as the stream input/output model: the most important contributions were perhaps the design of a lazy evaluator [Henderson et al. 76], the recognition of the practical importance of lazy data structures [Friedman et al. 76], and an examination of the relationship between co-routines and networks of parallel processes [Kahn et al. 77]. Only in the 1980s did serious exploration begin into the basic principles and feasibility of the implementation of purely functional interactive programs. The primary goal of much of this research was to prototype the main features of full operating systems, for example [Jones 84, Abramsky et al. 85, Stoye 85]. Some idea of the direction of this research will be given in section 7.6 of this chapter.

7.2 LAZY EVALUATION AND STREAMS FOR INPUT AND OUTPUT

In this section we introduce the basic techniques which enable us to write interactive functional programs.

7.2.1 Lazy evaluation, streams and processes

Consider the following function definitions, which may be used to compute a well known function of natural numbers:

sequence :: *num* → [*num*]
sequence n   = [ ], **if** *n* = 0
                 = *n* : *sequence*(*n*−1),   **otherwise**

multiply :: *num* → [*num*] → *num*
multiply p [ ]   = *p*
multiply p (*x* : *xs*) = *multiply* (*x*×*p*) *xs*

factorial :: *num* → *num*
factorial n = *multiply* 1 (*sequence n*)

Many programs are more easily understood when functions are written in an equational, pattern matching style. Hence the notation used here, and elsewhere in this chapter, is based on that used [Bird et al. 88]; we also use their notation for type descriptions. However, for convenience we adopt a few minor extensions: we allow lambda expressions, conditional expressions and we use "!" as an infix constructor for head strict lists (see later this section).

If we attempt to evaluate the expression *factorial* 3 using an *eager* evaluation strategy, then the course of events can be outlined as follows:

factorial 3
⇒ *multiply* 1 (*sequence* 3)
⇒ *multiply* 1 (3 : *sequence* 2) ⇒ ...
⇒ *multiply* 1 [3,2,1]
⇒ *multiply* (3×1) [2,1]
⇒ *multiply* 3 [2,1] ⇒ ...
⇒ *multiply* 6 [ ]
⇒ 6

At each step, an *innermost* reducible expression is selected for evaluation. The key observation that we should make is that the *entire* intermediate list, [3,2,1], is constructed *before* the multiplication is started; this is a direct consequence of the innermost selection strategy.

Alternatively, we may adopt a *lazy* evaluation strategy *with respect to the list processing components of the evaluation* (retaining eager evaluation for subtractions and multiplications); here is an outline of the course of events:

factorial 3

⇒ *multiply* 1 (*sequence* 3)

⇒ *multiply* 1 (3 : *sequence* 2)

⇒ *multiply* (3×1) (*sequence* 2)

⇒ *multiply* 3 (*sequence* 2)

⇒ *multiply* 3 (2 : *sequence* 1)

⇒ *multiply* (2×3) (*sequence* 1) ⇒ ...

⇒ *multiply* 6 (1 : *sequence* 0)

⇒ *multiply* (1×6) (*sequence* 0) ⇒ ...

⇒ *multiply* 6 [ ]

⇒ 6

Here, at each step when there is no eager − or × to perform, an *outermost* reducible expression is selected for evaluation. This is quite subtle: when the whole expression has the form *multiply* 3 (*sequence* 2) the application of *multiply* is outermost but not reducible since the second argument must pattern match with $x : xs$ or [ ]. Hence *sequence* 2 is in fact the outermost *reducible* expression. Looking at the overall pattern of the computation, the key observation is that no sooner has an inner expression of the form *sequence n* been evaluated as far as $n : sequence(n−1)$, than its evaluation is suspended, and *multiply* is applied once to consume the value of *n*; when *multiply* has performed as much work as it can, only then does evaluation of $sequence(n−1)$ proceed (only to be suspended again, almost immediately!). This may seem an unnatural mode of program execution to many programmers: imperative languages traditionally use a form of eager evaluation, with only "call-by-name" (now rather rare) approximating lazy evaluation; however, lazy evaluation is now a simple fact of life for most functional programmers.

In the example of lazy evaluation, *sequence* appears to produce the intermediate list incrementally, and "on demand"; *multiply* appears to cause the "demand", and to consume the intermediate list incrementally as it is produced. Thus we have what is in effect a form of *coroutine execution* [Conway 63], with execution alternating between a producer *sequence*, and a consumer *multiply*. This suggests that we can view the expression *multiply* 1 (*sequence n*) as a short *pipeline*, as shown in Fig 7.1, in which *sequence* produces a stream of messages (the numbers) which are sent for consumption by *multiply*:

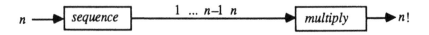

Fig 7.1 A simple pipeline

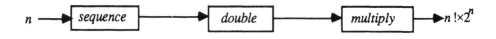

Fig 7.2 An extended pipeline

This observation is rather more than a pleasant illusion: the correspondence between such compositions of lazily evaluated functions and information processing pipelines is very close. For example, should we wish to double every number before multiplying them together, as shown in Fig 7.2, then this is encoded as

$f\, n = multiply\ 1\ (double\ (sequence\ n))$

or, more elegantly, using the function composition operator "·" :

$f = (multiply\ 1) \cdot double \cdot sequence$

where $double :: [num] \to [num]$
       $double\ [\ ]$ $= [\ ]$
       $double\ x : xs$ $= (2{\times}x) : double\ xs$

There is a very attractive similarity between the pipeline structure and the functional composition of its individual information processing elements. We obtain two important payoffs from this way of looking at functional program evaluation: firstly, the mechanism of lazily evaluated lists can be adapted to deal with interactive input and output in functional programs; secondly, with pipelines (extended later to general networks) we are offered a powerful program design paradigm, with no additional linguistic baggage to be taken into account. We shall investigate these two assertions in more detail below.

[Henderson 80] discusses networks of processes as solutions for a number of problems. This view of computation is closely related to the work on coroutines and networks of parallel processes in [Kahn et al. 77].

First, however, some technical scene setting, and a little terminology. We shall assume lazy evaluation as standard, that is an *outermost* evaluation strategy. This means, in particular, that the list constructor ":" does not evaluate its arguments [Friedman et al. 76], and that function arguments are not evaluated unless required (for example for pattern matching at function call).

The lazy lists carrying messages between the processing elements of pipelines and networks will be called *streams*. However, in the case of streams and stream processing functions we need more control over the evaluation than that usually afforded by lazy evaluation, both to ensure that the computation proceeds in an operationally useful way, and to enable a better intuitive grasp of the computation induced by a program. For example, if we define the function

$$f x : xs = e$$

and then apply it to some (previously unevaluated) expression, then because ":" is lazy the attempt to pattern match $x : xs$ with the argument will not force x or xs to be evaluated before the decision to evaluate e is taken. However, if the intention is that $x : xs$ is a stream in which x is the next message then it may not be appropriate, or intuitive, to make the decision to evaluate e until we know that x is available (or furthermore that it has a particular structure itself). Of course, it is quite acceptable that xs remains unevaluated since it represents "messages yet to be received". Thus streams will be constructed not by ":", but by *head strict cons*, denoted by "!". Head strict cons is given the following operational interpretation: $e_1 ! e_2$ forces the evaluation of e_1 but suspends the evaluation of e_2, building a stream whose first message (its head) is the value of e_1, and whose subsequent messages (its tail) are contained in e_2. We require "!" to be *hyperstrict* in its first argument, that is that messages must be *fully* evaluated; thus no stream producing function can "promise" the next message, by preparing a slot in the stream for it, without being able to "deliver" that message immediately. For example, if we apply the function defined by

$$f x ! xs = e$$

then e will not be selected for evaluation until the first message x is available for processing immediately.

Streams may be unterminated data structures, since they may represent indefinitely long interactions between a producer and a consumer; hence the recursive functions processing them may not have "base cases" to terminate the recursion. We have a distinction between process communication channels and internal data structures; we would not normally expect to use "!" to contruct the latter. For example, using these conventions, the function for doubling each number passing through a pipeline would be encoded as:

double :: *stream num* $\rightarrow$ *stream num*
double x ! xs = $(2 \times x)$! *double xs*

Functions which either produce one or more streams, or consume one or more streams, or do both, we shall call *processes*; we shall use this term to cover both the definitions of such functions, and their particular instantiations in pipelines and networks.

In pipelines the operational effect is as follows: the producer of a stream is suspended until the consumer of that stream "demands" the next message (usually by matching it against an argument of the form $x ! xs$); the producer then performs only enough computation to supply the next message, and is once again suspended; the consumer processes, and the cycle is repeated.

7.2.2 Interactive programs

Let us imagine that individual keystrokes at a terminal's keyboard generate numbers to be processed by some program. Consider evaluating a call of the stream version of *double* in the following way:

The user nominates *double* as the program to be executed.

As its implicit argument we provide a special expression *keyboard*, which denotes a stream containing all the numbers entered at the keyboard, and in the order in which they are entered. *keyboard* is a suspended stream producing process, and plays the role of a hardware input port register: when the consumer of its stream demands the next message, *keyboard* obtains the next available number from the keyboard buffer (waiting if none is available), and constructs a stream with this number at the head, and a suspended call of itself in the tail. *keyboard* can be thought of *very informally* as the following process:

$keyboard :: ( ) \rightarrow stream\ num$
$keyboard ( ) =$ "next number" $!\ keyboard ( )$

We perform outermost reductions until the evaluation has the form $n ! e$, where n is a fully evaluated number, and e is a suspended expression containing a further call of *double*. At this point n is ready for output, so we display it on the screen, and then move on to the tail of the stream e, to which we further apply outermost reduction, repeating the cycle as necessary. (Note: At this point the number n and the stream constructor cell associated with it may well have had their final reference discarded and may be recycled by the garbage collector.) Thus screen driving amounts to sending the output stream of *double* to a special consumer process which acts as a hardware output port register. The screen driver could be thought of *very informally* as the following process:

$screen :: stream\ num \rightarrow ( )$
$screen\ x ! xs =$ "display x and then" $screen\ xs$

The course of events will be an interaction between the program and the user:

"execute *double*" — implicit application to keyboard stream
⇒ *screen* (*double keyboard*) — keyboard buffer must be inspected
⇒ *screen* (*double* (3 ! *keyboard*)) — user has entered 3
⇒ *screen* ((2×3) ! *double keyboard*)
⇒ *screen* (6 ! *double keyboard*) — output is ready, display 6 on screen
⇒ *screen* (*double keyboard*) — continue computation
⇒ *screen* (*double* (5 ! *keyboard*)) ⇒ ... — user has entered 5
⇒ *screen* (10 ! *double keyboard*) — display 10 on screen
⇒ *screen* (*double keyboard*) ⇒ ... — and so on

We have an interactive functional program which performs input and output: it is a trivial pipeline whose source and sink are hardware ports, and whose computational part is what we earlier called a process. This is represented in Fig 7.3.

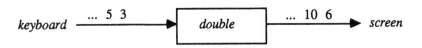

Fig 7.3 A simple system performing terminal I/O

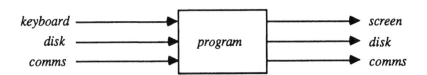

Fig 7.4 Multiple I/O devices

We thus have a pattern for expressing interactive programs functionally. This idea extends quite naturally to other I/O devices: we may use processes with one input stream per hardware input port, and one output stream per hardware output port, to produce the system in Fig 7.4. Here the process *program* has the type:

$$program :: (stream\ \alpha, stream\ \beta, stream\ \gamma) \rightarrow (stream\ \alpha', stream\ \beta', stream\ \gamma')$$

Of course, the sequences of messages to be used for performing disk and communications I/O will be more complex than those required for terminal I/O, but the principle of directing the messages via input and output streams holds good.

7.3 AN INTERACTIVE TEXT EDITOR

A less trivial example of an interactive program is a text editor: the editor has input streams from the keyboard and the disk, and output streams to the screen and the disk.

For simplicity we assume that the disk supports a structured file store, and that the text of a file is a list of characters: sending the disk the message *Get f* causes it to respond with the contents of file *f* as the next message on the input stream from the disk, or the response *Error* if the file does not exist; sending the disk the message *Put f c* causes the list of characters *c* to become the new contents of file *f* and there is no response.

The user can request that the contents of a particular file be fetched for editing, that the current text be edited, and that the current text be stored as the contents of some file. We assume that the input from the keyboard is pre-parsed into appropriate command messages; if required this could be achieved by inserting a parsing process between the keyboard port and the editor process.

The handling of the text to be edited is based on a simple idea exploited in [Sufrin 81]: the text is split up into a pair comprising the list of characters to the left of the "cursor" and the list of characters to the right. Implementations are given for two edit actions "*move one character to the right*" and "*delete the character to the right of the cursor*". Fig 7.5 shows the I/O stream connections required by the editor.

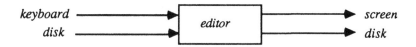

Fig 7.5 The editor's I/O stream connections

Here is one possible functional encoding of this text editor:

Types:

edit_action	::= *Move_Right* l *Delete_Right* l ...
file_name	== [*char*]
text	== [*char*]
keyboard_msg	::= *Fetch file_name* l *Do edit_action* l *Store file_name*
screen_msg	::= *Line* [*char*]
to_disk_msg	::= *Get file_name* l *Put file_name text*
from_disk_msg	::= *Contents text* l *Error*
process	::= (*stream keyboard_msg*, *stream from_disk_msg*)
	→ (*stream screen_msg*, *stream to_disk_msg*)

Functions:

>   *editor* :: *process*
>   *editor* = *edit* ([ ],[ ])

>   *edit* :: *(text, text)*→ *process*
>   *edit t* ((*Fetch f*) ! *kb, from_disk*) = (*scr*, (*Get f*) ! *to_disk*)
>   **where** *response* ! *from_disk'* = *from_disk*
>   (*scr, to_disk*)   = *recv response*
>   *recv* (*Contents t'*) = ((*Line* "Ready") ! *scr, to_disk*)
>   **where** (*scr, to_disk*) = *edit* ([ ], *t'*) (*kb, from_disk'*)
>   *recv Error*   = ((*Line* "No such file") ! *scr, to_disk*)
>   **where** (*scr, to_disk*) = *edit* ([ ], *t*) (*kb, from_disk'*)
>   *edit t* ((*Do a*) ! *kb, from_disk*) = (*response* ! *scr, to_disk*)
>   **where** (*response, t'*)   = *do_edit a t*
>   (*scr, to_disk*) = *edit t '* (*kb, from_disk*)
>   *edit* (*lt,rt*) ((*Store f*) ! *kb, from_disk*) =
>   ((*Line* "Done") ! *scr*, (*Put f* (*lt*++*rt*) ! *to_disk*))
>   **where** (*scr, to_disk*)   = *edit t* (*kb, from_disk*)
>   :
>   *edit t* (*other* ! *kb, from_disk*) = ((*Line* "Bad command") ! *scr, to_disk*)
>   **where** (*scr, to_disk*)   = *edit t* (*kb, from_disk*)

>   *do_edit* :: *edit_action* → (*text, text*) → (*screen_msg, (text, text)*)
>   *do_edit Move_Right* (*lt, c : rt*) = (*Line* "Done", (*lt*++[*c*], *rt*))
>   *do_edit Delete_Right* (*lt, c : rt*) = (*Line* "Done", (*lt, rt*))
>   :
>   *do_edit other t*   = (*Line* "Bad edit action", *t*)

The editor is written in a very direct style: the dependence of the program on a recursive computation involving tuples of streams is quite explicit. This may be seen as the traditional approach to writing functional programs; it does not attempt to exploit more recent developments in functional programming style.

An advantage that may be claimed for this direct style is that it makes the adopted model of streams for input and output quite apparent – nothing is hidden (this is in contrast to the alternative style that we shall look at in section 7.4). However, we have to set against this advantage the disadvantage that a substantial proportion of the program text is devoted to the management of the streams and tuples of streams: decomposing them, constructing them and directing them from their producers to their consumers; moreover, in the "*Do a*" and "*other*" clauses of *edit* the disk streams appear explicitly, although they have no immediate rôle in these clauses. If we were to examine other programs written in this style, we would discover that the strategies of stream management were largely the same in each case.

In the next section we shall see one way in which the power of functional programming can be harnessed to reduce this aspect of the complexity of the program text: we introduce a more appropriate level of abstraction for handling input and output which allows the programmer to concentrate on the more important program design issues.

7.4 REPACKAGING STREAMS: HIGHER ORDER FUNCTIONS AND CONTINUATIONS

To provide a more convenient interface for interactive processes we may propose that the programmer should have access to a library of higher order functions. [Thompson 86] suggests a number of such functions which also allow the maintenance of a state through the computation. Similar functions are also suggested in [Bird et al. 88].

7.4.1 A basic set of interface functions

In order to illustrate the general principle we present here a simple set of functions suitable for reprogramming the text editor more elegantly.

The text editor consumes two input streams (of messages from the keyboard and disk) and produces two output streams (of messages to the screen and disk). We require at least four interface functions to allow sending and receiving on all streams: *receive_keyboard*, *receive_disk*, *send_screen*, *send_disk*. Each of these constructs a *process* which performs the necessary action at the head of its input or output streams, and whose subsequent stream processing is determined by a *continuation parameter*. In the case of receiving, the continuation parameter is applied to the message which has been received, which may thus influence the subsequent stream processing activity.

We may define the interface functions as follows:

receive_keyboard : (*keyboard_msg* → *process*) → *process*
receive_keyboard c (*msg* ! *kb*, *from_disk*) = *c msg* (*kb*, *from_disk*)

receive_disk : (*from_disk_msg* → *process*) → *process*
receive_disk c (*kb*, *msg* ! *from_disk*) = *c msg* (*kb*, *from_disk*)

$send\_screen : screen\_msg \rightarrow process \rightarrow process$
$send\_screen\ msg\ c\ (kb, from\_disk) = (msg\ !\ scr, to\_disk)$
$\quad\quad\quad\quad\quad$ **where** $(scr, to\_disk) = c\ (kb, from\_disk)$

$send\_disk : to\_disk\_msg \rightarrow process \rightarrow process$
$send\_disk\ msg\ c\ (kb, from\_disk) = (scr, msg\ !\ to\_disk)$
$\quad\quad\quad\quad\quad$ **where** $(scr, to\_disk) = c\ (kb, from\_disk)$

Assuming that keyboard and screen messages are numbers, then the interactive program *double* from section 7.2 can be rewritten as:

$double :: process$
$double\ = receive\_keyboard$
$\quad\quad\quad\quad (\lambda x.\ send\_screen\ (2 \times x)\ double)$

The program has been reduced to its essential components: "read a value", "call it x", "print $2 \times x$", and repeat this behaviour. We are able to express a basically imperative behaviour in a clean, apparently imperative, way without leaving the purely functional framework. However, there is perhaps no great gain in this simple example; moreover the disk streams are not used.

Let us assume temporarily that disk files hold a list of numbers and that keyboard messages are numbers. Then we can write a program which obtains the contents of the disk file called *data*, displays on the screen the product of each number that it contains and a new number obtained from the keyboard and then halts:

$sums : process$
$sums = send\_disk\ (Get\ "data")$
$\quad\quad\quad\quad (receive\_disk\ \lambda(Contents\ xs).\ dosums\ xs)$

$dosums : [num] \rightarrow process$
$dosums\ [\ ] = stop$
$dosums\ x : xs = receive\_keyboard$
$\quad\quad\quad\quad\quad\quad (\lambda y.\ send\_screen\ (x \times y)\ (dosums\ xs))$

where *stop* is a process termination function which produces two empty output streams:

$stop : process$
$stop\ ss = ([\ ] , [\ ])$

Note how the higher order functions, and the structure of their types, has allowed us to avoid much administrative clutter that would otherwise have been required in order to deal with the tuples of streams. Instead we are able to concentrate our attention on the more important aspects of the program. For example, *dosums* contains no mention of the disk streams; they are correctly handled, in the background, by the interface functions.

The *sums* program makes use of a common idiom: the disk is sent a request, and its response is immediately awaited. This handshaking form of interaction can easily be given its own interface function:

request_disk : to_disk_msg → (from_disk_msg → process) → process
request_disk msg c = send_disk msg (receive_disk c)

and *sums* may be recoded as

sums = request_disk (Get "data")
  (λ(Contents xs). dosums xs)

7.4.2 The text editor: an improved version

Here we present the editor described in section 7.3 redesigned to exploit the interface functions defined in section 7.4.1.

Types:

edit_action	::= *Move_Right I Delete_Right I ...*
file_name	== *[char]*
text	== *[char]*
keyboard_msg	::= *Fetch file_name I Do edit_action I Store file_name*
screen_msg	::= *Line [char]*
to_disk_msg	::= *Get file_name I Put file_name text*
from_disk_msg	::= *Contents text I Error*
process	::= *(stream keyboard_msg, stream from_disk_msg)*
	→ (stream screen_msg, stream to_disk_msg)

Functions:

editor :: process
editor = edit ([ ],[ ])

$edit :: (text, text) \rightarrow process$
$edit\ t = receive\_keyboard\ (edit\_step\ t)$

$edit\_step :: (text, text) \rightarrow keyboard\_msg \rightarrow process$
$edit\_step\ t\ (Fetch f) = request\_disk\ (Get f)\ recv$
       where $recv\ (Contents\ t') =$ $send\_screen\ (Line\ "Ready")$
                                                $(edit\ ([\ ],t'))$
                     $recv\ Error$ $=$ $send\_screen\ (Line\ "No\ such\ file")$
                                                $(edit\ t)$
$edit\_step\ t\ (Do\ a) = send\_screen\ response\ (edit\ t')$
          where $(response, t')$ $= do\_edit\ a\ t$
$edit\_step\ (lt, rt)\ (Store f) =$ $send\_disk\ (Put f\ (lt ++ rt))$
                                        $(send\_screen\ (Line\ "Ready"))$
                                        $(edit\ (lt, rt)))$

$\vdots$

$edit\_step\ t\ other =$ $send\_screen\ (Line\ "Bad\ command")$
                          $(edit\ t)$

$do\_edit :: edit\_action \rightarrow (text, text) \rightarrow (screen\_msg, (text, text))$
$do\_edit\ Move\_Right\ (lt, c : rt)\ = (Line\ "Done", (lt++[c], rt))$
$do\_edit\ Delete\_Right\ (lt, c : rt)\ = (Line\ "Done", (lt, rt))$
$\vdots$

$do\_edit\ other\ t$ $= (Line\ "Bad\ edit\ action", t)$

In this form the editor is considerably easier to understand than when the detailed stream processing was exposed. The essential control structure of the program is explicit, and is reminiscent of imperative code; for example, to process a "*Store*" command the editor sends the new file contents to the disk, then notifies the user, and then is ready to continue editing with the text unchanged.

Note that the interface functions are used *only* in organization of the overall program evaluation; they are not appropriate, and are not practically useable, where manipulation of data structures is called for. For example, if *do_edit* were to provide a pattern matching search and replace option, then the ordinary power of functional programming would almost certainly prove to give the best solution to this.

7.4.3 Generalizing the interface functions

We have seen a collection of interface functions suitable for a restricted program execution environment with two input streams and two output streams. In a general purpose programming environment there will be many devices or many software subsystems. Any particular program will have the potential to communicate with any of these producers or consumers of data, but will need to access only a subset of them. It seems undesirable to provide a library containing specially named interface functions for each potential communication channel, and it will certainly not be possible if the collection of devices and subsystems may change dynamically. Thus it is necessary to provide general interface functions which allow access to any available communication channels.

We outline here two possible solutions. Filling out the details is left as an exercise for the reader. The solutions share the characteristic that a small fixed set of interface functions is provided, for example *receive*, *send* and *request*, and that these take one argument representing *all* input streams and deliver a result representing *all* output streams; an additional argument identifies the stream to be used for each particular action.

In the first solution, collections of streams are represented by an association list, and individual streams are identified by their associated names.

In the second solution, the input to and output from a process are single streams of messages tagged with the name of their source or intended destination, and individual "streams" (which no longer exist as such) are identified by their tags.

Whichever solution is adopted, it is quite feasible to hide the exact details behind the interface, and the programmer need not be concerned with the low level details since each implementation has the *same* interface.

7.5 PROCESS NETWORKS, PARALELLISM AND NON-DETERMINISM

In the preceding sections we have been discussing process *pipelines*. We may generalize these to *process networks*; in these we have a collection of processes communicating via streams, as before, but we no longer restrict ourselves to linear connections. Two particular consequences of this generalization are that streams may be duplicated (all messages go to all destinations), and that cycles may be introduced. The individual processes in a pipeline or network may be executed in parallel; there can be no deleterious interference between such parallel activities, since the data dependences of results on inputs are encoded explicitly in functional programs, and these dependences ensure correct synchronization. In the context of operating systems we often need to service requests from programs and the external environment on a first-come-first-served basis; to permit this *non-determinism* we need to introduce an extra facility into our functional language, and several options are available. These issues are discussed in the following sections.

7.5.1 Process networks

Consider extending the editor from section 7.4.2. Imagine that we will be editing the texts of programs in some programming language. Whenever we store the text of a program in a file, we would like it to be compiled automatically; the compiled code (or some set of error messages) should also be stored in a file on the disk, and we would like a message to appear on the screen informing us of the successful completion, or failure, of the compilation.

The major components of this system are the editor and the compiler; the editor is as in section 7.4, and the compiler is a process with a single input stream of texts to be compiled (it must receive a copy of all messages in the disk output stream from the editor, and should compile the contents of *Put* messages) and two output streams: one to the disk containing compiled programs, and one to the screen. There are two small, but vital, components in this system: two independent streams of messages (from the editor and the compiler) must be *merged* into a single stream directed to the screen, and, similarly, two streams must be merged into a single stream directed to the disk. Thus we have the network in Fig 7.6.

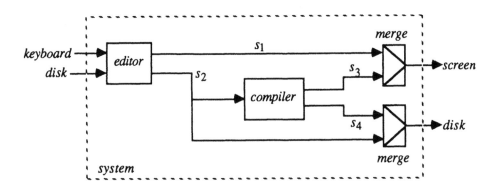

Fig 7.6 A process network: linking the editor and a compiler

We may define this network functionally as follows:

system :: (*stream keyboard_msg, stream from_disk_msg*)
$$\rightarrow (\textit{stream screen\_msg, stream to\_disk\_msg })$$

$$system(kb, from\_disk) = (screen, to\_disk)$$
$$\textbf{where} \quad (s_1, s_2) = editor \ (kb, from\_disk)$$
$$(s_3, s_4) = compiler \ s_2$$
$$screen \quad = merge \ s_1 \ s_3$$
$$to\_disk = merge \ s_4 \ s_2$$

This illustrates how a network structure may be encoded by a collection of equations in a **where** clause. Details of the *compiler* have been omitted, as they offer no additional insight into the structure of process networks. The two processes labelled *merge* combine the messages from their two input streams into a single output stream in a first-come-first-served fashion; this is problematical for functional languages, and we discuss it further in section 7.5.3.

Clearly we could consider this to be a very crude design for what might be a primitive operating system. In the section 7.6 we examine a more general approach to an operating system structure which may be extended smoothly with new facilities, in contrast to the rather *ad hoc* way in which the system above acquired a new subsystem.

7.5.2   Parallelism

Functional languages do not usually contain special constructs for the expression of parallel evaluation; such constructs could not, in any case, affect the result of a program and would only have the status of providing pragmatic hints to a compiler. There is no semantic problem associated with the *automatic* introduction of parallel evaluation, since there can be no deleterious interference between parallel activities. The reason for this is that all the essential data dependences are encoded in a functional program, and *any* evaluation scheme which respects these dependences will exhibit correct synchronization. There are a number of ways in which parallel evaluation can be exploited; for an overview of research in this area see [Peyton Jones 89].

An obvious source of parallelism in process networks is the individual processes; each may be executed independently, either timesharing one processor or on several processors, and synchronization occurs through the passage of messages on the streams between them. The other main source of parallelism is in the simultaneous evaluation of the arguments of function calls – especially "functions" such as *merge*, discussed below.

7.5.3   Non-determinism

Before we proceed, we must address a deeper question: what is the exact nature of the *merge* process used in Fig 7.6? Operationally it is quite easy to describe our requirements of *merge*: since, we will assume, the editor and compiler processes will be executing concurrently, the messages on *merge*'s input streams will become available only at unpredictable *relative* times; we require the messages to be transmitted by *merge* on a first-come-first-served basis. It is impossible to define this process in the functional language that we have been using so far. [Abramsky et al. 85] and [Stoye 85] take *merge* as a new primitive. Here we shall adopt a solution closer to McCarthy's **amb** [McCarthy 63]: we allow a function to be defined using non-exclusive ("overlapping") equations, that is equations in which more than one left hand side may match some calls of the function. When more than one equation matches a call, then the one that matches against the arguments which were computed *earliest* is selected.

Using this approach, *merge* may be defined as follows:

$$merge \;::\; stream \; \alpha \; \rightarrow \; stream \; \alpha \; \rightarrow \; stream \; \alpha$$
$$merge \; (x \,!\, xs) \; ys \; = \; x \,!\, merge \; xs \; ys$$
$$merge \; xs \; (y \,!\, ys) \; = \; y \,!\, merge \; xs \; ys$$
$$merge \; [\,] \; ys \qquad = ys$$
$$merge \; xs \; [\,] \qquad = xs$$

The first equation will be selected if the first input stream has a message available before the second stream has a message available, or if it arrived earlier in the case that they both have a message available. The second equation will be selected under symmetrical conditions. The third and fourth equations deal with streams which terminate, in an obvious way. This is intuitively reasonable in a parallel environment in which the arguments of *merge* are evaluated in parallel.

Thus *merge* is what is called a *non-deterministic* process since it appears to make a random choice between its arguments; however we have imposed a stronger condition, as we require that the choice is time dependent rather than random. Unfortunately, whether we adopt random or time dependent choice, with this step we lose an elegant formal property of the language, namely "referential transparency", and program transformations must be carried out with great care.

In a language which displays the property of referential transparency, we expect to be able to replace a single evaluation of an expression by a re-evaluation at each point where its value is required (and *vice versa*), without altering the result of the computation (provided that the computation terminates). In other words, we expect

$x+x$ **where** $x = e$

and $e+e$

to have the same value, that is $2 \times e$. In implementation terms, this means that implementing β-reduction by copying (i.e. by substitution) gives the same result as by graph reduction (in which e is *not* copied); in program transformation, it means that we have a great deal of flexibility because fold/unfold transformations do not change the set of values that may result from evaluation of an expression.

The problems associated with a loss of referential transparency can be demonstrated by the following simple example. Using overlapping equations we may define the operator *amb*:

   amb $x \, y = x$
   amb $x \, y = y$

Thus *amb* returns whichever of its arguments it detects has been evaluated first. Unfortunately the equivalence discussed above no longer holds if e contains a call of *amb*. For example:

   $x+x$ **where** $x = amb \, e_1 \, e_2$ may evaluate to $2 \times e_1$ or $2 \times e_2$

and $(amb \, e_1 \, e_2) + (amb \, e_1 \, e_2)$ may evaluate to $2 \times e_1$ or $2 \times e_2$ or $e_1 + e_2$

since in the latter case there are multiple independent evaluations of e_1 and e_2 and each *amb* might make a different choice (especially in a parallel environment).

We shall use *merge* only in a restricted way so as to contain this problem. Our strategy for containing the problem is to use non-determinism only in those places where it is precisely an implementation of requirements, such as *merging* to the screen, above; the capability for writing non-deterministic functions will be available only to the "systems programmer", and not to "users". We discuss the issue further in the last section of this chapter. This is a controversial issue, but the requirements for which *merge* is a candidate solution certainly arise in operating system design, and so we must adopt *some* workable solution and learn to apply it in a disciplined way. The *merge* function is a workable solution: it allows us to isolate the sources of non-determinism in a system to clearly identified locations, and to produce transparent system structures.

Other appproaches to the provision of non-deterministic processing have been proposed. [Burton 88] describes the use of *trees* of *decisions* to determine and record the non-deterministic choices made by any expression; programs have much the same form as here, but extra arguments are required to transmit *trees* of *decisions* to functions. [Stoye 85] uses a *sorting office* to provide non-determinism and centralized control in a process network; the sorting office is outside any individual process, and is the *sole* non-deterministic element.

7.6   AN OPERATING SYSTEM STRUCTURE

Our aim in this section is to outline a design for a multiprogramming operating system for a single user workstation. The system should make it possible to create processes and to kill processes; processes should be able to terminate and disappear from the system; there should be a well organized message passing regime for inter-process communication; and there should be a structured file system, and thus the operating system will have to manage a disk. The topic of operating systems properly covers many other issues, primarily those of resource management (resource sharing, mutual exclusion and monitors) and system design principles (layered architectures and virtual machines for resource abstraction), for example see [Brinch Hansen 73]. In the limited space available we identify two specific areas for consideration: the overall operating system structure and the architecture of a file system; the latter will require us to look briefly at low level device I/O. The design of the file system will indicate how a layered architecture may be realised; other operating system services may be implemented similarly using the basic process and communication facilities.

7.6.1   The network design

The system uses a dynamically reconfigurable network in the shape of a ring, with all user processes and devices attached as shown in Fig 7.7. Such a design was suggested in [Abramsky 82] and we adopt this approach with a few minor extensions.

Each of the user and operating system processes is a stream processing function in the sense of section 7.2.1, with the input and output streams of each connected in a specific way to form the ring. *All* communication between user and operating system processes occurs via the ring, and so there is no possibility of communication or interference between processes apart from that which is explicitly programmed to occur via the ring. The basic characteristics of functional stream processing ensure that messages are transmitted *atomically*; this means that the lower level synchronization problems which must be solved in operating system implementation do not arise.

Each process is allocated a unique process identifier, of type *pid*, which is used for a variety of purposes including system calls and message passing. Process identifiers may only be created and allocated by the process manager *pm*.

Process communication is via streams of messages tagged with *pids*. The convention is adopted that each message in the system is tagged with both the *pid* of the sender and that of the destination process. The packages sent around the ring are therefore of type (*pid, pid, mesg*). The system attaches source tags and strips destination tags from messages before their arrival. The view of a user process is that each incoming message is tagged with its origin only and each outgoing message is tagged with its destination only. Thus user processes are of type:

$$process = stream(\ pid,\ mesg) \rightarrow stream(\ pid,\ mesg).$$

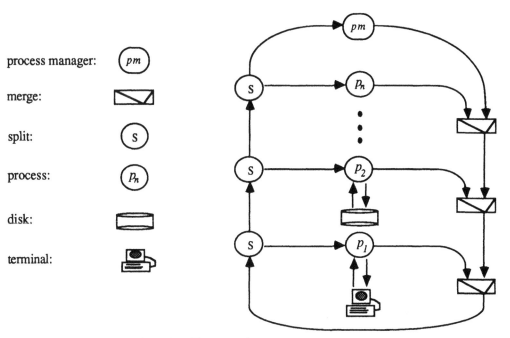

process manager: *pm*

merge:

split: *S*

process: p_n

disk:

terminal:

Figure 7.7 The operating system structure

The network is made up of four types of node: (i) processes $p_1 .. p_n$, (ii) *merges*, (iii) *splits*, and (iv) the process manager *pm*.

The processes $p_1 .. p_n$ may be simple user processes or operating system services such as the file store with devices and device drivers attached.

Device driver processes have streams to and from their specific devices in addition to their network links. In Fig 7.7 process p_1 is a terminal driving process; it receives service requests from other processes, and returns responses, via the ring. Requests serviced by the terminal driver could be *Get_Line*, *Put_Line*, etc; the assembly and disassembly of suitable network messages would be dealt with by standard interface functions similar to those examined in section 7.4. Process p_2 is a file system server; it receives high level, file oriented service requests, carries out appropriate low level actions through communication with the disk, and returns suitable high level responses via the ring.

In Fig 7.7 processes $p_3 .. p_n$ are user programs. Each communicates with the rest of the system via single input and output streams. Messages on these streams are tagged with source and destination *pids*; again this level of detail is handled by the standard interface functions. A program such as the editor in section 7.4.2 is suitable for use as a user process, though it would need modification to explicitly request (and parse) keyboard input.

Each *merge* is a version of the function given in section 7.5.3, modified to merge messages from a process into the ring. The modifications are extra control structures for message tagging and process termination. *merge* takes three arguments: the first is the *pid* of the process with which it is associated, the second a stream of messages from the ring and the third is the stream of messages from the process with which it is associated:

$$merge :: pid \rightarrow stream\ (pid, pid, mesg) \rightarrow stream\ (pid, mesg)$$
$$\rightarrow stream\ (pid, pid, mesg)$$

merge myid ring ((destid, msg) ! proc)
$$= (destid, myid, msg)\ !\ merge\ myid\ ring\ proc$$
merge myid ((destid, sourceid, msg) ! ring) proc
$$= (destid, sourceid, msg)\ !\ ring, \quad \textbf{if } destid = myid \wedge msg = Stop$$
$$= (destid, sourceid, msg)\ !\ merge\ myid\ ring\ proc, \quad \textbf{otherwise}$$
merge myid ring [] = (myid, pm, Stop) ! ring

The first equation for **merge** handles the case where a message comes from the process associated with that *merge*. These messages are tagged with the *pid* of the sender and passed around the ring. The second equation handles a message coming from the ring. A message for another process must be passed on around the ring. A *Stop* message, reserved for system use, sent to the local process indicates that *merge* should detach that process from the ring: *merge* returns its *ring* argument, relays the *Stop* to its partner *split* and becomes transparent to the system. When the process wishes to terminate normally, its output stream will end with []. The *merge* function handles this by sending a *Stop* message to the *split* associated with the process and reconfiguring to pass on messages transparently round the ring. The definition of *merge* again relies on overlapping equations, and the use of head strict constructor "!" ensures that messages are available before sending them.

Each process has a *split* associated with it to filter off messages with its *pid* on. The destination tag of messages for the local process are stripped away. The input to *split* is the *pid* of its local process and the stream of messages from the ring. Upon receiving a *Stop* signal, relayed by its corresponding *merge*, *split* reconfigures to pass all messages on round the ring in a transparent way and relays the *Stop* message to *pm*. Its output is a pair composed of the stream of ring messages, and the stream of messages for its associated process. Thus *split* is:

$split :: pid \rightarrow stream(pid, pid, mesg) \rightarrow (stream(pid, pid, mesg), stream(pid, mesg))$
$split\ myid\ ((destid, sourceid, msg)\ !\ ring)$

$=$	$((destid, sourceid, Stop)\ !\ ring, []),$	**if** $destid = myid \wedge msg = Stop$
$=$	$(r, (sourceid, msg)\ !\ p),$	**if** $destid = myid$
$=$	$((destid, sourceid, msg)\ !\ r, p),$	**otherwise**

where $(r, p) = split\ myid\ ring$

The process manager, *pm*, manages process creation and deletion, process identifiers and various other system calls and errors. It maintains a pool of available process identifiers. The special process identifier *pmid* is reserved for the process manager. Messages arriving at the process manager are already tagged with their origin and destination. Thus *pm* is of type:

$$pm :: pidpool \rightarrow stream(pid, pid, message) \rightarrow stream(pid, pid, message)$$

We do not give details here of the implementation of the process identifier pool. We assume the existence of a type *pidpool* (which could, for example, be implemented as a list), and two functions *addpid* and *getpid* for managing the process identifier pool:

$$addpid : pid \rightarrow pidpool \rightarrow pidpool$$
$$getpid : pidpool \rightarrow (pid, pidpool)$$

addpid adds the given process identifier to the pool, returning the updated pool; *getpid* extracts an unused process identifier from the pool, and returns the identifier and the updated pool.

The code below shows the action taken for process creation. When a process *myid* wishes to create a process, it sends the message *Create f* to the process manager, where *f* is the function describing the process to be created. The new process is created by reconfiguring the ring as shown in Fig 7.8. The *pid* of the new process is returned to the parent in a message of the form *New newid*:

$pm\ oldpool\ ((pmid, myid, Create f)\ !\ ring) = s$

where s	$=$	$merge\ newid\ o_1\ o_2$
o_1	$=$	$(myid, pmid, New\ newid)\ !\ pm\ newpool\ s_1$
o_2	$=$	$f\ s_2$
(s_1, s_2)	$=$	$split\ newid\ ring$
$(newid, newpool)$	$=$	$getpid\ oldpool$

Before:

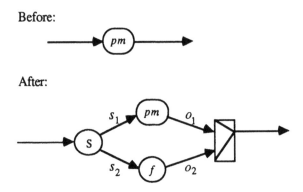

After:

Figure 7.8 Process creation

As described above, process termination causes the *split* associated with that process to send a *Stop* message to *pm*. This causes *pm* to add the *pid* of the terminated process to the process identifier pool as follows:

$$pm\ oldpool\ ((pmid, myid, Stop)\ !\ ring) = pm\ newpool\ ring$$
$$\textbf{where}\ newpool\ = addpid\ myid\ oldpool$$

When requested by a process *myid* to kill a process *pid*, i.e. on receipt of the message *Kill pid*, the process manager takes the following action: the special message *Stop*, only available to the system, is sent to the *merge* and *split* associated with the process *pid*, which causes them to reconfigure in the manner described above. This simplified example does not provide for any system security: here any process may kill any other whose *pid* it knows; protection information could be maintained by *pm*, since it knows about all process creation and deletion and also the process hierarchy. We do not address these issues here.

$$pm\ pool\ ((pmid, myid, Kill\ pid\ )\ !\ ring\ ) = s$$
$$\textbf{where}\ s\qquad = response\ !\ pm\ pool\ ring$$
$$response\ = (pid, pmid, Stop\ )$$

Once the *split* associated with a terminated process has reconfigured itself, messages addressed to that process will not be removed from the ring and will eventually arrive at the process manager. In such circumstances it is desirable that the process which sent the message should be informed that the process it is sending to has terminated. This is another function performed by *pm*. A message arriving at *pm* with a destination tag other than *pmid* causes *pm* to send a message to the sender indicating a system error, i.e. that the process no longer exists.

pm pool ((*destid, myid, mesg*) ! *ring*) = *s*
　　　　where *s* = (*myid, pmid, Syserr NO_SUCH_PROCESS*) ! *pm pool ring*

In this case *myid* is the *pid* of the process attempting to send to a terminated process, and *Syserr NO_SUCH_PROCESS* indicates the nature of the error.

7.6.2　Low level disk control, and a simple file system

We first consider a design for a functional low level disk controller. Using the low level disk controller a file system can then be built to service the rest of the operating system. The disk and the file system are one process node in the network as shown in Fig 7.7. The internal structure of the node is shown in Fig 7.9:

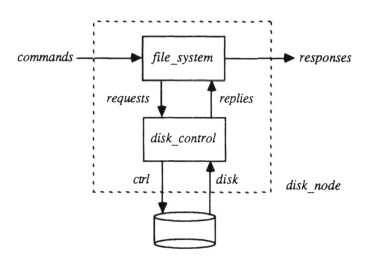

Figure 7.9 The file system server

Messages from and to the ring on the *commands* and *responses* streams are at the file I/O level; the *requests* and *replies* streams carry communications at a block I/O level and the *disk* and *ctrl* streams at a device control level. We will only look at the *disk_control* process here.

The physical disk interface from the functional program is via control streams although actual block reads and writes will be performed using Direct Memory Access. All DMA accesses are made via an area of memory, one block long, reserved for DMA access. The use of an intermediate area of fixed memory for DMA access is normal practice, and makes the design easier to generalize to concurrent use of discs using a larger DMA area. The disk is controlled using two streams: *disk* and *ctrl*. Low level block access will be performed using a disk block type:

$block == [char]$

where the length of [char] is the same as that of a disk block.

We assume that we have a hardware disk controller which can respond to six instructions:

Track t :	Move the disk head to track *t*.
Sector s:	Select sector *s* for disk access.
Read :	Read the currently selected block into the DMA area.
Write :	Write from the DMA area to the currently selected block.
Get :	Return the contents of the DMA area on the *disk* stream.
Put b :	Put the *block b* into the DMA area.

We can now define the type of items on the *ctrl* stream to the disk:

$disk\_out ::= Read \mid Write \mid Track\ num \mid Sector\ num \mid Get \mid Put\ block$

The *Read* and *Write* instructions return status values on the *disk* stream and *Get* returns a *block*; we assume that the other instructions always succeed, and give no response. Therefore, replies from the disk on *input* can be of two types, either a status value indicating whether an action was successful, or a *block* transferred from the DMA area. Thus the type of data on the input stream is:

$disk\_in ::= Status\ num \mid Block\ block$

With these instructions, it is now possible to read and write disk blocks to and from the functional program. A read from the block at track 5, sector 7 would be achieved by the following sequence:

$(Track\ 5)\ !\ (Sector\ 7)\ !\ Read\ !\ Get\ !\ ...$

to which we would expect the reponse:

$(Status\ OK)\ !\ (Block\ data)\ !\ ...$

where *OK* is the code for a successful *Read* and *data* is a block representing the contents of the DMA area.

To write the *block data* to track 5, sector 7:

(Track 5) ! *(Sector 7)* ! *(Put data)* ! *Write* ! ...

Only *Write* returns a status in this case, so successful execution should result in the response:

(Status OK) ! ...

Using these primitives it is possible to design the process *disk_control*: this is a simple function to provide the abstraction of a contiguous list of *block*s avoiding the need to deal with tracks and sectors. Requests are made by the *file_system* to *disk_control* on a stream of items of type:

disk_requests ::= Read block_id | Write block block_id

where   *block_id == num*

and replies to the *file_system* are a stream of messages of type *disk_in*. The function is shown below:

disk_control ((Read blk) ! requests) disk = (replies, ctrl)
　　　　where *replies =* **if** *stat = OK* **then** *(Block data)* ! *next_replies*
　　　　　　　　　　　　　　　　　　else *(Status stat)* ! *next_replies*
　　　　　　(Status stat) ! *(Block data)* ! *rest   = disk*
　　　　　　ctrl   = sct ! *trk* ! *Read* ! *Get* ! *next_ctrl*
　　　　　　sct   = (Sector (blk **mod** *SECTORS_PER_TRACK))*
　　　　　　trk   = (Track (blk **div** *SECTORS_PER_TRACK))*
　　　　　　(next_replies, next_ctrl) = disk_control requests rest

disk_control (Write text blk ! *requests) disk = (replies, ctrl)*
　　　　where *replies = status* ! *next_replies*
　　　　　　status ! *rest   = disk*
　　　　　　ctrl   = sct ! *trk* ! *(Put text)* ! *Write* ! *next_ctrl*
　　　　　　sct   = (Sector (blk **mod** *SECTORS_PER_TRACK))*
　　　　　　trk   = (Track (blk **div** *SECTORS_PER_TRACK))*
　　　　　　(next_replies, next_ctrl) = disk_control requests rest

The function *disk_control* illustrates the principle of constructing a device driver to provide a more useable abstraction of a physical device. Furthermore, Fig 7.9 shows a process *file_system* which provides a high level of abstraction as the main programming interface; this would itself be made up of a number of processes in a similar configuration, each one providing another level of abstraction, allowing a layered decomposition of the problem. Such levels of abstraction would be: management of disk blocks in a heap, simple file structures and finally a fully structured file system with protection and hierarchies. Clearly these layers would need to maintain directories, disk allocation maps and so on; this information itself could and probably would, be held on the disk and would be accessed as required. Assuming that we have a process *file_system* implemented, then the *disk_node* configuration can be set up:

$$disk\_node :: stream\ (pid, mesg) \rightarrow stream\ disk\_in$$
$$\rightarrow (stream\ (pid, mesg), stream\ disk\_out)$$

$disk\_node\ commands\ disk\ =\ (responses, ctrl)$

where $(replies, ctrl)$ $= disk\_control\ requests\ disk$
$\quad\quad (responses, requests)$ $= file\_system\ commands\ replies$

Despite the fact that we have not given a definition of *file_system* here, it should be appreciated by the reader that this is a "well understood", although perhaps non trivial, programming task.

7.7   DISCUSSION

We have demonstrated how the stream input/output model can provide a semantically adequate basis for designing interactive functional programs and functional operating systems. We have seen its uniformity and flexibility when applied to system structuring, device driving and program interfacing. However, as we saw in section 7.3, it does not always lead to great elegance and clarity in the detailed coding of programs. This has had the effect of slowing down the introduction of such facilities into practical functional programming systems.

One solution to these problems was suggested in section 7.4: we supply a package of functions which simply hide the details of stream manipulation from the programmer; they are designed with the intention of allowing the elimination of all explicit references to streams from process definitions − all that remains are the messages and the source and destination identifiers. In fact, if we go a little further, we could *insist* that the programmer use these (or similar) functions for stream handling. The programmer would then be unaware of the details of a program's stream interface − whether single stream, multiple stream, or any other method convenient for the operating system. These ideas may be packaged in various ways; they are surveyed in [Jones et al. 89].

We draw an important conclusion from the observations made in this section: we are building, within a purely functional framework, facilities which enable a natural encoding of sequential input and output control; for all other aspects of programs, standard functional programming techniques must still be employed. These facilities are identical to those features of imperative languages which deal with the same problem; but we have none of the difficult features of traditional imperative languages such as side-effects and dangerous aliasing. To some functional programmers this trend seems culturally disturbing: they seem to be unwilling to accept that a sequential programming paradigm may be the natural solution to certain problems, and they seek to reject the use of functional programming techniques to encode directly such a paradigm. However, we may turn this argument around: there is a wide body of experience which suggests that many problems (or aspects of them) have an essentially sequential nature, and it is an excellent demonstration of the power of functional languages that we can build new, purely functional, program components which allow us to express this essence cleanly and simply in the structure of our programs. The next chapter contains a detailed comparison of the imperative and the functional styles and shows how state-oriented problems can be solved naturally in the purely functional framework.

REFERENCES

[Abramsky 82] S. Abramsky. Dynamically reconfigurable process networks: an applicative approach. Internal Report, Computer Systems Laboratory, Queen Mary College, London, 1982.

[Abramsky et al. 85] S. Abramsky, R. Sykes. A virtual machine for applicative multiprogramming. Proc. Conf. on Functional Programming Languages and Computer Architecture, pp. 81-98, LNCS 201, Springer Verlag, 1985.

[Bird et al. 88] R. Bird, P. Wadler. Introduction to Functional Programming. Prentice Hall International, Series in Computer Science, 1988.

[Brinch Hansen 73] P. Brinch Hansen. Operating Systems Principles. Prentice Hall, 1973.

[Burton 88] F. W. Burton. Non-determinism with referential transparency in functional programming languages. Computer Journal, Vol. 31, No. 3, pp. 243-247, 1988.

[Conway 63] J. Conway. Design of a separable transition diagram compiler. CACM, Vol .6, pp. 396-408, 1963.

[Friedman et al. 76] D. P. Friedman, D. S. Wise. Cons should not evaluate its arguments. Proc. 3rd Int. Coll. on Automata, Languages and Programming, pp. 257-284, 1976.

[Harper et al. 86] R. Harper, D. MacQueen, R. Milner. Standard ML. LFCS-86-2. Laboratory for Foundations of Computer Science, University of Edinburgh, March 1986.

[Henderson et al. 76] P. Henderson, J. H. Morris. A lazy evaluator. Proc. 3rd Conf. on Principles of Programming Languages, pp. 95-103, January 1976.

[Henderson 80] P. Henderson. Functional Programming: Application and Implementation. Prentice Hall International, Series in Computer Science, 1980.

[Johnsson 87] T. Johnsson. Compiling Lazy Functional Languages. PhD thesis, Chalmers University of Technology, Göteborg, 1987.

[Jones 84] S. B. Jones. A range of operating systems written in a purely functional style. Programming Research Group Technical Monograph PRG-42, Oxford University, September 1984.

[Jones et al. 89] S. B. Jones, A. F. Sinclair. Functional programming and operating systems. Computer Journal, Vol. 32, No. 2, pp. 162-174, April 1989.

[Kahn et al. 77] G. Kahn, D. B. MacQueen. Coroutines and networks of parallel processes. Information Processing 77, North Holland, 1977.

[MASCOT] The handbook of Mascot. Mascot Supplies Association, RSRE, Malvern.

[McCarthy 60] J. McCarthy. Recursive functions of symbolic expressions and their computation by machine. CACM, Vol. 3, No. 4, pp. 184-195, 1960.

[McCarthy et al. 62] J. McCarthy, P. W. Abrahams, D. J. Edwards, T. P. Hart, M. I. Levin. LISP 1.5 Programmer's Manual. MIT Press, 1962.

[McCarthy 63] J. McCarthy. A basic mathematical theory of computation. In: Computer Programming and Formal Systems (P. Braffort, D. Hirschberg eds.), pp 33-70, North-Holland, 1963.

[Peyton Jones 89] S. L. Peyton Jones. Parallel implementations of functional programming languages. Computer Journal, Vol. 32, No. 2, pp. 175-186, April 1989.

[Stoye 85] W. Stoye. The Implementation of Functional Languages using Custom Hardware. PhD Thesis, University of Cambridge, December 1985.

[Sufrin 81] B. Sufrin. Formal specification of a display editor. Programming Research Group Technical Monograph PRG-21, Oxford University, 1981.

[Thompson 86] S. Thompson. Writing interactive programs in Miranda. Computing Laboratory Report No. 40, University of Kent at Canterbury, August 1986.

[Turner 87] D. A. Turner. An Introduction to Miranda. In: The Implementation of Functional Programming Languages (S. L. Peyton Jones ed.), Prentice Hall International, Series in Computer Science, 1987.

CHAPTER 8

FOR IMPERATIVE PROGRAMMERS

Daniel Le Métayer

8.1 INTRODUCTION

We advocated in the first chapter the choice of purely functional languages as the basis formalism for future programming environments and all the analysis and transformation techniques described in this book rely on a purely functional language. However our approach may still be unconvincing to programmers or software engineers who are used to imperative languages. One reason is that even if several implementations of "functional" languages [Gordon et al. 79, Abelson et al. 85, Turner 85, Cousineau et al. 88] are now available and adopted by more and more users (mainly in the academic world), most of these languages are not purely functional (in the sense that they allow some form of side-effect) and the (relative) success of a language like LISP (whose name is often associated with the keyword "functional") has contributed to the spread of a misleading perception of functional languages. Most LISP dialects provide some form of assignment, so it would be more fair to describe them as imperative languages with powerful function manipulation facilities. This shows that the separation between imperative languages and functional languages is not so clear: in fact there is a large spectrum of languages which provide more or less powerful function manipulation facilities and more or less powerful imperative features. Other widespread languages such as ML [Gordon et al. 79, Cousineau et al. 88] and MIRANDA [Turner 85] are much closer to the definition of a pure functional language. However ML possesses the assignment statement (which turns out to be hardly necessary and could probably be abandoned) and an escape mechanism; furthermore ML and MIRANDA contain unrestricted forms of input/ouput (through the use of read and write pseudo-functions) which can be used to perform side-effects. Actually this is a crucial issue since input/ouput is in essence a form of side-effect and side-effects are clearly prohibited in functional languages. Furthermore it is clear that if functional languages are ever to be used on a wide scale, they must be able to deal with the demand for natural input/output facilities. So in order to convince the reader that the functional approach is realistic, and as a consequence that the tools proposed in this book are relevant, we have to answer the following questions:

(1) Why are presently used "functional" languages systematically polluted by imperative features destroying the semantic simplicity of the language and making program manipulation more difficult? Is there any fundamental reason for this state of affairs, or should we consider that this situation is only temporary and that real languages will become closer to the pure model in the future?

(2) How could convenient input/output facilities be integrated in a clean way within a functional language?

Actually these two points are closely related since the answer to question (2) is a preliminary step towards an answer to question (1). Question (2) has been thoroughly studied in the previous chapter which describes a clean integration of input/output facilities within a purely functional language. In this chapter we try to tackle the first question in the light of a more general study of the relationship between the functional paradigm and the imperative paradigm. In section 8.2 we consider denotational semantics as a way of translating imperative programs into functional programs. Section 8.3 compares imperative languages and functional languages in the light of program construction and program correctness proof and explains the intrinsic superiority of the latter in this respect. Section 8.4 tackles the efficiency issue; it is shown that the program transformation and program analysis techniques made possible by the functional approach can be used to derive efficient programs from correct programs. In section 8.5 we examine the lessons learned from these investigations and we show that syntactic constructs may be introduced in order to express in a more natural way history-sensitive computations within a purely functional framework. We stress that these constructs do not allow the construction of programs in an imperative style, but rather extend a little the syntax of a functional language to give to the programmer the illusion of using some restricted forms of imperative facilities. We show that these "imperative looking" programs can be analysed using the techniques described in the previous chapters. In conclusion we review different proposals for integrating functional and imperative programming and show that, in contrast to our approach, they all rely on an extension of the purely functional model.

8.2 DENOTATIONAL SEMANTICS

In chapter 2 we introduced denotational semantics as a methodology for specifying the meaning of programs in terms of mathematically defined functions acting on particular domains [Schmidt 86]. We shall not dwell on domain theory and least fixpoints here but rather focus on the translation rules allowing us to derive a function from an imperative program. Let us consider the syntax of a small imperative language:

$$P ::= PR \text{ in } (I_1,..., I_n) \text{ out } (O_1,..., O_m) \ C \qquad\qquad \text{Programs}$$

$$C ::= C_1 ; C_2 \ | \ \text{if } B \text{ then } C_1 \text{ else } C_2 \text{ end} | \ I := E \ |$$
$$I_1[I_2] := E \ | \ \text{while } B \text{ do } C \text{ end} \qquad\qquad \text{Commands}$$

$$E ::= E_1 + E_2 \ | \ minimum \ (E_1, E_2) \ | \ maximum \ (E_1, E_2) \ |$$
$$I_1[I_2] \ | \ I \ | \ N \qquad\qquad \text{Expressions}$$

$$B ::= E_1 = E_2 \ | \ E_1 > E_2 | \ \text{not } B \qquad\qquad \text{Boolean expressions}$$

$$I ::= identifier \qquad\qquad \text{Identifiers}$$

$$N ::= numeral \qquad\qquad \text{Numerals}$$

In the program definition PR in $(I_1,..., I_n)$ out $(O_1,..., O_m) \ C$, PR is the name of the program, $I_1,..., I_n$ are identifiers representing the arguments of the program and $O_1,..., O_n$ stand for the result of the program; C represents the text of the program. In expression $I_1[I_2]$, I_1 is supposed to be an array identifier and I_2 an identifier corresponding to an acceptable index. The denotational semantics of a program

$$PR \text{ in } (I_1,..., I_n) \text{ out } (O_1,..., O_m) \ C$$

is a function from the domain D^n (D containing numbers and arrays) to $D^m_\perp$; $D_\perp$ is defined as $D \cup \{\perp\}$, where $\perp$ is a special value representing undefined results. In order to understand the domains associated with commands, we should think a little about the effect of an assignment: such a statement makes use of a data structure which is not explicitly mentioned in the syntax and which is usually called the store; the net effect of an assignment is a modification of the store; in functional terms, a command is a function from the domain of stores to itself ($S \rightarrow S$) and a store is a function from identifiers to values ($Identifiers \rightarrow D$). In contrast to commands, expressions do not modify the store but they use it since they may involve identifiers; so they are associated with functions of type $S \rightarrow D$. In the same way the denotation of a boolean expression has the type $S \rightarrow Bool$. Following [Schmidt 86] we can now define the semantic functions for our small language ($[\![\ ]\!]$ surrounds expressions in the source language syntax):

$$P: Program \rightarrow D^n \rightarrow D^m_\perp$$
$$P \ [\![PR \text{ in } (I_1,..., I_n) \text{ out } (O_1, ..., O_m) \ C]\!] =$$
$$\lambda(v_1,...,v_n).$$
$$\text{let } s_1 = (update \ [\![I_1]\!] \ v_1 \ newstore) \text{ in}$$
$$...$$
$$\text{let } s_n = (update \ [\![I_n]\!] \ v_n \ s_{n-1}) \text{ in}$$
$$\text{let } s' = C \ [\![C]\!] \ s_n \text{ in}$$
$$((access \ [\![O_1]\!] \ s'), ..., (access \ [\![O_m]\!] \ s'))$$

C: *Command -> Store -> Store*

$C [\![C_1 ; C_2]\!] = \lambda s.\ C [\![C_2]\!]\ (C [\![C_1]\!]\ s)$ (1)

$C [\![$ **if** B **then** C_1 **else** C_2 **end** $]\!] =$

        $\lambda s.$ **if** $B [\![B]\!]\ s$ **then** $C [\![C_1]\!]\ s$ **else** $C [\![C_2]\!]\ s$

$C [\![I_1[I_2] := E]\!] = \lambda s.\ update\ [\![I_1]\!]$

        $(modify\ (access\ [\![I_1]\!]\ s)\ (access\ [\![I_2]\!]\ s)\ (E [\![E]\!]\ s))\ s$

$C [\![I := E]\!] = \lambda s.update\ [\![I]\!]\ (E [\![E]\!]\ s)\ s$ (2)

$C [\![$ **while** B **do** C **end** $]\!] =$

        letrec $f = \lambda s.$ **if** $B [\![B]\!]\ s$ **then** $f\ (C [\![C]\!]\ s)$ **else** s (3)

E: *Expression -> Store -> D*

$E [\![E_1 + E_2]\!] = \lambda s.\ (E [\![E_1]\!]\ s)\ plus\ (E [\![E_2]\!]\ s)$

$E [\![minimum\ (E_1, E_2)]\!] = \lambda s.\ minimum\ (E [\![E_1]\!]\ s, E [\![E_2]\!]\ s)$

$E [\![maximum\ (E_1, E_2)]\!] = \lambda s.\ maximum\ (E [\![E_1]\!]\ s, E [\![E_2]\!]\ s)$

$E [\![I_1[I_2]]\!] = \lambda s.\ value\ (access\ [\![I_1]\!]\ s)\ (access\ [\![I_2]\!]\ s)$

$E [\![I]\!] = \lambda s.\ access\ [\![I]\!]\ s$

$E [\![N]\!] = \lambda s.\ N [\![N]\!]$

B: *Boolean expression -> Store -> Boolean*

$B [\![E_1 = E_2]\!] = \lambda s.\ (E [\![E_1]\!]\ s)\ equals\ (E [\![E_2]\!]\ s)$

$B [\![E_1 > E_2]\!] = \lambda s.\ (E [\![E_1]\!]\ s)\ greaterthan\ (E [\![E_2]\!]\ s)$

$B [\![$ **not** $B]\!] = \lambda s.$ **not** $(B [\![B]\!]\ s)$

N: *Numerals -> D*

N is a function yielding the value of a numeral. Functions *newstore*, *access* and *update* are used respectively to create a new store, to access the value of an identifier in a store and to modify the value associated with an identifier in a store. They are defined in the following way:

    newstore: Store

        newstore $= \lambda i.\ \bot$

    access: Identifiers -> Store -> D

        access $= \lambda i.\ \lambda s.\ (s\ i)$

    update: Identifiers -> D -> Store -> Store

        update $= \lambda i.\ \lambda n.\ \lambda s.\ (\lambda j.\ ($**if** $j = i$ **then** n **else** $(s\ j)))$ (4)

The store yielded by *update* is similar to the store argument s except that it returns the value n for the identifier i; *modify* and *value* are array manipulation functions: (*modify a i v*) yields an array a' similar to a except that $a'[i] = v$, and (*value a i*) yields $a[i]$. In a denotational semantics, these equations would be complemented with a definition of least fixpoints in order to give a precise meaning to the **letrec** construction used in the rule for C ⟦**while** B **do** C **end**⟧; however this point is not relevant here and we shall rather look at the function associated with an imperative program as a functional program. We are particularly interested in the study of the translation rules to understand how some essential imperative constructs can be mirrored quite naturally in the functional framework.

Rule (1) defines the semantics of the sequentiality operator; it shows that sequentiality can be expressed within the purely functional framework by function composition: if we define $(f \circ g) \, x$ as $f(g(x))$, rule (1) can be rewritten as: C ⟦$C_1 ; C_2$⟧ $= C$ ⟦C_2⟧ $\circ \, C$ ⟦C_1⟧. Even in the absence of explicit sequencing in the functional language, this composition expresses the fact that C_1 has to be executed before C_2 since C_1 builds the state which is necessary to execute C_2. In other words, the explicit sequencing in the imperative language has been translated into a logical dependency in the functional language. Rule (2) is the semantics of assignment; it is possible to express the meaning of this statement because the state itself is incorporated within the functional expression. We can say that in some sense an operation may be considered as a side-effect or not, depending on the level of the observation: an assignment may produce a side-effect in an imperative language because it may have an effect on an implicit data structure which is outside the statement itself, but if this data structure is integrated within the expression the side-effect disappears (for the good reason that there is no "side" any longer). Rule (3) shows that iterations can be simulated in a functional language by (left-) recursive functions. Rule (4) describes the functional counterpart of a state modification; let us take a small example to illustrate this point:

$$C \, ⟦X := 4 ; X := 5⟧ = \lambda s. \, C \, ⟦X := 5⟧ \, (C \, ⟦X:=4⟧ \, s)$$

$$C \, ⟦X := 4⟧ \; = \lambda s. \, update \, ⟦X⟧ \, (E \, ⟦4⟧ \, s) \, s$$

$$\qquad\qquad = \lambda s. \, update \, ⟦X⟧ \, 4 \, s$$

$$\qquad\qquad = \lambda s. \, \lambda j \, . \, (\text{if } j = ⟦X⟧ \text{ then } 4 \text{ else } (s \, j))$$

$$C \, ⟦X := 5⟧ \; = \lambda s. \, update \, ⟦X⟧ \, (E \, ⟦5⟧ \, s) \, s$$

$$\qquad\qquad = \lambda s. \, update \, ⟦X⟧ \, 5 \, s$$

$$\qquad\qquad = \lambda s. \, \lambda j \, . \, (\text{if } j = ⟦X⟧ \text{ then } 5 \text{ else } (s \, j))$$

so: $C \, ⟦X := 4 ; X := 5⟧$

$$\qquad\qquad = \lambda s. \, \lambda j \, . \, (\text{if } j = ⟦X⟧ \text{ then } 5 \text{ else } (\text{if } j = ⟦X⟧ \text{ then } 4 \text{ else } (s \, j)))$$

$$\qquad\qquad = \lambda s. \, \lambda j \, . \, (\text{if } j = ⟦X⟧ \text{ then } 5 \text{ else } (s \, j))$$

In a functional language, an expression is never modified but the evolution of the state is simulated through the use of lambda expressions allowing us to mask part of the old state; the old value of the assigned identifier still belongs to the expression but it is no longer accessible.

We illustrate now the rules defined above through a small example; we consider a program M computing the minimum element of an array a containing n elements $(n \geq 1)$:

M **in** (a, n) **out** (min)

 $j := 1;$

 $min := a[j];$

 while $j < n$ **do**

    $j := j+1;$

    $min := minimum\ (min, a[j])$

    end

The rules defined above associate this program with the following function:

$\lambda(N_1, N_2).$

 let $s = update\ [\![a]\!]\ N_1\ newstore$ **in**

 let $s = update\ [\![n]\!]\ N_2\ s$ **in**

 let $s = update\ [\![j]\!]\ 1\ s$ **in**

 let $s = update\ [\![min]\!]\ (value\ (access\ [\![a]\!]\ s)\ (access\ [\![j]\!]\ s))\ s$ **in**

 letrec

  $f = \lambda s.$

   if $((access\ [\![j]\!]\ s) < (access\ [\![n]\!]\ s))$

   then

    $f\ (\textbf{let}\ s = update\ [\![j]\!]\ (plus\ 1\ (access\ [\![j]\!]\ s))\ s$ **in**

     $update\ [\![min]\!]$

     $minimum\ (access\ [\![min]\!]\ s, value\ (access\ [\![a]\!]\ s)\ (access\ [\![j]\!]\ s)))$

   else s

 in

 let $s = f\ s$ **in**

 $(access\ [\![min]\!]\ s)$

The lessons learned from the denotational semantics will be useful in section 8.4 when we shall propose a way to provide the illusion of imperative facilities in a purely functional language. Let us now investigate further the correspondence between the two models through the study of the compilation of functional languages.

8.3 CORRECTNESS CONSIDERATIONS

The theoretical qualities of the functional model described in the first chapter may look unconvincing to a software engineer whose main concern is to develop programs. In this section we attempt to demonstrate that the basic properties of functional languages have extremely beneficial consequences in terms of program construction and program proof. It was claimed a long time ago that programming should be a goal-oriented activity [Wirth 71, Dijkstra 72a, Dijkstra 72b, Gries 81]. This means that:

(1) programs should be proven rather than tested because *"program testing can be a very effective way to show the presence of bugs, but it is hopelessly inadequate for showing their absence"* [Dijkstra 72a];

(2) *"the program and the proof should be developed hand-in-hand, with the proof usually leading the way"* [Gries 81].

We describe the construction of a program along these lines successively in the imperative framework and in the functional framework; we consider the problem of finding the maximum, the minimum and the average of a non-empty set of numbers. In order to avoid any bias we represent the set by an array in the imperative language and by a list in the functional language. A formal specification of the problem may be:

> **find** min, max, av **such that**
> $(\forall\, x \in Set, min \leq x)$ **and** $(min \in Set)$ **and** $\qquad\qquad$ (S)
> $(\forall\, x \in Set, max \geq x)$ **and** $(max \in Set)$ **and**
> $av = (\Sigma\, x \in Set) / card(Set)$

8.3.1 The imperative case

Let us consider the imperative case first; we can reformulate the specification to take into account the array representation of sets; let a denote an array of size n:

> **find** min, max, av **such that** $\qquad\qquad$ (Sa)
> $(\forall\, i \in [1,n],\ min \leq a[i])$ **and** $(\exists\, i \in [1,n]\ min = a[i])$ **and** $\qquad$ (Sa_1)
> $(\forall\, i \in [1,n],\ max \geq a[i])$ **and** $(\exists\, i \in [1,n]\ max = a[i])$ **and** $\qquad$ (Sa_2)
> $av = (\Sigma\, i \in [1,n], a[i]) / n$ $\qquad\qquad$ (Sa_3)

The usual strategy for deriving a program is to weaken the specification predicate in order to develop a loop; there are several ways to weaken a predicate; the most useful ones are:

(1) to delete a conjunct and

(2) to replace a constant by a variable.

For instance, starting with $((Sa_1)$ **and** (Sa_2) **and** $(Sa_3))$ we can delete (Sa_2) and (Sa_3) and attempt to derive a program from (Sa_1) alone. (Sa_1) can be weakened by substituting a new variable j for the constant n; we get

$$(Sa_1) = (Sa_1') \text{ and } (Sa_1'')$$
$$(Sa_1') = (j \leq n \text{ and } \forall \, i \in [1,j], \ min \leq a[i]) \text{ and } (\exists \, i \in [1,j], \ min = a[i])$$
$$(Sa_1'') = (j \geq n)$$

Assignments $j := 1$ and $min := a[1]$ obviously establish (Sa_1'); the strategy consists now in developing a loop with (Sa_1') as invariant (the property that is true before and after each iteration of the loop) and (Sa_1'') as variant (the property that will be established after the last iteration of the loop). A loop **while** B **do** C **end** is determined by a condition B and a command C; for the variant to hold at the exit of the loop, we should have:

$$(\textbf{not } B) \text{ and } (Sa_1') \implies (Sa_1'')$$

that is to say

$$(\textbf{not } B) \text{ and } (Sa_1') \implies (j = n)$$

A straightforward choice for B is $(j < n)$. The purpose of the loop is to make progress towards the validation of the variant. This progress is measured by an integer function of the state called the termination function which represents an upper bound of the number of iterations still to be performed. Each iteration must strictly decrease the value of the termination function. In our example, termination is characterized by the property $(j \geq n)$; the loop begins with $(j = 1)$, so a candidate for the termination function is $f(state) = n - j$. Since n is a constant, a natural way to decrease the value of f is to increment j; however $j := j+1$ is not sufficient since it could invalidate the invariant (Sa_1'); for (Sa_1') to be maintained, min has to be modified in such a way that

$$\forall \, i \in [1,j'], \ min' \leq a[i] \tag{1}$$

where j' and min' denote the new values of j ($j' = j+1$) and min; from the invariant we know that:

$$\forall \, i \in [1,j], \ min \leq a[i]$$

It is clear that a sufficient condition for (1) to hold is:

$$min' = minimum \, (min, \, a[j])$$

So we have developed the following loop:

```
while (j<n) do
        j := j+1;
        min := minimum (min, a[j])
        end
```

The same derivation can be carried out for specifications (Sa_2) and (Sa_3) and we obtain the following program:

```
mma₁ in (a, n) out (min, max, av)
    j := 1;
    min := a[j];
    while (j<n) do
            j := j+1;
            min := minimum (min, a[j])
            end;
    j := 1;
    max := a[j];
    while (j<n) do
            j := j+1;
            max := maximum (max, a[j])
            end;
    j := 1;
    sum := a[j];
    while (j<n) do
            j := j+1;
            sum := sum + a[j]
            end;
    av := sum / n
```

Let us remark that other programs could have been derived as well from the same specification. In fact each decomposition of the specification could potentially lead to a different solution; for example another way to weaken (Sa) could be to replace the constant n by a variable j directly; this would lead to the development of a single loop for the evaluation of min, max and sum; let us call this second program mma_2:

mma_2 **in** (a, n) **out** (min, max, av)

    $j := 1;$

    $min := a[j];$

    $max := a[j];$

    $sum := a[j];$

    while $(j<n)$ **do**

                 $j := j+1;$

                 $min := minimum\ (min, a[j]);$

                 $max := maximum\ (max, a[j]);$

                 $sum := sum + a[j]$

                 end;

    $av := sum\ /\ n$

This program is probably closer to what an imperative programmer would naturally write; it looks more efficient than the first one because it entails only one array traversal; however it may be argued that the first one is better structured because it separates the three logically different problems of evaluating the minimum, the maximum and the sum. This argument will become clear when we look more closely at the formal correctness proof of these programs.

According to the principles stated at the beginning of this section, the correctness proofs should be established hand-in-hand with the construction of the program. We have indeed used a proof of the program to guide the construction of mma_1 above; however the proof has been given in a very informal way and we come back to it now to show how it can be described more formally. To this aim, we use Hoare's logic [Hoare 69] which is an axiomatic semantics where axioms and inference rules specify the behaviour of language constructs. Informally interpreted, a proposition P $\{C\}$ Q (where P and Q are boolean functions of the state) says that if P holds before the evaluation of C and if C terminates then Q holds after the evaluation of C. P is called the precondition and Q the postcondition. The axioms for assignment (1), the rules for the sequentiality (2) and the **while** statement (3) and a basic property of preconditions (4) can be stated in the following way:

$$(P [E/x]) \{x := E\} \ P \tag{1}$$

$$\frac{P \{C_1\} Q, \ Q => R, \ R \{C_2\} S}{P \{C_1 ; C_2\} S} \tag{2}$$

$$\frac{(P \textbf{ and } B) \{C\} \ P}{P \ \{\textbf{while } B \textbf{ do } C \textbf{ end}\} \ (\textbf{not } B) \textbf{ and } P} \tag{3}$$

$$\frac{P_1 \{C\} Q, \ P_2 => P_1}{P_2 \{C\} Q} \tag{4}$$

It should be clear from the program development example above that P and B in rule (3) correspond respectively to the invariant and the negation of the variant of the loop. Let us consider for example the proof that the first loop in mma_1 establishes property (Sa_1'). We first prove the correctness of the body of the loop:

$$(Sa_1') \textbf{ and } (j \neq n) \quad \{j := j+1; min := minimum(min, a[j])\} \quad (Sa_1')$$

that is to say:

$(j < n)$ **and**		$(j \leq n)$ **and**
$(\forall \ i \in [1,j], \ min \leq a[i])$ **and**	$\{j := j + 1;$	$(\forall \ i \in [1,j], \ min \leq a[i])$ **and**
$(\exists \ i \in [1,j], \ min = a[i])$	$min := minimum(min, a[j])\}$	$(\exists \ i \in [1,j], \ min = a[i])$

From rule (1) we have:

$(\forall \ i \in [1,j], \ minimum(min, a[j]) \leq a[i])$		$(\forall \ i \in [1,j], \ min \leq a[i])$
and	$\{min := minimum(min, a[j])\}$	**and**
$(\exists \ i \in [1,j], \ minimum(min, a[j]) = a[i])$		$(\exists \ i \in [1,j], \ min = a[i])$

Using (1) again we have:

$(\forall\, i \in [1,j+1],\ minimum(min, a[j+1]) \le a[i])$
$\qquad$ **and** $(j+1 \le n)$ **and**
$(\exists\, i \in [1,j+1],\ minimum(min, a[j+1]) = a[i])$

$(\forall\, i \in [1,j],\ minimum(min, a[j]) \le a[i])$
$\qquad$ **and** $(j \le n)$ **and**
$(\exists\, i \in [1,j],\ minimum(min, a[j]) = a[i])$

$\{j := j+1\}$

We have:

$$(\forall\, i \in [1,j+1],\ (minimum(min, a[j+1]) \le a[i])\ \textbf{and}\ (j+1 \le n)\ \textbf{and}$$
$$(\exists\, i \in [1,j+1],\ minimum(min, a[j+1]) = a[i]))$$
$$<=>$$
$$(j < n)\ \textbf{and}$$
$$((\,a[j+1] > min)\ \textbf{and}\ (\forall\, i \in [1,j],\ min \le a[i])\ \textbf{and}\ (\exists\, i \in [1,j],\ min = a[i]))\ \textbf{or}$$
$$((a[j+1] \le min)\ \textbf{and}\ (\forall\, i \in [1,j],\ a[j+1] \le a[i]))$$
$$<=$$
$$(j < n)\ \textbf{and}\ (\forall\, i \in [1,j]\ min \le a[i])\ \textbf{and}\ (\exists\, i \in [1,j]\ min = a[i])$$
$$<=>$$
$$(Sa_1')\ \textbf{and}\ (j \ne n)$$

So from rule (4) we have:

$$((Sa_1')\ \textbf{and}\ (j \ne n)) \qquad \{j := j+1;\ min := minimum(min, a[j])\} \qquad (Sa_1')$$

We can now apply rule (3) and we obtain:

(Sa_1')
```
{while (j≠n)  do
    j := j+1;
    min := minimum (min, a[j])
 end}
```
$(j = n)$ **and** (Sa_1')

Since $(Sa_1) = ((j = n)\ \textbf{and}\ (Sa_1'))$, we have proved the correctness of the loop; in order to complete the correctness proof of this part of the program, it remains to show that the initialization sequence (j:=1; min:=$a[1]$) establishes the invariant (Sa_1'). This proof can be carried out by two applications of rule (1) and one application of rule (2).

This concludes our study of program development in the imperative framework. Let us now see how a functional program can be derived from the same specification.

8.3.2 The functional case

The specification can be reformulated in terms of lists in the following way:

> **find** *min, max, av* **such that** $\hspace{4cm}$ (SI)
> $(\forall\ x \in List,\ min \leq x)$ **and** $(min \in List)$ **and**
> $(\forall\ x \in List,\ max \geq x)$ **and** $(max \in List)$ **and**
> $av = (\Sigma\ x \in List) / length(List)$

Following the stepwise refinement strategy [Wirth 71], we can state that a solution of a specification like (**find** v_1, v_2, v_3 **such that** $P_1(l, v_1)$ **and** $P_2(l, v_2)$ **and** $P_3(l, v_3)$) should be a function of the form:

$$f(l) = (f_1(l), f_2(l), f_3(l))$$

such that $P_1(l, f_1(l))$ **and** $P_2(l, f_2(l))$ **and** $P_3(l, f_3(l))$. Applying this strategy to the specification above, we try to derive a function of the form:

$$mma(l) = (min(l), max(l), av(l))$$

such that

> $(\forall\ x \in l,\ min(l) \leq x)$ **and** $(min(l) \in l)$ **and** $\hspace{2cm}$ (SI$_1$)
> $(\forall\ x \in l,\ max(l) \geq x)$ **and** $(max(l) \in l)$ **and** $\hspace{2cm}$ (SI$_2$)
> $av(l) = (\Sigma\ x \in l) / length(l)$ $\hspace{4cm}$ (SI$_3$)

A specification of the form (**find** $min(l)$ **such that** $(\forall\ x \in l,\ P(min(l), x))$ **and** $(min(l) \in l)$) can be refined into a list-traversal function:

$$min\ (l) = \textbf{if}\ null\ (tail(l))\ \textbf{then}\ f_1(l)\ \textbf{else}\ f_2\ (head(l),\ min(tail(l)))$$

The case $null(tail(l))$ corresponds to a singleton list; the only solution complying with $(min \in l)$ is $f_1(l) = head(l)$; now, if we assume that $min(tail(l))$ yields a correct result, that is to say a value m such that

$$\forall\ x \in tail(l),\ m \leq x$$

f_2 should return a value m' such that

$\forall \, x \in l \, , \, m' \leq x$ $\Longleftrightarrow$

$\forall \, x \in tail(l) \, , \, m' \leq x$ and $m' \leq head(l)$ $\Longleftarrow$

$m' \leq m$ and $m' \leq head(l)$ $\Longleftarrow$

$m' = minimum \, (head(l), m)$

This suggests the function $f_2 \, (x, y) = minimum \, (x, y)$; so we have derived the program:

$$min \, (l) = \textbf{if } null \, (tail(l)) \textbf{ then } head(l) \textbf{ else } minimum \, (head(l), min(tail(l)))$$

To derive the program *max* we can notice that (Sl_2) can be obtained from (Sl_1) by substitution of *max* for *min*; this similarity should be reflected in the resulting program. In fact, we can even embody the common structure of the two programs within a higher-order list-traversal function *lt*:

$$lt \, (f) \, (l) = \textbf{if } null(tail(l)) \textbf{ then } head(l) \textbf{ else } f \, (head(l), lt \, (f) \, (tail(l)))$$

It turns out that the third program exhibits the same structure again, and we have the following definition for *mma*:

$$mma \, (l) = (min(l), max(l), av(l))$$
$$min \, (l) = lt \, (minimum) \, (l)$$
$$max \, (l) = lt \, (maximum) \, (l)$$
$$av \, (l) = (lt \, (add) \, (l)) \, / \, length(l)$$
$$lt \, (f) \, (l) = \textbf{if } null(tail(l)) \textbf{ then } head(l) \textbf{ else } f \, (head(l), lt \, (f) \, (tail(l)))$$

Let us now come back to the correctness proof of the program *min*; the argument used in the derivation of the else part of the body suggests a proof by structural induction [Manna et al. 73]: the assumption that *min* applied to an argument smaller than l yields a correct result was used to deduce that f_2 should be the *minimum* function; the correctness proof of *min* by structural induction is straightforward indeed:

(1) the basis of the induction is the case $(length(l) = 1)$; the definition of *mma* indicates that the result is $head(l)$ which is obviously correct with respect to (Sl_1).

(2) the induction hypothesis is

$$(\forall \, x \in tail(l), \, min(tail(l)) \leq x) \textbf{ and } (min(tail(l)) \in tail(l))$$

from this property we have to prove

$(\forall\ x \in l,\ minimum(head(l),\ min(tail(l))) \le x)$ **and** $(minimum(head(l),\ min(tail(l))) \in l)$

which is straightforward.

Let us now show how this proof can be carried out in a completely different way. We should first point out that a predicate like

$$P(l, m) = (\forall\ x \in l,\ m \le x)$$

can be expressed as a boolean function:

$check\ (l, m) =$ **if** $null\ (tail(l))$ **then** $m \le head(l)$ **else** $(m \le head(l))$ **and** $check\ (tail(l), m)$

so proving that $P(l, min(l))$ holds amounts to showing that:

$$\forall\ l,\ check\ (l, min(l)) = true$$

This suggests that we could use correctness preserving transformations to show that the expression $check(l, min(l))$ can be reduced to $true$. To this aim we use the folding/unfolding technique introduced in chapter 5. We introduce the definition $f(l) = check(l, min(l))$:

$f(l) = check(l, min(l))$
$\quad =\quad$ **if** $null\ (tail(l))$
$\qquad$ **then** $check\ (l, head(l))$
$\qquad$ **else** $check\ (l, minimum\ (head(l), min(tail(l))))$

by unfolding the definition of min and using the distributivity of the conditional;

$\quad =\quad$ **if** $null\ (tail(l))$
$\qquad$ **then** $head(l) \le head(l)$
$\qquad$ **else** $check\ (l, minimum\ (head(l), min(tail(l))))$

by unfolding the definition of $check$ and using the distributivity of the conditional;

$\quad =\quad$ **if** $null\ (tail(l))$
$\qquad$ **then** $true$
$\qquad$ **else** $minimum\ (head(l), min(tail(l))) \le head(l)$ **and**
$\qquad\qquad\qquad check\ (tail(l), minimum\ (head(l), min(tail(l))))$

by unfolding the definition of *check* and using the distributivity of the conditional;

$$= \textbf{if } null\ (tail(l))$$
$$\textbf{then } true$$
$$\textbf{else } check\ (tail(l),\ minimum\ (head(l),\ min(tail(l))))$$

by using properties of *minimum* and **and**.

Unfortunately *check* $(tail(l),\ minimum\ (head(l),\ min(tail(l))))$ is not exactly an instantiation of the body of f, so no folding can be performed. This suggests the following generalization:

$$g(l,m) = check\ (l,\ minimum\ (m,\ min(l)))$$

f can be defined from g in the following way:

$$f(l) = g(l,\ min(l))$$

Starting from $g(l,m)$ we can carry out the same transformations as above and get:

$$g(l,m) \quad = \quad \textbf{if } null\ (tail(l))$$
$$\textbf{then } true$$
$$\textbf{else } check\ (tail(l),\ minimum\ (m,\ minimum\ (head(l),\ min(tail(l)))))$$
$$= \textbf{if } null\ (tail(l))$$
$$\textbf{then } true$$
$$\textbf{else } check\ (tail(l),\ minimum\ (minimum\ (m,\ head(l)),\ min(tail(l))))$$

using the associativity of *minimum*; so, by folding:

$$g(l,\ m) = \quad \textbf{if } null\ (tail(l))$$
$$\textbf{then } true$$
$$\textbf{else } g\ (tail(l),\ minimum\ (m,\ head(l)))$$

The second argument of g is clearly not useful and we can set:

$$g(l,m) = h(l)$$
$$h(l) = \textbf{if } null\ (tail(l))\ \textbf{then } true\ \textbf{else } h\ (tail(l))$$
So: $\quad h(l) = true$
and $\quad f(l) = g(l,\ min(l)) = h(l) = true$

We have proven by program transformation within the functional framework that *min* is correct with respect to property P ($\forall x \in l$, $min(l) \leq x$); the second part of the specification ($min(tail(l)) \in tail(l)$) can be tackled in the same way.

8.3.3 Comparison of the imperative paradigm and the functional paradigm

We can now continue our comparison of the imperative and the functional paradigms in the light of the program developments and the the program proofs described above. We discard for the time being efficiency considerations which are the topic of the next section. We shall also attempt to avoid the dissimilarities which are only due to the syntactic idiosyncrasies of the formalisms. It should be clear from the program derivations presented here that the two paradigms induce two completely different ways of reasoning. The imperative framework requires proofs which are in essence "dynamic" in the sense that they mimic the execution of the program. A formula in Hoare's logic describes a property of the state after the execution of a command if an initial property holds before the execution. This operational reasoning makes proofs unnecessarily complicated because the sequentiality expressed in an imperative program is often not relevant to the logic of the program. For example in the program mma_1 the three loops may logically be executed in any order and the modification of *min* could precede the adjustment of j as well. It is true that some form of multiple assignment may alleviate this problem; however the separation between a world of statements and a world of expressions precludes the possibility of assignments like

$$(min, max\ sum) := (\textbf{while} \ldots \textbf{do} \ldots \textbf{end}, \textbf{while} \ldots \textbf{do} \ldots \textbf{end}, \textbf{while} \ldots \textbf{do} \ldots \textbf{end})$$

Furthermore there is no doubt about the fact that imperative languages encourage a pervasive use of sequentiality. One may argue that the proof of the functional program by structural induction on the length of the list is very similar to the proof of the loop in the imperative case (with index j playing the role similar to the *length* primitive). We contend however that the ways of reasoning underlying these two proofs are very different since structural induction proceeds in terms of static properties of functions, with no consideration about the computation steps. A proof in the imperative framework has to handle a succession of small adjustments to the state whereas in the functional framework the basic level of reasoning is the function call.

Since any command may *a priori* access any variable, the predicates of Hoare's logic must be functions of the whole state; for large programs the number of variables may become huge, which makes proofs less tractable. Of course some kind of analysis can be carried out to select only the relevant parts of the state; however this adds yet another level of complexity to the proof. In some sense we can say that imperative programming overspecifies the flow of control (since it introduces much more sequentiality than required by the logic of the program) and underspecifies the data dependency (since all variables are contained in an unstructured state). These two features tend to make correctness proofs more laborious: in order to extract the logic of the program it is necessary to destructure the flow of control imposed by the imperative program and to deduce a more structured data organization.

Let us come back to the small program M defined in section 8.2 to illustrate this point:

M **in** (a, n) **out** (min)
    $j := 1;$
    $min := a[j];$
    while $j < n$ **do**
            $j := j+1;$
            $min := minimum\ (min,\ a[j])$
        end

The rules defined in section 8.2 associate this program with the following function:

$\lambda(N_1, N_2).$
    let $s = update\ [\![a]\!]\ N_1\ newstore$ **in**
    let $s = update\ [\![n]\!]\ N_2\ s$ **in**
    let $s = update\ [\![j]\!]\ 1\ s$ **in**
    let $s = update\ [\![min]\!]\ (value\ (access\ [\![a]\!]\ s)\ (access\ [\![j]\!]\ s))\ s$ **in**
    letrec
      $f = \lambda s.$
          if $((access\ [\![j]\!]\ s) < (access\ [\![n]\!]\ s))$
          then
              $f\ (\textbf{let}\ s = update\ [\![j]\!]\ (plus\ 1\ (access\ [\![j]\!]\ s))\ s$ **in**
                     $update\ [\![min]\!]$
                     $minimum\ (access\ [\![min]\!]\ s,\ value\ (access\ [\![a]\!]\ s)\ (access\ [\![j]\!]\ s)))$
          else s
    in
    let $s = f\ s$ **in**
    $(access\ [\![min]\!]\ s)$

An equivalent and more natural functional program could be:

$M' = \lambda(a, n). f\,1\,(value\ a\ 1)$
    where $f = \lambda j\ min$. **if** $j < n$ **then** $f\,(j+1)\,(minimum\ min\ (value\ a\ j))$ **else** min

M and M' can be seen as the incarnations of two different programming styles within the same language. To derive M' from M we have (1) to destroy the explicit (and unnecessary) sequencing imposed by let expressions and (2) to replace the monolithic state by independent values which can be passed as arguments to functions. The logical dependencies between these values is made explicit via argument passing. For instance a and n are not passed as arguments to f since they are global "constants" for this function; on the other hand each recursive call of f requires different values of j and min, so these values are passed as arguments to f. To summarize, we can say that functional programming tends to promote locality which is a crucial issue as far as correctness proofs are concerned; powerful program manipulation techniques are available because it is possible to reason about a sub-expression independently of the rest of the expression.

Another noticeable point illustrated by the functional program development described above is the possibility of performing proofs by program transformations within the functional framework itself. This is not feasible in the imperative framework because no powerful transformation technique such as fold/unfold is available (we have seen in the introduction that even the replacement of an expression by its value is not always safe).

It should also be clear from the program derivation described in this section that systematic program development by stepwise refinement and modularity fits very well with the functional approach [Hughes 89]; it is possible to build a program lt embodying the common structure of min, max and sum (section 8.3.2) because functions are treated as ordinary values and because there is no separation between a world of statements and a world of expressions; this is a significant advantage for the promotion of modularity.

8.4 EFFICIENCY CONSIDERATIONS

The arguments put forward in the previous section may still be unconvincing to a programmer paying a great deal of attention to the efficiency of his programs. For example, we pointed out in section 8.3 that program mma_2 which combines the three loops within a single loop would probably be more straightforward for an imperative programmer; on the other hand, the function manipulation facilities of a functional language would encourage a solution like mma which entails several list traversals. Here again, the powerful program transformation techniques offered by the functional framework can be turned to account to solve the problem. Let us show how the original version of mma can be transformed into a more efficient program by folding/unfolding.

$mma(l) = (min(l), max(l), av(l))$

    $= (lt \ (minimum) \ (l), lt \ (maximum) \ (l), (lt \ (add) \ (l)) \ / \ length(l))$

by unfolding *min*, *max* and *av*; we introduce a new definition:

$mma'(l) = (lt \ (minimum) \ (l), lt \ (maximum) \ (l), (lt \ (add) \ (l)))$

    $= ($**if** $null(tail(l))$ **then** $head(l)$ **else** $minimum \ (head(l), lt \ (minimum) \ (tail(l))),$

        if $null(tail(l))$ **then** $head(l)$ **else** $maximum \ (head(l), lt \ (maximum) \ (tail(l))),$

        if $null(tail(l))$ **then** $head(l)$ **else** $add \ (head(l), lt \ (add) \ (tail(l))))$

by unfolding *lt*;

$=$ **if** $null(tail(l))$

      then $(head(l), head(l), head(l))$

      else $(minimum \ (head(l), mi), maximum \ (head(l), ma), add \ (head(l), su))$

      where

        $(mi, ma, su) = (lt \ (minimum) \ (tail(l)), lt \ (maximum) \ (tail(l)), lt \ (add) \ (tail(l)))$

(property of the conditional and abstraction)

$=$ **if** $null(tail(l))$

      then $(head(l), head(l), head(l))$

      else $(minimum \ (head(l), mi), maximum \ (head(l), ma), add \ (head(l), su))$

            where $(mi, ma, su) = mma' \ (tail(l))$

folding *mma'*; *mma* can be defined from *mma'*:

$mma(l) = (mi, ma, su/length(l))$ **where** $(mi, ma, su) = mma'(l)$

We have obtained a new version of *mma* which is more efficient than the original one because it involves a single list traversal. Another possible reservation about this program is the fact that it uses recursion whereas the straightforward imperative solution is based on a less expensive loop. One solution to get out of this problem is again to resort to program transformation. We have seen in section 8.2 that a loop is expressed in a functional language as a tail-recursive function. A traditional technique for transforming a non-tail-recursive function into a tail-recursive one is to generalize the original function by the introduction of new arguments [Arsac et al. 82]. Chapter 5 contains an example describing the derivation of an iterative form of factorial using this technique.

Let us now show how it can be applied to the function *mma'*; we define the function *mma"* as a generalization of *mma'* in the following way:

$$mma''(l, mi, ma, su) = (minimum(mi, mi'),\ maximum(ma, ma'),\ add(su, su'))$$
$$\textbf{where } (mi', ma', su') = mma'\ (l)$$

Unfolding the definition of *mma'* and using the distributivity of the conditional we get:

$mma''(l, mi, ma, su) =$
    if $null(tail(l))$
    then $(minimum(mi, head(l)),\ maximum(ma, head(l)),\ add(su, head(l)))$
    else $(minimum(mi,\ minimum\ (head(l), mi')),$
                       $maximum(ma,\ maximum\ (head(l), ma')),$
                       $add(su,\ add\ (head(l), su')))$
        where $(mi', ma', su') = mma'\ (tail(l))$

Using the associativity of *minimum, maximum* and *add,* we get:

$mma''(l, mi, ma, su) =$
    if $null(tail(l))$
    then $(minimum(mi, head(l)),\ maximum(ma, head(l)),\ add(su, head(l)))$
    else $(minimum(minimum\ (mi, head(l)), mi'),$
                     $maximum(maximum\ (ma, head(l)), ma'),$
                   $add(\ add\ (su, head(l)), su'))$
        where $(mi', ma', su') = mma'\ (tail(l))$

So:

$mma''(l, mi, ma, su) =$
    if $null(tail(l))$
    then $(minimum(mi, head(l)),\ maximum(ma, head(l)),\ add(su, head(l)))$
    else $mma''(tail(l),\ minimum\ (mi, head(l)),\ maximum\ (ma, head(l)),\ add\ (su, head(l)))$

by folding of the definition of *mma"*.

We have obtained, after several transformations, a program which behaves very much like the imperative solution described in section 8.3. The arguments *l, mi, ma* and *su* play the role of the state and the program proceeds by iteration, each step performing modifications of the state. This example shows that it is possible to start with a program which is well structured and can be easily proven correct and to transform it into an equivalent but more efficient version; this last version is far less readable than the original one but this fact is irrelevant since the transformation is carried out only for the purpose of implementation.

Another usual restriction with respect to efficiency is the fact that functional programs are profligate consumers of processing time spent on the management of heap storage. This criticism is based on two straightforward observations:

(1) functional programs make pervasive use of lists which require dynamic allocation and collection;

(2) functional languages prevent the user from expressing explicitly that memory can be reused.

Let us consider for example a program to compute the sum of the squares of the elements of a list; a functional programmer may want to separate the issues of evaluating the squares and computing the sum and may write:

sumsquares (l) = sum (squares (l))
squares (l) = **if** *null(l)* **then** *nil* **else** *cons(square(head(l)), squares(tail(l)))*
sum (l) = **if** *null(l)* **then** 0 **else** *head(l) + sum(tail(l))*

This separation of concerns is valuable from a logical viewpoint but it entails the construction of an unnecessary intermediate list; this construction, and all the resulting heap manipulations, can be avoided by a simple program transformation:

sumsquares (l) = sum (squares (l))
    = **if** *null(l)* **then** *sum(nil)* **else** *sum(cons(square(head(l)), squares(tail(l))))*

    by unfolding *squares* and using the distributivity of the conditional;

    = **if** *null(l)* **then** 0 **else** *square(head(l)) + sum (squares(tail(l)))*

    by unfolding *sum*;

    = **if** *null(l)* **then** 0 **else** *square(head(l)) + sumsquares(tail(l))*

    by folding *sumsquares*;

We obtain a new version of sumsquares with no intermediate list construction. [Wadler 81] contains a set of rules to make this transformation systematic.

These transformations alleviate the problem of dynamic memory allocation; the problem of memory reuse is tackled in chapter 4 which describes an analysis technique allowing us to compile the garbage collection of cells.

The conclusion of these remarks is that the functional style encourages the construction of clear, modular, and provable programs; correctness is considered as the primary concern in program development; when a correct version of the program has been built, efficiency issues can be tackled within the functional framework by program transformation. The functional paradigm favours a clear separation of concerns whereas the imperative programming style tends to mix the two issues, or even to put efficiency concerns before correctness considerations.

8.5 HISTORY-SENSITIVE PROGRAMMING IN A PURELY FUNCTIONAL LANGUAGE

In the previous sections we have praised the advantages of functional programming according to various criteria. However the question raised in the introduction remains unanswered: if functional languages do really possess such outstanding qualities, why are they so little used in practice and why are the very few functional languages polluted by impure features? The reason which is most often put forward to justify such a situation is the inability to express certain kinds of optimizations (for example memory reuse) in a purely functional language [Schwarz 78, Josephs 86, Sturgis 88]. Let us remark that the same arguments were also used some years ago to rehabilitate **goto** [Knuth 74]. It should be clear from the previous section that we are not ready to accept these arguments, especially nowadays when many functional program optimization methods exist [Darlington et al. 76, Burstall et al. 77, Wadler 81, Arsac et al. 82, Partsch et al. 83, Feather 87] (see also chapter 4 for the presentation of one optimization method) and efficient implementation techniques begin to be available [Cardelli 84, Cousineau et al. 88] (chapter 6 is devoted to the description of a compilation technique).

Let us now consider better arguments for the introduction of impure features within a functional language. We do not mention the input/output problem here since chapter 7 presents several ways to introduce input/output in a functional language via the use of streams and continuations. There is no reason to reject the argument that the solution to certain problems may be more naturally described in terms of states and state transitions. We know that such behaviour can be modelled in the functional framework by the introduction of arguments representing the state, but it is not clear whether this would lead to very readable and tractable programs. To illustrate this issue, we consider a text editing program taking as input a text and two patterns and returning a new text in which each occurrence of the first pattern has been replaced by the second pattern; additional information is returned: the place in the original text where the first occurrence of the pattern was found, the place where the last occurrence was found, the number of occurrences of the pattern found in the text and the number of occurrences of the pattern corresponding to a full word in the original text (the word separator being the space). In an imperative language close to the one defined in section 8.2, a solution following that in [Dromey 82] can be (the text being represented by an array of size *textlength*):

textedit$_{imp}$ **in** (*text, textlength, pattern, patternlength, newpattern, newpatternlength*)
        out (*newtext, firstoc, lastoc, nboc, nbocfw*)

```
i := 1; j:= 1; k := 0; firstoc := 0; lastoc := 0; nboc := 0; nbocfw := 0;
while  i ≤ textlength - patternlength + 1  do
   if text[i+j-1] = pattern[j]
   then j := j+1;
        if j > patternlength
        then      for l = 1 to newpatternlength do
                         k := k+1;
                         newtext[k] := newpattern[l]
                      end
                  if firstoc = 0 then firstoc := i end;
                  if text[i-1] = space and text[i+j-1] = space
                         then nbocfw := nbocfw+1 end;
                  lastoc := i; i := i + patternlength;
                  nboc := nboc+1; j := 1
        end
   else
        k := k+1;
        newtext[k] := text[i];
        i := i+1;
        j := 1
   end
end;
while i ≤ textlength  do
        k := k+1;
        newtext[k] := text[i];
        i := i+1
end
```

The most natural solution to the same problem in the functional framework might be the following (the text being represented by a list):

textedit $_{func1}$(text, pattern, newpattern) =
 (replace(text, pattern, newpattern), firstoc(text, pattern, 1), lastoc(text, pattern, 1, 1),
  nboc(text, pattern), nbocfw(text, pattern))
where
replace(text, pattern, newpattern) =
 if *null(text)*
 then *nil*
 else
  if *match(text, pattern)*
  then *conc(newpattern, replace(remove(text, pattern), pattern, newpattern))*
  else *cons(head(text), replace(tail(text), pattern, newpattern))*
firstoc(text, pattern, n) =
 if *null(text)* **or** *match(text, pattern)*
 then *n*
 else *firstoc(tail(text), pattern, n+1)*
lastoc(text, pattern, n, m) =
 if *null(text)*
 then *n*
 else
  if *match(text, pattern)*
  then *lastoc(remove(text, pattern), pattern, m, m + length(pattern))*
  else *lastoc(tail(text), pattern, n, m+1)*
nboc(text, pattern) =
 if *null(text)*
 then *0*
 else
  if *match(text, pattern)*
  then *1 + nboc(remove(text, pattern), pattern)*
  else *nboc(tail(text), pattern)*

nbocfw(text, pattern) =
   if *null(text)*
   then 0
   else
      if *match(text, pattern)* **and** *(next(text, pattern) = space)*
      then 1 + *nbocfw(remove(text, pattern), pattern)*
      else *nbocfw(nextword(text), pattern)*

match(text, pattern) =
   if *null(pattern)*
   then *true*
   else if *null(text)*
      then *false*
      else   **if** *head(text)* ≠ *head(pattern)*
           then *false*
           else *match(tail(text), tail(pattern))*

remove(text, pattern) =
   if *null(pattern)*
   then *text*
   else *remove(tail(text), tail(pattern))*

next (text, pattern) =
   if *null(pattern)*
   then
      if *null(text)*
      then *space*
      else *head(text)*
   else *next (tail(text), tail(pattern))*

conc (text$_1$, text$_2$) =
   if *null(text$_1$)*
   then *text$_2$*
   else *cons (head(text$_1$), conc(tail(text$_1$), text$_2$))*

nextword(text) =
   if *null(text)*
   then *nil*
   else
      if *head(text) = space*
      then *tail(text)*
      else *nextword(tail(text))*

This program is satisfactory from a conceptual point of view because it entails a nice separation of concerns which makes it easy to understand. However it may seem a bit heavy because it involves the definition of a rather large number of functions, each one being built on the same model (a walk through the text looking for occurrences of the pattern) but with some differences. These differences make it difficult to define a higher-order function embodying the common model. Some people may find it more natural to evaluate the result by a single walk through the text; this strategy yields the following program:

textedit $_{func2}$(*text, pattern, newpattern*) = *replace* (*text, nil*, 1, 0, 0, 0, 0, *true*)
where
    replace (*text, newtext, i, firstoc, lastoc, nboc, nbocfw, separator*) =
    if *length*(*text*) < *length*(*pattern*)
    then (*conc* (*newtext, text*), *firstoc, lastoc, nboc, nbocfw*)
    else if *match* (*text, pattern*)
        then

                if *separator* **and** (*next* (*text, pattern*) = *space*)
                then
                replace (*remove* (*text, pattern*), *conc* (*newtext, newpattern*),
                      i+length(*pattern*), (**if** *firstoc* = 0 **then** *i* **else** *firstoc*), *i*,
                      nboc+1, *nbocfw*+1, *false*)
                else
                replace (*remove* (*text, pattern*), *conc* (*newtext, newpattern*),
                      i+length(*pattern*), (**if** *firstoc* = 0 **then** *i* **else** *firstoc*), *i*,
                      nboc+1, *nbocfw, false*)
        else
                replace (*tail*(*text*), *conc* (*newtext, cons*(*head*(*text*), *nil*))), *i*+1,
                      firstoc, lastoc, nboc, nbocfw, (*head*(*text*) = *space*))
  match(*text, pattern*) =
    if *null*(*pattern*)
    then *true*
    else
        if *head*(*text*) ≠ *head*(*pattern*)
        then *false*
        else *match*(*tail*(*text*), *tail*(*pattern*))
  remove(*text, pattern*) =
    if *null*(*pattern*)
    then *text*
    else *remove*(*tail*(*text*), *tail*(*pattern*))

next (text, pattern) =
    if *null(pattern)*
    then *head(text)*
    else *next (tail(text), tail(pattern))*
conc ($text_1$, $text_2$) =
    if *null($text_1$)*
    then *$text_2$*
    else *cons (head($text_1$), conc(tail($text_1$), $text_2$))*

separator is a boolean value indicating whether the character preceding the current chain is a space or not.

We do not return here to a comparison of the imperative model and the functional model in terms of correctness or efficiency since these issues have already been discussed in the previous sections. Let us rather assess these three programs from a software engineering viewpoint. Deciding which of these two programs is the more natural is a highly subjective matter; a programmer used to imperative languages will probably appreciate the first one: he will not see the point of defining intermediate functions like *match*, *next*, *remove* and *conc*; he will not like the introduction of so many functions in *textedit$_{func1}$* or function calls with so many arguments in *textedit$_{func2}$*. Furthermore the multiple traversal of the source text (through functions *match*, *next*, *remove* and *conc*) will look completely artificial to him since it would be easy to get all the information in one pass. On the other hand, a functional programmer will appreciate the separation of concerns in his programs: the problems of matching the two patterns and removing the first pattern are logically different, even if they may be solved in a very similar way. This issue is related to the already mentioned contrast between operational and denotational reasoning.

There is one reason, however, for which the functional programmer may find his second program a bit awkward: it is not easy to write and to manipulate functions with so many arguments.

First it may seem unnatural to need to supply a recursive function call with all its arguments when most of them have not been "changed" from the previous recursive call (the last call of *replace* above is an example of such a situation); more serious is the fact that it is very difficult to mentally manage the correspondence between the formal and the actual arguments when there are so many of them; for example in the first recursive call of *replace* it is not obvious that the value *i* is the fifth argument and so corresponds to the argument *lastoc*. However, this drawback is related to the application itself; it is likely that certain problems may be more naturally expressed in terms of states and state transitions and the text editing problem probably belongs to this category. The eight arguments of the function *replace* can be seen as a representation of the state and each function call entails some modifications of this state. We believe that the clumsiness of $texteditfunc2$ is mainly a matter of textual appearance; we propose now some syntactic facilities (or macrocombinators) allowing a more elegant writing of state oriented programs in a functional language.

$$(x := e_1) \; e_2 \equiv (\lambda x. \; e_2) \; e_1 \qquad (\equiv \textbf{let } x = e_1 \textbf{ in } e_2) \qquad (1)$$

$$e_1 \; ; e_2 \equiv e_1 \; e_2 \qquad\qquad ; \text{ associating to the right} \qquad (2)$$

$$\textit{label: } e \equiv \quad \textbf{letrec } \textit{label } x_1 \dots x_n = e$$

$$\textbf{in } \textit{label } x_1 \dots x_n \qquad\qquad (3)$$

where $x_1 \dots x_n$ are the free variables of e

$$\textit{call label} \equiv \textit{label } x_1 \dots x_n \qquad \text{in a context where } \textit{label } x_1 \dots x_n = e \qquad (4)$$

$$\textit{exit} \equiv (x_1, \dots , x_n) \qquad\qquad \text{in a context where the immediately}$$

surrounding label definition is

$$\textit{label } x_1 \dots x_n = e$$

The notation **letrec** $label \; x_1 \dots x_n = e$ **in** $label \; x_1 \dots x_n$ is used here as a shorthand for:

  let $label = ($ **letrec** $label = \lambda \, x_1 \dots x_n. \, e \,)$ **in** $label \; x_1 \dots x_n$

The symbol $\equiv$ can be read as "is equivalent to" or "is macro-expanded into".

  These definitions turn to account the lessons drawn from section 8.2. We have seen that denotational semantics uses lambda abstraction to express the state in a functional way; this is precisely what (1) does; for example

$$x := 1;$$
$$y := 2;$$
$$x + y$$

is equivalent to

  let $x = 1$ **in** (**let** $y = 2$ **in** $(x + y)$)

which is equivalent to 3.

The only interest of the ";" feature is to give to programs the usual imperative appearance. This operator is right-associative because $e_1; e_2; e_3$ is intended to mean $e_1; (e_2 \; ; e_3)$ rather than $(e_1; e_2) \; ; e_3$. (3) and (4) provide a means to define and call a function without supplying its arguments explicitly; the implicit arguments are the free variables of the expression representing the body of the function. The simulation in the functional framework of a loop modifying variables is a function taking these variables as arguments. For example a definition of factorial in this notation could be:

fact: $m := 1$;

loopfact: **if** $n = 1$

               then m

               else $m := m \times n$;

                     $n := n - 1$;

                     (*call loopfact*)

According to the rules defined above, this definition is macro-expanded into:

letrec *fact* $n =$

       let $m = 1$ **in**

       letrec *loopfact* $n\ m =$

          if $n = 1$

          then m

          else   **let** $m = m \times n$ **in**

                 let $n = n - 1$ **in**

                 (*loopfact* $n\ m$)

       in (*loopfact* $n\ m$)

because n is the only free variable in the body of *fact* and n, m are the free variables in the body of *loopfact*; this function is equivalent to:

letrec *fact* $n =$

       letrec *loopfact* $n\ m =$ **if** $n = 1$ **then** m **else** (*loopfact* $(n - 1)\ (m \times n)$) **in**

       (*loopfact* n 1)

Let us now show how these macro-combinators can be turned to account to produce a more concise solution to our text editing problem; program *textedit$_{func2}$* can be reformulated in the following way:

$textedit_{func3}(text, pattern, newpattern) =$

$\quad i := 1; firstoc := 0; lastoc := 0; nboc := 0; nbocfw := 0; separator := true;$

$\quad$ *replace*:

$\qquad$ **if** $length(text) < length(pattern)$

$\qquad$ **then** $(conc\ (newtext, text), firstoc, lastoc, nboc, nbocfw)$

$\qquad$ **else** **if** $match\ (text, pattern)$

$\qquad\qquad$ **then** **if** $separator$ **and** $(next\ (text, pattern) = space)$

$\qquad\qquad\qquad$ **then**

$\qquad\qquad\qquad\qquad text := remove\ (text, pattern);$

$\qquad\qquad\qquad\qquad newtext := conc\ (newtext, newpattern);$

$\qquad\qquad\qquad\qquad firstoc := (\textbf{if } firstoc = 0 \textbf{ then } i \textbf{ else } firstoc);$

$\qquad\qquad\qquad\qquad lastoc := i;$

$\qquad\qquad\qquad\qquad i := i + length(pattern);$

$\qquad\qquad\qquad\qquad nboc := nboc+1;$

$\qquad\qquad\qquad\qquad nbocfw := nbocfw+1;$

$\qquad\qquad\qquad\qquad separator := false;$

$\qquad\qquad\qquad\qquad (call\ replace)$

$\qquad\qquad\qquad$ **else**

$\qquad\qquad\qquad\qquad text := remove\ (text, pattern);$

$\qquad\qquad\qquad\qquad newtext := conc\ (newtext, newpattern);$

$\qquad\qquad\qquad\qquad firstoc := (\textbf{if } firstoc = 0 \textbf{ then } i \textbf{ else } firstoc);$

$\qquad\qquad\qquad\qquad lastoc := i;$

$\qquad\qquad\qquad\qquad i := i + length(pattern);$

$\qquad\qquad\qquad\qquad nboc := nboc+1;$

$\qquad\qquad\qquad\qquad separator := false;$

$\qquad\qquad\qquad\qquad (call\ replace)$

$\qquad\qquad$ **else**

$\qquad\qquad\qquad text := tail(text);$

$\qquad\qquad\qquad newtext := conc\ (newtext, cons(head(text), nil));$

$\qquad\qquad\qquad i := i + 1;$

$\qquad\qquad\qquad separator := (head(text) = space);$

$\qquad\qquad\qquad (call\ replace)$

This example shows how the imperative style and functional style may be freely mixed within an expression. The notation introduced here makes more obvious the correspondence between the formal and the actual arguments of a function call; for example it becomes clear now that the value of the argument *lastoc*, in the first call of *replace*, is *i*. Before each recursive call only the arguments whose value has been "changed" from the previous call, are explicitly assigned.

The notation introduced here can be seen as a way to give to purely functional programs an imperative appearance or alternatively as a means to write restricted forms of imperative programs that can be macro-expanded into functional programs. So this notation can be used to apply the program analysis technique described in chapter 5 to analyse restricted forms of imperative programs. For instance the imperative style definition of fact introduced above has been macro-expanded into the function:

> **letrec** *fact n* =
>   **letrec** *loopfact n m* = **if** *n* = 1 **then** *m* **else** (*loopfact* (*n* - 1) (*m* × *n*)) **in**
>   (*loopfact n* 1)

This function can be analysed using the technique defined in chapter 5. We obtain:

> *Cfact* (*n*) = 1 + *Cloopfact*(*n*, 1)
> *Cloopfact* (*n*, *m*) = **if** *n* = 0 **then** 0 **else** 1 + *Cloopfact* ((*n* - 1), (*m* × *n*))

The second argument being useless, we have:

> *Cloopfact* (*n*, *m*) = *Cloopfact'*(*n*)
> *Cloopfact'*(*n*) = **if** *n* = 0 **then** 0 **else** 1 + *Cloopfact'*(*n* - 1)

Applying the recursion induction principle we obtain:

> *Cloopfact'* (*n*) = *n*
> *Cloopfact* (*n*, *m*) = *n*
> *Cfact* (*n*) = 1 + *n* ~ *n*

Let us emphasize that the notation presented here should not be seen as an encouragement to write programs in an imperative style. The imperative facilities provided here are limited; for example the (*call label*) expression does not act like a jump instruction but rather like a function call with implicit arguments. The assignment facility is restricted in the sense that it is effective only within an explicit continuation. For example the expression:

> **let** *x* = 5 **in**
>   (*x* := 0; *x* + 1) + *x*

returns the value 6 and not 1 because the assignment $x := 0$ is effective only within its continuation, which is $(x + 1)$ here. This may be clearer if we put the above expression into its expanded form:

$$\textbf{let } x = 5 \textbf{ in } (\textbf{let } x = 0 \textbf{ in } x + 1) + x =$$
$$(\textbf{let } x = 0 \textbf{ in } x + 1) + 5 =$$
$$1 + 5 = 6$$

This example shows that our notation does not invalidate referential transparency. In some sense we could say that we allow assignments but not side-effects. If the intended value for the above expression was 1, we should have written:

$$\textbf{let } x = 5 \textbf{ in } (x := 0; ((x + 1) + x))$$

indicating that the scope of the assignment includes the two occurrences of x. The traditional functional notation for this expression is

$$\textbf{let } x = 5 \textbf{ in } (\textbf{let } x = 0 \textbf{ in } ((x + 1) + x)) =$$
$$\textbf{let } x = 0 \textbf{ in } ((x + 1) + x) =$$
$$((0 + 1) + 0) = 1$$

So the use of assignment is tied to the use of continuations; we believe that this constraint reduces the risk of seeing functional programs denatured by a pervasive use of assignment.

To our knowledge, the only case where such an imperative notation may be useful is when the application itself is state-oriented like the text editing problem studied above. Another typical example within the field of computer science is the construction of a compiler; such a program handles several dozens of variables (symbol table, stack frame, source code, compiled code, ... each of these data structures being described by an array, a bound and a current index). Each recursive call modifies only a few variables; in such cases it would be very convenient to specify only the modified variables instead of supplying each function with a huge and untractable collection of arguments.

8.6 RELATED WORKS

In comparison with other approaches suggested for integrating the imperative and the functional paradigms [Schwartz 78, Gifford et al. 86, Josephs 86, Felleisen et al. 87, Lucassen et al. 88, Sturgis 88], our solution is the only one which does not introduce any extension to the functional model. [Gifford et al. 86, Lucassen et al. 88] present a class of languages, called *fluent languages*, permitting programmers to mix functional and imperative computations in a single program; side-effects must be declared as part of the type of the program; side-effect assertions are checked by the system and they determine the sublanguage to which an expression must be confined. It is argued that fluent languages retain the benefits of imperative languages and functional languages by allowing to describe each part of a program within the best suited sub-language. However this solution does not fulfill our requirement for better structured and provable programs since it does not favour any programming style in particular. In contrast to this approach, we put deliberately emphasis on functional programming and show how imperative programming can be cast into this framework.

[Felleisen et al. 87] presents an extension of lambda-calculus with assignments and describes a rewriting semantics for a version of this language. The rewriting semantics is possible because the store is integrated within the expression itself; so the rewriting is not really carried out on the original (with side-effects) expressions, but rather on equivalent expressions representing their semantics. The criticism raised about the previous approach can be addressed to this proposal as well because it seems to favour a free introduction of assignments within expressions.

[Schwartz 78, Sturgis 88] also allow the mixing of imperative statements and functional expressions but in a much more restricted way and mainly for the purpose of efficiency. These proposals rely on the functional model and allow the introduction of primitive functions (such as *cons*) achieving some kind of side-effect (typically destructive update). The system is responsible for the verification that these side-effects are safe, that is to say that they do not change the meaning of the program. So this approach is better in the sense that it favours the functional model and it separates correctness and efficiency issues. However it does not provide any answer to the problem of writing state-oriented programs. Actually these works may be more easily related to the technique described in chapter 4 which seems more ambitious in the sense that it tries do deduce the safe side-effects without any information from the user.

Efficiency is also the reason put forward in [Josephs 86] to justify an extension to functional languages allowing a form of side-effects; side-effects are made possible because arguments are considered as logical variables and a lazy evaluation mechanism is assumed. For example, in contrast to our proposal, the expression

$$(x := 0; x + 1) + x$$

returns 1 because the evaluation of a free variable like the last occurrence of x is suspended until an expression is assigned to it. This clearly shows that the extension proposed destroys referential transparency; in our notation, the expression is undefined.

The spirit of the proposal described in [Williams et al. 88] is closer to the approach taken in this chapter since it provides a means of describing input/output side-effects in a purely functional way (in a lazy version of FP) without compromising the elegance of programs. All programs map a pair whose first element is an ordinary object and whose second element encodes the status of input/output ports. Assignments can obviously not be represented as in usual languages since there are no variables in FP but they can be simulated by write and read operations.

8.7 FUNCTIONAL PROGRAMMING IS NOT A MIRAGE

Let us first sum up the content of this book. The first chapter is a study of the software development process. A comparison of imperative languages and functional languages shows that the latter are better suited to formal program construction. Chapter 2 contains a more formal introduction to functional programming and the presentation of two widespread functional languages: LISP and ML. Denotational semantics is used to show the relationship between imperative languages and functional languages. The significance of functional languages for formal program manipulation is illustrated with examples of program transformation. For a long time, functional languages had the reputation of being very inefficient. In order to convince potential users, proponents of functional languages have to show that this problem is only temporary. It is clear that functional languages, not being based on the von Neumann model, it is more difficult to implement them efficiently on traditional computers. We believe that the inherent qualities of functional languages, the availability of powerful program manipulation methods, can be exploited to design efficient implementation techniques. We present in the rest of the book several analysis and transformation methods supporting this claim. Chapter 3 introduces *abstract interpretation*, a program analysis technique which is widely used in the functional framework. This technique is applied in chapter 4 to compile the memory management in a first order functional language. This compilation may have drastic effects on the execution time since memory allocation and collection represent often an important part of the execution time of functional programs. Chapter 5 introduces several program transformation techniques and applies them to the complexity analysis of functional programs. The system ACE, which implements these techniques is briefly described. Chapter 6 shows how the compilation of functional programs can be described entirely by program transformation in the functional framework. A correct and efficient compiler has been built along these lines. The second main objection which is often raised against functional languages is their inablity to express input/output or state-oriented problems. Chapter 7 and 8 deal respectively with these two aspects and show that solutions can be found in the purely functional framework: streams or continuations can be used to express input/output in a purely functional language and syntactic facilities can be provided to make the description of state manipulating programs easier.

Let us now sum up the conclusions of the comparison between the imperative paradigm and the functional paradigm carried out in this book:

(1) Referential transparency, which is the fundamental property of functional languages, can be turned to account to develop powerful program proof techniques. The important point is that functional programming tends to promote locality which is a crucial issue because it makes it possible to reason about a sub-expression independently of the rest of the expression.

(2) The apparent inefficiency of functional programs is due to a clean separation of correctness concerns and efficiency concerns. Powerful program analysis and program transformation techniques can be used to solve this problem.

(3) Some problems may be more naturally expressed in terms of state transitions but a notation can be provided to describe these programs in an elegant way within the functional framework.

These conclusions may be seen as the justification of the approach taken in this book. We hope that they may help to convince the reader of the significance of functional languages both from a research and from a practical point of view.

REFERENCES

[Abelson et al. 85] H. Abelson et al. The revised revised report on Scheme or an uncommon Lisp. MIT AI Memo No. 848, August 1985.

[Arsac et al. 82] J. Arsac, Y. Kodratoff. Some techniques for recursion removal from recursive functions. ACM TOPLAS, Vol. 4, No. 2, pp. 295-322, April 1982.

[Backus 78] J. Backus. Can programming be liberated from the von Neumann style? A functional style and its algebra of programs. CACM, Vol. 21, No. 8, pp. 613-641, August 1978.

[Burstall et al. 77] R. M. Burstall, J. Darlington. A transformation system for developing recursive programs. JACM, Vol. 24, No. 1, pp. 44-67, January 1977.

[Cardelli 84] L. Cardelli. Compiling a functional language. Proc. ACM Conf. on LISP and Functional Programming, ACM, pp. 208-217, 1984.

[Cousineau et al. 88] G. Cousineau , G. Huet. The CAML primer. LIENS Research Report 88-3, 1988.

[Darlington et al. 76] J. Darlington, R. M. Burstall. A system which automatically improves programs. Acta Informatica, No. 6, pp. 41-60, 1976.

[Dijkstra 72a] E. W. Dijkstra. The humble programmer. CACM Vol. 15, No. 10, pp. 491-502, October 1972.

[Dijkstra 72b] E. W. Dijkstra. Notes on structured programming. In Structured Programming. O. J. Dahl, E. W. Dijkstra, C. A. R. Hoare, Academic Press, 1972.

[Dromey 82] R. G. Dromey. How to solve it by computer. Prentice-Hall International, Series in Computer Science, 1982.

[Feather 87] M. S. Feather. A survey and classification of some program transformation approaches and techniques. In Program specification and transformation. L. G. L. T. Meertens (ed.), North-Holland, pp. 165-195, 1987.

[Felleisen et al. 87] M. Felleisen, D. P. Friedman. A calculus for assignments in higher-order languages. Proc. 14th ACM Symp. on Principles of Programming Languages, pp. 314-325, 1987.

[Gifford et al. 86] D. K. Gifford, J. M. Lucassen. Integrating functional and imperative programming. Proc. ACM Conf. on LISP and Functional Programming, pp. 28-38, 1986.

[Gordon et al. 79] M. J. Gordon, R. J. Milner. and C. P. Wadsworth. Edinburgh LCF. LNCS 78, Springer Verlag, 1979.

[Gries 81] D. Gries. The science of programming. Springer Verlag, 1981.

[Henderson 80] P. Henderson. Functional programming: application and implementation. Prentice-Hall International, Series in Computer Science, 1980.

[Hoare 69] C. A. R. Hoare. An axiomatic basis for computer programming. CACM Vol. 12, No. 10, pp. 576-580, October 1969.

[Hughes 89] J. Hughes. Why functional programming matters. Computer Journal. Vol. 32, No. 2, pp. 98-107, 1989.

[Josephs 86] M. D. Josephs. Functional programming with side-effects. Science of Computer Programming, Vol. 7, pp. 279-296, 1986.

[Knuth 74] D. E. Knuth. Structured programming with go to statements. Computing Surveys. Vol. 6, No. 4, pp. 261-301, December 1974.

[Lucassen et al. 88] J. M. Lucassen, D. K. Gifford. Polymorphic effect systems. Proc. 15th ACM Symp. on Principles of Programming Languages, pp. 47-57, 1988.

[Manna et al. 73] Z. Manna, S. Ness, J. Vuillemin. Inductive methods for proving properties of programs. CACM, Vol. 16, No. 8, pp. 491-502, August 73.

[McCarthy 60] J. McCarthy. Recursive functions of symbolic expressions and their computation by machine. CACM, Vol. 3, No. 4, pp. 184-195, April 1960.

[Partsch et al. 83] H. Partsch and R. Steinbrüggen. Program transformation systems. Computing Surveys, Vol. 15, No. 3, pp. 199-236, 1983.

[Schmidt 86] D. A. Schmidt. Denotational semantics. Allyn and Bacon, 1986.

[Schwarz 78] J. Schwarz. Verifying the safe use of destructive operations in applicative programs. Proc. 3rd int. Symp. on Programming, Dunod Informatique, pp. 395-411, 1978.

[Sturgis 88] H. E. Sturgis. Maintaining the illusion of a functional language in the presence of side effects. XEROX Research Report CSL-88-2, Palo Alto, 1988.

[Turner 85] D. A. Turner. Miranda: a non-strict functional language with polymorphic types. Proc. Conf. on Functional Programming Languages and Computer Architecture, LNCS 201, Springer Verlag, pp. 1-16, 1985.

[Wadler 81] P. Wadler. Applicative style programming, program transformation and list operators. Proc. Conf. on Functional Programming Languages and Computer Architecture, ACM, pp. 25-32, 1981.

[Williams et al. 88] J. Williams and E. L. Wimmers. Sacrificing simplicity for convenience: Where do you draw the line? Proc. 15th ACM Symp. on Principles of Programming Languages, pp. 169-179, 1988.

[Wirth 71] N. Wirth. Program development by stepwise refinement. CACM, Vol. 14, No. 4, pp. 221-227, 1971.